SHORT-TERM
PSYCHOANALYTIC PSYCHOTHERAPY
FOR ADOLESCENTS WITH DEPRESSION

Developments in Psychoanalysis Series

Series Editors: Peter Fonagy, Mary Target, and Liz Allison

Tavistock Clinic Series

Series Editors: Margot Waddell and Jocelyn Catty

SHORT-TERM PSYCHOANALYTIC PSYCHOTHERAPY FOR ADOLESCENTS WITH DEPRESSION

A Treatment Manual

Simon Cregeen, Carol Hughes, Nick Midgley,
Maria Rhode, & Margaret Rustin

Edited by
Jocelyn Catty

KARNAC

First published in 2017 by
Karnac Books
118 Finchley Road
London NW3 5HT

British Library Cataloguing in Publication Data

A C.I.P. for this book is available from the British Library

ISBN: 978–1–78220–352–0

Edited, designed, and produced by Communication Crafts

Printed in Great Britain

www.karnacbooks.com

CONTENTS

ABOUT THE EDITOR AND AUTHORS   ix

ACKNOWLEDGEMENTS   xi

SERIES EDITORS' PREFACE   xiii

FOREWORD   xv

INTRODUCTION   1

Depression in adolescence   4
Treatment of adolescent depression   6
STPP and the IMPACT trial   7
The manual: STPP in practice   8

CHAPTER ONE

Psychoanalytic views of adolescent depression   11

Psychoanalytic theories of depression   12
Developmental considerations   25
*Towards a psychoanalytic formulation of depression
for adolescents*   34

CHAPTER TWO

Psychoanalytic child psychotherapy: principles and evidence   37

Psychoanalytic psychotherapy with children and young people   38

The evidence for psychoanalytic psychotherapy with children and young people   42

CHAPTER THREE

Short-Term Psychoanalytic Psychotherapy
for adolescent depression: framework and process   53

Principles, aims, and techniques of STPP   53

Case management, collaborative working, and psychiatric issues   74

Referral for STPP   78

CHAPTER FOUR

The stages of treatment in
Short-Term Psychoanalytic Psychotherapy   85

The early stages of STPP   86

The middle stages of STPP   104

The ending stages of STPP   112

Post-treatment contact   124

CHAPTER FIVE

Work with parents and carers   127

Principles of psychoanalytic work with parents and carers   127

Parent work in STPP   134

Setting-up, reviews, communication, and routine outcome monitoring   142

The process of parent work in STPP   146

Common themes, difficulties, and variations   156

Working with adopted and looked-after children and their carers   159

CHAPTER SIX

Supervision of Short-Term Psychoanalytic Psychotherapy   167

Principles and aims of psychoanalytic supervision   168

STPP supervision: the framework and process   173

Dealing with risk   176
Problems of management in STPP supervision   177
Supporting therapists' management of countertransference   177
Parallel process in supervision   179
Supervision of parent work   181

CHAPTER SEVEN
Short-Term Psychoanalytic Psychotherapy in clinical practice   185
Managing psychiatric difficulties and risk   185
Some common problems   189

AFTERWORD   213

ABOUT THE ASSOCIATION OF CHILD PSYCHOTHERAPISTS   219

REFERENCES   221

INDEX   247

ABOUT THE EDITOR AND AUTHORS

Jocelyn Catty is a Child and Adolescent Psychotherapist, working with adolescents in a Child and Adolescent Mental Health Service (CAMHS) in South London, and an adult psychotherapist in independent practice. She is Research Lead for the doctoral training in Child Psychotherapy at the Tavistock Centre and co-editor of the Tavistock Clinic Series. She was previously Senior Research Fellow in Mental Health at St George's, University of London, with a special interest in the therapeutic alliance, and has published in social psychiatry, psychotherapy, and English literature..

Simon Cregeen is Head of Child and Adolescent Psychotherapy in Manchester and Salford CAMHS, Central Manchester NHS Foundation Trust, and a clinical tutor on the doctorate training at the Northern School of Child and Adolescent Psychotherapy, Leeds. He has a particular interest in work with parental couples, looked-after children and young people, adoptive families, and their networks. He has published a number of papers.

Carol Hughes, now retired, had a long career as a Consultant Child and Adolescent Psychotherapist within the NHS and social care. She worked for several teaching hospitals and in CAMHS clinics in

London, Kent, and Cambridge for very many years. She was a founding member of the STPP steering group for the IMPACT trial.

Nick Midgley is Academic Course Director of the doctorate in Child and Adolescent Psychotherapy at the British Psychotherapy Foundation/Anna Freud Centre and Lecturer in the Research Department of Clinical Educational and Health Psychology, UCL. He has edited and written several books, including *Child Psychotherapy and Research* (2009), *Minding the Child* (2012), and *Reading Anna Freud* (2013), and is currently involved in a number of research projects related to the therapeutic needs of children, especially those in foster care.

Maria Rhode is Emeritus Professor of Child Psychotherapy at the Tavistock Clinic and the University of East London. She is co-editor of *Psychotic States in Children* (1997), *The Many Faces of Autism* (2004), and *Invisible Boundaries: Psychosis and Autism in Children and Adolescents* (2006) and a contributor to *Childhood Depression: A Place for Psychotherapy* (ed. J. Trowell, 2012). She is currently working on an early intervention project for toddlers with communication difficulties.

Margaret Rustin is a child, adolescent, and adult psychotherapist and an Associate of the British Psychoanalytical Society. She was Head of Child Psychotherapy at the Tavistock Clinic from 1985 to 2007 and has taught extensively in Europe and elsewhere. She was co-editor of *Closely Observed Infants* (1989) and has maintained a deep interest in the observational roots of child psychotherapy. She has written many books and papers about child psychotherapy and, with Michael Rustin, two books on the application of psychoanalytic ideas to literature. Her most recent book, co-edited with Simonetta Adamo, was *Young Child Observation: A Development in the Theory and Method of Infant Observation* (2014). *Reading Klein,* which she has co-authored with Michael Rustin, will be published in the New Library of Psychoanalysis Series in 2017. She has a private practice and continues to supervise many child psychotherapists.

ACKNOWLEDGEMENTS

Our thanks to Ian Goodyer and the Principal Investigators of the IMPACT (Improving Mood with Psychoanalytic and Cognitive Therapies) trial for their support in the development of the original version of this manual, for their permission to publish this revised version, and for providing us with the opportunity to participate in the study. Key aspects of the manual (particularly chapters 1, 3, and 4) were inspired by and draw upon an unpublished treatment manual written by Judith Trowell in conjunction with Maria Rhode, which was used in an earlier study of the treatment of childhood depression (Trowell et al., 2007).

In preparing this manual for publication, we have gained enormously from the feedback given by all the child psychotherapists and supervisors who worked on the IMPACT trial. In particular, we have been indebted to Rajni Sharma and Jannie Hollins, who contributed essential clinical vignettes and invaluable thinking, and to therapists who participated in a day-long meeting organized by the authors to share their experiences. Yael Yadlin provided invaluable scholarly assistance.

We are also grateful to Peter Fonagy, Mary Target and Liz Allison, Series Editors of the Developments in Psychoanalysis series, and to Margot Waddell and Jocelyn Catty, Series Editors of the Tavistock

Clinic Series, for their encouragement in publishing this manual. We have also benefited hugely from the support of the Association of Child Psychotherapists (ACP) in the UK, both in encouraging the publication of this manual and for promoting the model of Short-Term Psychoanalytic Psychotherapy (STPP) which it describes. The ACP's STPP Implementation Group, which has been working to promote the introduction of STPP across the UK, has been led by Rajni Sharma by kind support of the Northern School of Child and Adolescent Psychotherapy.

Finally, and above all, we are deeply grateful to the young people and families who participated in the IMPACT trial, who gave us the most important feedback possible: their experience of STPP.

Simon Cregeen, Carol Hughes, Nick Midgley,
Maria Rhode, & Margaret Rustin

SERIES EDITORS' PREFACE

This manual for Short-Term Psychoanalytic Psychotherapy for adolescents with depression represents the combined efforts of a great many people: the principal investigators of the IMPACT trial led by Ian Goodyer and including two of us (Peter Fonagy and Mary Target); the many child psychotherapists who participated in the study as therapists to the young people involved or as supervisors of the clinical work; and, of course, the team of authors of the manual, who also guided the psychoanalytic work in the study as its steering group: Simon Cregeen, Carol Hughes, Nick Midgley, Maria Rhode, and Margaret Rustin.

The IMPACT trial was, from the outset, a collaborative endeavour for the psychoanalytic child psychotherapy profession in the UK. The authors, the therapists in the study, and the manual itself represent the wide range of clinical work undertaken by psychoanalytic child psychotherapists here, within the post-Kleinian, Anna Freudian, and Independent traditions. The study also represents clinical child psychotherapy as undertaken across the UK, being conducted in London, East Anglia, and Manchester. The child psychotherapists in the study were all members of the Association of Child Psychotherapists in the UK (details of which can be found at the end of this book).

As Series Editors of the Developments in Psychoanalysis Series and of the Tavistock Clinic Series, we are delighted to be launching this book as a joint publication. Both series have long histories of contributing to the clinical, theoretical, and research literature on psychoanalysis and psychoanalytic psychotherapy with children, adolescents, and adults. The Developments in Psychoanalysis series highlights advances in psychoanalysis that seek to meet the intellectual challenge of complementing our new understanding of genetics and neuroscience with a systematic and scholarly exploration of questions of meaning and interpretation, while also allowing our psychoanalytic understanding of the mind to be informed by scientific, philosophical, and literary enquiry. Similarly, the Tavistock Clinic Series has for many years made available the clinical and empirical approaches that are most influential at the Clinic (now the Tavistock and Portman NHS Trust), setting out new perspectives in the understanding and treatment of psychological disturbance in children, adolescents, and adults, both as individuals and as families.

As a treatment manual, this book is certain to contribute to both the research and the clinical literature on Short-Term Psychoanalytic Psychotherapy, both in its careful thought about the nature and origin of severe depression in children and young people and in describing in such vivid detail the work of psychoanalytic child psychotherapists in theory and in practice. We can only agree with Anne Alvarez that the book is "more than a manual". Rather, it is one that "contributes to the 'science of the art' of psychotherapy".

London, July 2016

FOREWORD

This treatment manual to support the use of Short-Term Psycho-analytic Psychotherapy for young people with depression was born out of the need to provide such a manual for use in a research study: the IMPACT trial (Goodyer et al., 2011). This study created the opportunity for a group of experienced child and adolescent psychotherapists to think through the nature of clinical involvement in a research study of time-limited therapy for adolescent depression with the demanding conditions of random allocation to the three treatment modalities. Work on the treatment model proved to be interesting as well as challenging. We found we shared a strong commitment that our manual would be closely based on established models of once-weekly psychotherapy, with parallel parent work and network liaison. Two of us had been part of an earlier study led by Judith Trowell (Trowell et al., 2007), and this informed our approach in important respects. In particular, we were convinced of the necessity for substantial clinical supervision for the therapists, being mindful that there would be considerable anxiety to be faced by the clinicians. Being part of an important research study with the need for audio-recording of sessions and the ongoing involvement of a research team, the high levels of depression and of risk in the patients referred to IMPACT, the time-limited nature of the therapy – all these factors were inevitably sources of anxiety for therapists. What we thought would perhaps surprise some was that our model privileged the focus on transference and countertransference phenomena as the central therapeutic tool despite the limited time available for the work.

How did it all turn out? The anxieties of the therapists about the short-term nature of the intervention were allayed once it was clear that we were building on a well-understood tradition of psychoanalytic once-weekly work. Indeed, the substantial theoretical background we described to support the model was greeted with pleasure. However, many felt themselves to be inexperienced whether in working with such severe cases or with the specific pathology of depression, or with the age-group, older adolescents being much in the majority. Most were uncertain how to handle the time limit clinically.

The patients were, of course, enormously varied in background, and the clinic context and team composition diverged considerably in different parts of the UK. In the cities, a wide range of ethnicities was represented, and, very broadly, two-parent families often seemed to be in a minority. Mental health difficulties across generations were frequent features, and family conflict was ubiquitous. As anticipated, themes of separation from family, uncertain and changing identities, and peer relationships often preoccupied the young people. Many had had repeated or recent losses, with the need for space to mourn important family figures being a crucial focus. The demands of adolescence in terms of individuation and greater personal responsibility and of academic achievement loomed large. Unresolved oedipal issues complicated adolescent sexual exploration, sometimes leading to sexual promiscuity and sometimes to withdrawal and isolation. As psychoanalytic theories of depression would suggest, problems with anger and aggression were frequent.

What is now possible is to build on this work in a number of ways. Child psychotherapists have found that they can indeed treat severely depressed adolescents, including those who self-harm or are at risk of suicide. The model of time-limited work can certainly be expected also to be appropriate for other groups of patients. Indeed, many of those seen in the research sample had at least one other diagnosis, and most of them struggled with profound anxieties. Whether or not there are future research studies on the scale of IMPACT, there is plenty of room to try out the model with the children and adolescents seen within CAMHS in a systematic way.

What the young people had to tell us about their experience of time-limited treatment has proved very thought-provoking. For example, one boy of 15 whose depression had prevented him attending school or sustaining peer relationships for many months commented four weeks before his last session, when he was reporting feeling much better and able to get to school on a daily basis: "They all think I am back to normal and don't realize things are still difficult for me. They have already forgotten what this last year has been like. They just want me to get right back into it, exams and all that. Get back to where I was before." When his therapist wondered how he felt about the sessions coming to an end, he nodded as she spoke about his fear of being forgotten by her, and of not having a memory of their work together inside him. Two weeks later, he returned to this theme, now able to speak directly about the end of the therapy. "I don't know how I will feel when it's finished. I can imagine I may not notice it for a while, but then I might find I will miss coming here." They were able to discuss how a review meeting a few months later could be useful to him.

If a wide take-up of STPP across the UK can gradually be achieved, there will be a good case to be made for STPP to be included within the scope of the Children and Young People's Improving Access to Psychological Therapies (CYP-IAPT) programme. This opportunity to build psychoanalytic thinking and practice into CAMHS teams and voluntary sector services for young people is indeed a precious one. The necessity for regular work with parents on family relationships is a particularly relevant feature given the increasing reluctance of CAMHS clinics to provide *treatment* for parents. STPP is a challenge to this culture of treating the child or adolescent as someone to be understood but also providing forms of education to parents which rarely take account of the emotional and developmental complexities of family life, including the unconscious features of parent–child relationships.

In the wider international context, the opportunity for linking the contribution of psychoanalytic child psychotherapy to public health outcomes for young people can be a source of optimism for child psychotherapists. It has been encouraging to find that there is active interest in STPP in both Europe and the United States, and this publication should enhance that. International collaboration can potentially expand and strengthen the all-important evidence base, drawing on both research and practice-based evidence. We hope that this book will provide encouragement and inspiration and provoke dialogue and experimentation.

Margaret Rustin

SHORT-TERM
PSYCHOANALYTIC PSYCHOTHERAPY
FOR ADOLESCENTS WITH DEPRESSION

Introduction

S hort-Term Psychoanalytic Psychotherapy (STPP) for adolescents is a model of psychoanalytic treatment combining 28 individual psychotherapy sessions for the adolescent or young person and seven sessions for the parents or carers, supported by supervision. As a treatment for young people with moderate to severe depression, it is rooted in psychoanalytic principles and practice and has evolved out of a long history of providing time-limited psychoanalytic work to adolescents in the UK. Its effectiveness for this group has been investigated empirically in three key Randomized Controlled Trials (RCTs), two of which are still ongoing. Individual STPP sessions with the young person are provided by a professional with a core clinical training in psychoanalytic psychotherapy with children and adolescents (referred to henceforth as a "child psychotherapist" or "therapist"). Parent work is provided by another professional who may be a child psychotherapist or by another colleague working in a psychoanalytically informed way. Supervision is provided by an experienced colleague.

Unlike many psychological therapies for depressed young people, STPP is designed for those whose depression is severe, and where the clinical picture is complicated by intergenerational difficulties, such as parental mental illness, or complex problems such as arise from multiple losses, early trauma, and serious developmental difficulties or compromised patterns of development. Child psychotherapists can work with such complex difficulties because of the depth and breadth of their training, experience of their own psychoanalysis, and close psychoanalytic supervision. STPP, like longer-term psychoanalytic psychotherapy, pays close attention to the transference relationship with the young patient, including the therapist's countertransference, which facilitates the understanding of unconscious anxiety and phantasy. It aims to enable the young person to relinquish ingrained patterns of emotional relating that have allowed depression to take hold. Unlike open-ended psychotherapy, STPP makes use of the time limit to bring to the surface issues relating to loss which are regarded as key to the development and maintenance of depression.

A young person offered STPP, as with other psychological therapies, is unlikely to know quite what to expect (Midgley et al., 2014) but will find him or herself presented with an opportunity: to think about his or her feelings with a therapist who is attentive, empathic, and able both to facilitate the expression of strong emotion and to tolerate this when the feelings expressed are negative, distressing, or hostile towards the therapist. This is crucial for young people with severe depression, as they frequently feel angry with themselves and those around them (Midgley et al., 2015) and experience profound guilt about such feelings. For some, knowing what they are feeling is difficult, and here the capacity of the child psychotherapist to work with unconscious feeling and phantasy and to facilitate communication with a "shut-down" or silent young person, or understand the play or drawings of a younger adolescent, is essential.

Parent work for STPP, like the direct clinical work with the young person, is founded on psychoanalytic principles. It aims to support the young person's therapy by facilitating the parent's or carer's understanding of their child and his or her difficulties, and it does so through a delicate process of attending to the painful areas of experience that may be thrown up in parents by their child's depression. Parents, whether intact couples, single parents, or in partnership with step-parents, are likely to be deeply worried by their adolescent child's depression and the range of behaviours that may accompany it. For some, difficulties in their own adolescent years will be evoked; for others, perhaps experience of fragility in their own mental health or that of a parent or sibling, or earlier experiences of losses or trauma, may be key. There may be acute worries about a young person's suicidal feelings or deliberate self-harm, and a parent may harbour guilty worries that some aspect of their parenting may be responsible. To have the opportunity to share such concerns with a therapist (the parent worker) who is able to focus on the adolescent child's difficulties and their impact on the parents and family, while bringing out the subtleties of the parents' response, is tremendously helpful for many. For some, who may struggle with acute anxiety about their child's therapy, being a point of contact and liaison between the young person's therapist and the parent(s), and potentially a source of understanding of the nature of the therapy and its likely significance to the young person, is also a key role for the parent worker. For carers of children "looked after" by the state, or for adoptive parents, all these anxieties may be present, but additional worries may be involved, such as a pressure to make up to the young people for difficulties in their life before being removed into "care" (such as abuse or neglect) and high levels of trauma in the young people from their early lives. The parent worker may also have a particular role to play in relationship to the wider network of care around the young person.

Underpinning both direct clinical work with the young person in STPP and parent work, psychoanalytic supervision plays a key role in supporting the therapist's and parent worker's understanding of the clinical picture and in providing a safe space in which countertransference experiences can be processed and understood. The frequency of supervision will vary depending on the experience of the STPP psychotherapist and on what is feasible within ordinary clinical practice. For therapists early in their careers or those starting out in using the STPP model, the opportunity to present a clinical STPP case fortnightly is ideal; for others, less frequent supervision and peer supervision may be appropriate. Child psychotherapists are, of course, trained to work with powerful unconscious projections coming from their young patients, or from families, and to understand the emotional reactions and sometimes disturbing associations this kind of clinical encounter arouses in them. The value of supervision lies partly in the opportunity to explore such complex and disturbing dynamics with an experienced colleague working at one remove from the direct therapeutic work with the patient. In the context of STPP for young people with severe depression, supervision is likely to be particularly important in helping to contain the powerful feelings aroused by the nature of the work, perhaps particularly the impact of early relational and other trauma and the closeness to anxieties about survival where suicidal feelings are present.

The 28-week model of STPP, while "short" compared to longer-term or open-ended psychoanalytic work, spans the majority of an academic year and is rarely seen as "short" by young people themselves, nor in the context of financially pressed public mental health services, where shorter (or "brief") treatments tend to predominate. It is sufficiently long, indeed, to give the young patient an experience of something substantial – a robust and in-depth treatment relationship with the psychotherapist – and to allow for the sense of a beginning, middle, and end. Within such a structure, the treatment can both develop and deepen, while issues around loss can be worked through as the time limit is held in mind (Molnos, 1995).

To set the scene for the detailed account of STPP for young people with depression given in this manual, we now briefly describe the nature and prevalence of depression in this age group and survey the range of treatments available for it. We then go on to describe the development of STPP and its use in three empirical studies, before giving an outline of the manual presented in this book.

Depression in adolescence

Studies have suggested that about 2.8% of children under the age of 13 years, and 5.6% of those between 13 and 18, suffer from some kind of depressive disorder (Costello, Erkanli, & Angold, 2006), with depression twice as common among girls as boys after the age of 13 (Birmaher et al., 2007). Yet until quite recently, it was assumed that young people did not experience clinical depression in the way that adults did, and that the mood swings and irritability seen in adolescents were just part of the normal developmental process, the "storm and stress" of being a teenager. The diagnosis of depressive disorders was only extended to children and adolescents in 1980, when the third edition of the *Diagnostic and Statistical Manual of Mental Disorders* (*DSM*) was published, following a series of studies in the 1970s (e.g., Weinberg, Rutman, Sullivan, Penick, & Dietz, 1973) that had begun to establish that clinical depression in young people is not the same as the normal strains of being a teenager and can also be differentiated from depression in adults.

According to the recent, fifth edition of the *DSM* (APA, 2013), a diagnosis of major depressive disorder in young people depends on signs of a pervasive shift towards sadness, irritability, loss of interest, or loss of pleasure over a minimum of a two-week period. To meet the diagnostic threshold, these symptoms need to be markedly different from how the young person usually is and to be causing clear impairment in the young person's life. Other symptoms that are considered to be potentially part of a diagnosis of major depressive disorder include loss of appetite, difficulty in sleeping (or waking up), reduced energy, low self-esteem, poor concentration, social withdrawal, and a sense of hopelessness. In severe instances, there may also be a strong sense of guilt and suicidal ideation. Unlike with adults, irritability is also noted as a significant symptom of depression in young people, and there are also some recognized differences in how depression may appear in children as opposed to older adolescents. In all circumstances, however, major depression is likely to have a significant effect on the young person's life, with the various different elements often interacting in such a way that the lived experience for the child or adolescent is one of feeling hopeless and helpless (Midgley et al., 2015).

There is also an increasing recognition that children and adolescents suffering from depression are likely to have a range of other difficulties, with levels of co-morbidity rated as between 50% and 80% (Birmaher et al., 2007). Depressed adolescents are most likely also to suffer from some form of anxiety disorder, but they may also present with disruptive disorders, substance abuse, eating difficulties, or emerging personality disorder. Depression leads to an increased risk of self-harm and suicidality (especially among boys), with one study suggesting that 7% of adolescents who experienced a depressive disorder went on to commit suicide as young adults (Weissman et al., 1999). Although there are relatively high rates of recovery from depressive episodes (which last on average between seven and nine months in young people), there is also a very high level of relapse, with as many as 70% of young people who experience depression having a further episode of depression within five years (Richmond & Rosen, 2005). The long-term consequences of depression in adolescence are also striking, with an increased risk of self-harm, suicide, depression, physical illness, substance misuse, and interpersonal problems in adulthood (Weissman et al., 1999).

Treatment of adolescent depression

Given the high rates of depression among young people, identifying effective treatments is clearly a priority. From a review of the existing evidence base, the National Institute for Health and Care Excellence (NICE) produced updated guidance on the treatment of depression in children and young people in 2015 (NICE, 2015), in which they recommend a stepped approach to care, in recognition of the different needs of young people depending on the nature of their depression and their personal circumstances. Where possible, the guidelines suggest that young people should be offered treatment on an outpatient or community basis, and a careful assessment should always be made, which includes attention to potential parental mental health issues. They also suggest that young people should be provided with psycho-education about sleep hygiene, the benefits of regular exercise, and a balanced diet. Where the depression is mild, a period of "watchful waiting" may be appropriate, or some form of non-directive supportive therapy or group Cognitive Behavioural Therapy (CBT). Where the depression is more moderate or severe, fluoxetine is the only form of antidepressant medication that is recommended; in all cases, the recommendation is that this should only be offered alongside some form of psychological therapy. Where the young person is non-responsive to treatment, careful review by a multidisciplinary team is recommended. Regarding the specific types of psychotherapy that are recommended, especially for moderate to severe depression that is not responsive to a brief intervention, the NICE guidelines suggest that individual CBT, interpersonal therapy, systemic family therapy, and psychodynamic child psychotherapy are all options that should be considered.

There are a number of areas where the guidance suggests that further research is necessary. There have been relatively few studies that have assessed the capacity of treatments to prevent relapse in the mid- to long term, despite the fact that epidemiological studies suggest relatively high rates of relapse for depression in young people. There are also ongoing controversies about the use of medication for young people, including concerns about higher levels of suicide in some studies; there have also been mixed findings about the relative merits of stand-alone treatments and combined ones (combining medication with psychotherapy). Fonagy and colleagues (2014) also note, crucially, that "the fact that 40–50% of the treated samples across trials of both medication and psychosocial interventions generally do not respond and remain depressed shows that we need to continue to develop more effective models of treatment, and that, in the meantime, a range of alternative approaches needs to be retained" (p. 118). The need to refine and to make available high-quality treatments that are both acceptable to young people and effective for more severely depressed children and adolescents – not only in the short term but also in the medium and long term – remains paramount.

STPP and the IMPACT trial

STPP was developed out of a long-standing commitment among child psychotherapists to providing time-limited psychoanalytic treatment to young people. Since the turn of the century, this tradition has converged with a commitment to testing the clinical effectiveness of such an approach through empirical studies. STPP thus evolved from a 30-session model of child and adolescent psychotherapy tested in two RCTs: one for children who had been sexually abused (Trowell et al., 2002), the other for children and young adolescents with depression (Trowell et al., 2007) (comparing it to group therapy and family therapy, respectively). The latter, which demonstrated not only the effectiveness of STPP by the end of treatment but its continued effect (or "sleeper effect") beyond the end of treatment to six-month follow-up, provided the precedent on the basis of which funding was provided for the much larger scale RCT of STPP, the IMPACT (Improving Mood with Psychoanalytic and Cognitive Therapies) trial. The IMPACT trial also drew on the Adolescent Depression Antidepressant and Psychotherapy Trial (ADAPT), which compared CBT with antidepressants to antidepressants alone in the treatment of young people with depression (Dubicka et al., 2008), which also set a valuable precedent for evaluating psychological therapies for depressed young people.

The IMPACT trial (Goodyer et al., 2011), involving 540 patients, is the largest RCT to date involving child and adolescent psychotherapy, covering three regions of the UK: North London, East Anglia, and the North West of England. The adolescents and young people involved, aged from 11 to 17 years, were randomly allocated to receive either STPP, CBT, or Specialist Clinical Care and were followed up at regular intervals, including at the end of treatment and at 86 weeks after their initial referral. Empirical findings from the trial were not available at the time of writing.

The manual: STPP in practice

This book is a descriptive treatment manual: a full description of what STPP is, its theoretical context, and how it may be used within ordinary clinical services for young people. While an earlier version of this manual was used in the IMPACT trial, the current manual has been written for use in routine clinical practice, by child psychotherapists usually working in multidisciplinary teams. STPP can also be offered in other settings, including independent practice, the voluntary sector, or in education, provided that issues concerning case management and risk are closely attended to.

While the acronym "STPP" has been used for other treatment models, particularly short-term psychodynamic psychotherapy for adults, we use it here for the model of short-term psychoanalytic psychotherapy that we describe. Likewise, we use the term "psychoanalytic" to describe this form of therapy throughout the book, regarding it as a more precise term than "psychodynamic" and denoting a particular form of therapy (in the UK, that practised by members of the ACP) within the broader school of "psychodynamic psychotherapy" or "psychotherapies". As is common practice in the psychoanalytic literature, we distinguish between unconscious "phantasy" and conscious "fantasy".

Chapter 1 gives an overview of different psychoanalytic theories and models of adolescent depression. STPP is not based on a single psychoanalytic theoretical model of depression but draws on a range of psychoanalytic theories combined with theories of child development; this chapter therefore aims to demonstrate the range of thinking that may be brought to bear on understanding young people with moderate to severe depression. Chapter 2 describes psychoanalytic work with children and young people: first its key principles and techniques, then the empirical evidence for psychodynamic psychotherapy in general and STPP in particular. Chapter 3 introduces the STPP model itself, along with a description of the relationship of STPP to case management and collaborative work in the context of a multidisciplinary clinic. It then describes usual referral processes for STPP within the multidisciplinary clinical setting. Chapter 4 delineates the stages of STPP, using a composite case to illustrate the principles of STPP work and common themes and issues that arise at each stage. In chapter 5, psychoanalytic parent work is described, using the same composite case along with other vignettes, while chapter 6 focuses on supervision for STPP. Where chapter 4 aims to illustrate the key principles of STPP in its tracing of one particular composite case, and thus perhaps runs the risk of idealizing the process, chapter 7 describes common difficulties arising in STPP in practice, including problems of non-attendance and treatment breakdown, as well as particular issues around psychiatric liaison and risk management. These difficulties are illustrated with vignettes drawing on the process of direct therapy with the young person and parallel parent work, supported by supervision.

All the vignettes and case studies described in this book are "composite cases", based on a wide range of clinical experiences of young people with severe depression, through direct clinical work and supervision and as reported through the supervisory processes of the IMPACT trial. The revision of this manual from its earlier incarnation as the treatment manual in a clinical trial also drew on the experiences of a large number of psychotherapists who used it in direct clinical work or supervision as part of the study.

In conclusion, it is worth noting that the experience of the child psychotherapists involved in the IMPACT trial – those in the steering group who prepared the manual, the therapists of the young people and their parents, and the supervisors – was that the focus on developing and testing out the model of STPP proved to be clinically valuable and professionally enriching. It brought together therapists working in very varied clinical settings, with a range of theoretical frameworks and different levels of experience, in a way that strengthened their grasp of technique and their conviction in the value of their work with the growing population of troubled young people.

CHAPTER ONE

Psychoanalytic views of adolescent depression

Psychiatric definitions of depression, such as the ones provided in the *DSM-5* (APA, 2013) and the International Classification of Diseases (*ICD-10*; WHO, 2010), are primarily based on manifest symptoms. In psychoanalytic psychotherapy, however, the focus is primarily on underlying psychodynamic and developmental issues, rather than on the manifest symptoms of depression. This is in line with research suggesting that depressive symptoms may well be a component of many different disorders, given the high levels of co-morbidity with other Axis I disorders (such as anxiety) and with Axis II disorders such as personality disorders (Fava et al., 1996). It is also in line with a study of depression in young people (Trowell et al., 2007) which reported high levels of co-morbidity with other conditions, particularly anxiety. These findings have important implications for both treatment and research, as different treatments may turn out to be differentially beneficial for different types of depression (Corveleyn, Luyten, & Blatt, 2005).

In therapeutic terms, psychoanalytic treatment aims to address the underlying dynamics of the disorder first and foremost, not just the symptoms *per se*. In focusing on such underlying dynamics, this form of therapy thus focuses on some of the vulnerabilities to depression, thereby offering not only symptomatic improvement but also the possibility of fostering greater resilience against the recurrence of depression. An effective theory of depression needs to encompass the many different forms that depression may take, including the various possible changes in cognition, mood, and other symptoms. In order to be clinically relevant, the theory needs also to speak meaningfully to the considerable co-morbidity with other types of disturbance, especially during adolescence, as well as both the internalizing and externalizing types of depression (Trowell et al., 2007).

This chapter begins by describing a range of psychoanalytic theories of depression. It then goes on to consider the importance of looking at depression in the context of adolescent development. It ends by offering a psychoanalytic formulation of some of the underlying psychodynamic processes and factors that are likely to make some adolescents vulnerable to depression and to suffer ongoing depression. These processes, which reflect the key theoretical concepts on which STPP is based, underpin the approach to treatment described in the following chapters.

Psychoanalytic theories of depression

The role of unconscious conflict and aggression

Conflict is inherent to human existence but is particularly intense during adolescence, especially with respect to adult authority figures, and often linked to depressive symptoms. Unconscious conflict may be particularly powerful in relation to feelings of aggression and hostility. Psychoanalytic authors, beginning with Freud in "Mourning and Melancholia" (1917e), are in agreement that depression is associated with fears about the consequences of aggression and the patient's conscious or unconscious fear of being unable to manage it appropriately. When such fears become overwhelming, the result may be guilt (Rado, 1928), hopelessness, and despair. In depression, there is a tendency to turn aggression against the self and a consequent failure to elaborate issues of identity in a satisfactory manner.

The focus on aggression in psychoanalytic theories of depression has been especially important in helping to make sense of the severe levels of self-reproach and self-criticism that can be found in many depressed patients, although there are ongoing debates within psychoanalysis about the role that aggression plays in the genesis of depression (Bleichmar, 1996). Bleichmar (1996) identifies four broad perspectives on the interaction between aggression and depression within psychoanalytic theory:

» aggression as a necessary universal feature and a fundamental causal agent present in every depression (e.g., Abraham, 1924; Klein, 1935);

» aggression as a causal agent of depression but as part of a larger process involving the frustration of particular desires and wishes, which leads to aggression being directed towards the self (e.g., Jacobson, 1972);

» aggression being present in certain cases but the central dynamic of depression being related more specifically to experiences of helplessness and loss of self-esteem (e.g., Bibring, 1953);

» aggression as a secondary phenomenon in depression understood as a response to failures of the object which leads to narcissistic rage (e.g., Kohut, 1977).

Early relationships

Abraham (1924) was the first psychoanalyst to highlight the particular importance in the vulnerability to depression of hostile elements in the early relationship to the mother, based either on temperament or on early experience. Drawing on his clinical experience with depressed adults, Abraham suggested that an experience of interpersonal loss or disappointment in adult life (especially in a love relationship) was experienced by some people as an unconscious repetition of an early childhood state of being wounded narcissistically (i.e., an injury to the sense of integrity of the self), thus evoking powerful feelings of hostility and aggression. In some cases, such aggressive feelings are experienced as unacceptable, and they evoke unmanageable feelings of guilt. The aggression may then be repressed and turned against the self, leading to merciless attacks on the patient's own self as well as feelings of guilt and lack of self-worth.

Abraham's focus on the connection between depression and the earliest mother–infant relationship was developed by Melanie Klein (1935, 1940), whose ideas helped to identify some of the typical anxieties and defence mechanisms found in the depressed patient. Klein (1946) proposed that the first months of life, for all infants, were characterized by the "paranoid-schizoid" defences against anxiety, in which the prime concern is for the survival of the self. Splitting of good and bad is necessary to overcome confusion but, when taken to extremes, can lead to an excessively black-and-white world view and an impoverishment of the personality. In the depressive position, which follows developmentally, good and bad aspects of the self and of significant others begin to be integrated, and this can lead to guilt about any hostility towards loved people. The main concern is for the survival of loved figures, both externally and internally, so that someone who has not overcome the anxieties of the depressive position may be preoccupied with loss and be frightened of forming attachments. These "depressive anxieties" (which are not the same as a state of depression) are resolved by making reparation during the "working-through" (Freud, 1914g) of the depressive position. This process is repeated throughout life, especially when external events arouse anxiety about loved ones.

When the adult patient has a depressive breakdown, Klein understood this in terms of an inability to tolerate (normal) depressive anxieties, especially those concerned with a sense of having irreparably damaged a loved person. Someone for whom guilt is intolerable may regress to the paranoid-schizoid position or adopt a "psychic retreat" (Steiner, 1993). The defences that are mobilized to manage the persecutory anxieties may limit the patient's capacities, especially to manage guilty feelings, which may become overwhelming. For the depressed patient struggling to maintain the depressive position, guilt and self-reproach are powerful. Equally, these patients lack confidence in their capacity to "repair" the situation and restore loved internal figures. This links with the sense of hopelessness and helplessness discussed by other psychoanalytic writers such as Bibring (1953).

The role of loss

The role of "object loss" in the aetiology of depression has been central to many psychoanalytic theories, alongside aggression. Freud (1917e) distinguished between "melancholia" (depression) and normal mourning, while suggesting that both could be understood as the ego's reaction to the loss of an important "object" (either an actual person or, for example, a political ideal). In mourning, a period of intense sadness and withdrawal from normal interests gradually leads to the bereaved person's acknowledgement that the loss he or she has suffered is irreversible, and that the loved person will not return. As an outcome of this mourning process, the lost, loved person becomes more securely established as an inner presence with whom the bereaved person can identify, so that his or her sense of self becomes enriched.

Freud contrasted this situation with that in pathological mourning, or "melancholia", where he noticed that the depressed person's feeling of worthlessness and self-reproaches were typically voiced in a way that sounded as though they were being addressed to another person. He posited that the melancholic person's internal situation reflected the way in which he or she had dealt with the loss of an emotionally important figure (generally a parent) towards whom profoundly ambivalent feelings were held. In Freud's striking phrase, the loss (either real or perceived) of such a relationship had a profound consequence: "the shadow of the object fell upon the ego" (1917e, p. 249). The aggression and reproaches originally aimed at the ambivalently loved object were now turned against the melancholic's own self. This notion of what was later termed the "ego-destructive super-ego" was elaborated by other authors (e.g., Bion, 1959; O'Shaughnessy, 1999) in relation to difficulties other than depression and has continued to be central to the way psychoanalysts have understood certain key aspects of the experience of depression. Recently, Green (2013), revisiting "Mourning and Melancholia", has argued that in melancholia the psyche rigidifies into inflexible postures. In some young people this seems marked, whereas for others it is an additional component in the background.

While Freud's ideas helped to make links between experiences of loss, self-directed aggression, and depression, it was clear that not all depression was precipitated by loss and that not all experiences of loss led to depression. Freud's work had offered a powerful account of the dynamics at play in depression, but it did not sufficiently address the question of why certain individuals appeared to be more susceptible to reacting to loss in a melancholic way, whereas others were able to pass through a period of more "healthy" mourning. For psychoanalysts, it was necessary to get a clearer idea of the particular vulnerabilities that certain individuals had that would make them more susceptible to a depressive reaction.

While the work of Freud, Abraham, and Klein helped to elucidate some of the mechanisms that lead to feelings of guilt and self-hatred in depression, other psychoanalytic thinkers have focused more on the sense of helplessness and powerlessness that is characteristic of some forms of depression. Bibring (1953) was one of the first psycho-analytic thinkers to see depression as a primary affect that could be evoked in certain threatening situations. As Lazar (1997) puts it, "he viewed rage turned against the self as less important than a sense of helplessness in the face of a loss of ideals and self-esteem" (p. 52).

More specifically, Bibring suggested that a loss of self-esteem and depressed feelings were a direct response when the ego was faced by frustration. While experiences of loss were common among Bibring's depressed patients, what defined the depression was a sense of the self as unable to attain certain goals, leading to a profound sense of impotence and helplessness (see also Haynal, 1977). As Bemporad, Ratey, and Hallowell (1986) put it, "what the depressive has lost was not necessarily a love object but also a set of aspirations or a view of one's self" (p. 168).

Bibring's ideas were elaborated by Sandler and Joffe (1965) in their extensive review of the case notes of children with depression seen for psychoanalytic treatment at the Anna Freud Centre in London in the post-war years. Sandler and Joffe agreed with Bibring that depression could be thought of as a basic emotion that was evoked when children were faced by the loss of something or someone whom they felt was central to their core sense of well-being. They emphasized that the significant thing was not the lost person *per se*, but, rather, the loss of a previous sense of self, a self whose well-being was associated with maintaining a link to a particular person. These children felt unable to do anything to repair this loss, leading to a self-representation as helpless and powerless that in turn was associated with a sense of apathy, inhibition, and hopelessness characteristic of depression. It is interesting to note the convergence of this idea with Klein's emphasis on the centrality of reparation (Klein, 1937).

There are certain similarities between Bibring's conceptualization and that of Bowlby (1960), who also saw depression as one stage in a natural sequence of responses to any experience of loss or separation from an important attachment figure. Sandler and Joffe (1965) hypothesized that some children were more vulnerable to depression than others because of pre-morbid personality characteristics, which one might hypothesize could be linked to Bowlby's ideas about the effect of different patterns of attachment on the way children manage separation and loss. Bowlby's work on the importance of secure attachment for the child's emotional development shows obvious parallels with psychoanalytic ideas concerning the importance of the balance between love and hostility: the defining characteristic of securely attached toddlers is the capacity to protest when left by their mothers, but then to allow themselves to be comforted. In insecurely attached toddlers, this balance cannot be attained or maintained. One might hypothesize that such an insecure attachment would make the developing child more vulnerable to depression, a hypothesis that is supported by recent longitudinal research (Halligan, Herbert, Goodyer, & Murray, 2004).

The psychoanalytic thinking of Bibring, Sandler and Joffe, Bowlby, and Haynal is useful in understanding the well-established link between traumatic experiences and depression. Certain traumatic experiences, including physical and emotional abuse or physical illness, may leave people feeling a profound sense that they are unable to influence their world in any meaningful way. This is consistent with Brown and Harris's (1978) finding that when traumatic experiences are identified in the histories of depressed adults, they tend to threaten profoundly that person's sense of identity and worth.

The death instinct

Primary aggression and destructiveness is a contested notion within psychoanalysis. Freud first proposed (1920g) and then developed (1930a, 1937c) the existence of a conflict between a life instinct and a death instinct, following clinical observations and based on his ideas regarding biology and philosophy. Central to his thinking was the idea that there is a primary destructiveness which involves a fusion of the life and death instincts. Although there have been many views on this idea, and indeed objections to it, it is an idea that has survived and been developed by subsequent thinkers and so needs consideration.

Freud's thinking was subsequently taken up by Klein, whose ideas were rooted in her clinical experience. She made a conceptual link between the death instinct and the development of a harsh superego (Klein, 1933), and she later considered that primitive envy was the most destructive manifestation of the death instinct (Klein, 1957), thus presenting a significant impediment to development. Klein linked the life instinct with feelings of love, and the death instinct with those of hate and destructiveness. She considered that the fear of annihilation was the primary anxiety: "Since the struggle between the life and death instincts persists throughout life, this source of anxiety is never eliminated and enters as a perpetual factor into all anxiety-situations" (Klein, 1948, p. 29).

As her thinking developed, Klein increasingly saw the manifestations of love and hate as being less derived from instincts and more associated with the interplay of object relations and thus subject to being projected into external and internal objects. Subsequent post-Kleinian psychoanalysts have developed thinking on the life and death instincts, especially in relation to narcissism, most notably Meltzer (1968), Rosenfeld (1971), Segal (1997a), and Feldman (2009).

In clinical work with depressed patients, we often see the conjunction of an identification with a lost object (Freud, 1917e) and persecution by a harsh superego. O'Shaughnessy describes the formation of this constellation:

> Freud described how in a melancholia, destructiveness is felt to be concentrated in the superego . . ., and four years later in 1927, Melanie Klein showed that the extreme and unreal destructiveness of the early superego is the result of the projection into it of the child's savage impulses. [O'Shaughnessy, 1986/2015, p. 88]

With patients who are in a state of melancholia, the identification with the lost and hated object is a narcissistic one and may include states of envy, grievance, possessiveness, and tyranny felt towards the object (Sodre, 2005). In melancholia, the dynamic combination of a severe superego and the narcissistic identification could be thought of as associated with the workings of the death instinct.

In her summary review of developments in Kleinian thought, Bott Spillius (1994) suggests that there are two, not mutually exclusive ideas in relation to the death instinct that are still prevalent in post-Kleinian thinking. One is that of a "strong tendency toward inherent destructiveness and self-destructiveness" which can lead the individual to "attack or turn away from potentially life giving relationships", with the associated wish to "oblate any awareness of desire that would impinge on their static and apparently self-sufficient state" (p. 341). The second idea is "what Rosenfeld [1987], following Freud, calls 'the silent pull of the death instinct'" (Bott Spillius, 1994, p. 341). In this, the individual is inexorably drawn towards "a nirvana-like state of freedom from desire, disturbance, and dependence" (p. 341). She suggests that it is "a false opposition" to try to determine whether such tendencies are "innate or acquired, inherent or defensive" and that, clinically, "what one can tell is how deep-rooted the patient's negative tendencies are in the present analytic situation" (p. 341).

Clinical work with some depressed patients reveals phantasies (which are sometimes made explicit) that suicide will bring about a relief from the pain of living and a belief that this peaceful state will be experienced, known, and enjoyed by them, albeit post-death. Such a state of mind also may include a sense of triumph over the object (and the world of the living) associated with an idealized sense of apparent self-sufficiency.

Psychotic depression

Winnicott's work represents an interesting bridge between theories that emphasize the mother–infant relationship and attachment, and the Freud/Klein tradition. He maps out ways in which the quality of maternal provision can impact on the individual's sense of self and of well-being, including the development of a "false self" when the baby is forced to pay premature attention to the mother's state of mind (Winnicott, 1948, 1960a). His description of maternal mirroring (Winnicott, 1967) and its effect on the sense of identity is highly relevant to the feeling of alienation and futility often reported by depressed people. This concerns the sense of self at a fundamental level, and it therefore links with what Winnicott (1963, p. 222) called "psychotic" or endogenous depression, in accordance with the distinction in common usage at that time between the "reactive" depression that is triggered by events and the "endogenous" depression that appears to have no immediately recognizable external cause, but that could actually be understood as a response to fundamental vulnerabilities in the patient's sense of self.

This concept of psychotic depression (which should not be confused with the psychiatric use of the term "psychosis") was further elaborated by Frances Tustin (1972), who linked it with some children's fundamental problems in establishing a viable sense of self when they realized that they were physically distinct from the caregiver. Such children's sense of catastrophe and of feeling beset by existential anxieties was often experienced physically: Tustin wrote about a "flop" type of depression and stressed that the children suffering from it could feel that the separateness of the caregiver robbed them of part of their own body (see also Winnicott, 1963). This "flop" type of depression is characterized by bodily collapse and the existential experience of being "gone" or of being swallowed up by a "black hole". Like Bick (1968, 1986), Tustin stressed these children's reliance on physical sensations they could generate themselves to provide a sense of continuing existence in the face of such profound anxieties. This is relevant to some depressed young people who can feel temporarily relieved by heightened physical activity or by the sensations induced by self-harm. Tustin also stressed the importance of the caregiver's ability to resonate with the child's extreme anxieties and to be able to tolerate them sufficiently so that they could be transformed into something more tolerable—the process that Bion (1962a) described as "containment" and which he thought was essential to the growth of the personality. In the absence of sufficient containment, Bion suggested that the child's frightening experiences, specifically the child's fear of dying, could not become known or indeed meaningful and therefore manageable; instead the child lost whatever degree of meaning it might have had, so that it was left with a sense of "nameless dread" (1962a, p. 96). Emanuel (2001) explores the relevance of this for patients whose sense of nameless dread manifests as a sense of having a "void" within them, describing the range of defences used to ward off contact with such "potentially annihilating terror" (p. 1069).

In this context, Green (1980) has highlighted the fundamental importance of the phantasy of "the dead mother". This internal mother is psychically "dead" or unresponsive, rather than dead in physical reality, with profound consequences for the patient's own sense of aliveness, including existential anxieties concerning the possibility of "going-on-being" (Winnicott, 1960b, p. 587) as well as anxieties relating to bodily integrity. Such existential anxieties were observed in virtually all the young people in one study of the treatment of childhood depression (Trowell, Rhode, Miles, & Sherwood, 2003; Rhode, 2011). In such cases, the depressed patient may feel to an extreme degree that their situation is hopeless and that life is pointless. They are typically preoccupied by the fear of containing nothing that could help them to live their lives; their inner presences seem to be dead and impossible to restore to life (Klein, 1935). Many suffer from existential anxieties about losing their identity and from fears about spilling out or falling forever that have been described by Winnicott (1949), Bick (1968), and Tustin (1986). This formulation provides a bridge between the view of depression in which the management of aggression is seen to be central and the view that stresses the importance of an impoverished sense of self. In such states, there is typically little or no sense of being in any way effective or of having an impact, and the appearance of realistic feelings of anger is an important step in the recovery process (Trowell et al., 2003).

The integration of psychoanalytic models of depression

It seems likely that the range of psychoanalytic models of depression that exist, as indicated in this brief survey, have developed in order to account for somewhat different aspects of depression. Authors with different theoretical backgrounds within the psychoanalytic field appear to be describing similar presentations in differing terms: for example, "narcissistic vulnerability" (Kohut, 1977), "unstable sense of self" (British Object Relations, e.g., Winnicott, 1960a, 1967; Bion, 1962a, 1962b), or "essential depression" (Paris Psychosomatic School, e.g., Smadja, 2005) may be different ways of describing the same underlying features of depression. Whether an integrated psychoanalytic model is feasible, accounting for the range and variety of depressive symptoms and the possibility of different psychodynamic features underlying apparently similar manifest behaviours and symptoms, is a moot point given the range of models developed to date and the need to do justice to the complexity of the subject under investigation. In Bleichmar's (1996) view, however, a "more integrated model can be useful in helping us gain a general orientation of which conditions are sustaining the depression in a particular patient. . . . If one were to detect that pathology resides basically in one [particular condition], then our therapeutic interventions would be primarily oriented towards modifying that area" (p. 950). A number of writers have attempted to produce such an integrated model, developing psychoanalytic aetiological models of depression that seem to have key elements in common.

From a review of many of the key psychoanalytic theories of depression, Busch, Rudden, and Shapiro (2004) have identified two broad models of depression: "those involving aggression towards others that is ultimately directed toward the self" and "those focusing on difficulties with self-esteem in patients whose expectations of themselves far exceed their capacity to live up to them" (p. 27). This distinction seems related to the distinction made by Bleichmar (1996) between "guilty depression" and "narcissistic depression". With "guilty depression", according to Bleichmar, the primary preoccupation is with the object's well-being, and the depression can be understood as related to guilt and a sense of responsibility for having attacked and damaged the ambivalently loved object. The outcome is a sense of the self as mean, bad, and potentially destructive, and the depressive symptoms can be understood as a response to this. In "narcissistic depression", the primary preoccupation is with the person's sense of self-worth, and the depression can be understood as related to a sense of narcissistic injury which leads to heightened self-criticism and hopelessness. The disturbance is understood as a reaction to experiences that puncture the person's grandiose fantasies, leading to a sense of humiliation and feelings of inadequacy. (See also Anastasopoulos, 2007.)

Supporting this latter view, Kernberg (1986) writes of a type of depression "which has more of the quality of impotent rage, or of helplessness-hopelessness in connection with the breakdown of an idealised self concept" (p. 294), while Kohut (1977) describes a form of depression where feelings of frustration in relation to narcissistic aspirations of the self are the core dynamic. A chronic sense of emptiness, seen as a result of failures in empathic parenting, was described by Kohut as the core depressive feature in some narcissistic patients. Rather than the emphasis being on guilt due to a sense of having damaged the object, in this type of depression, according to Kohut, there is a greater focus on the subject's own sense of narcissistic fragility, with subsequent feelings of shame and humiliation (see also Milrod, 1988). These could well be compared to Winnicott (1967) on failures of maternal mirroring; Tustin (1986) and Green (1980) on an inadequately constituted sense of self, and the Paris school (Smadja, 2005) on "essential depression".

Rosenfeld (1960) sees narcissistic fragility of the ego as an important factor in depression, alongside the failure to deal with the anxieties of the depressive position. He suggests that this fragility comes about through the projection of parts of the self that the patient feels cannot be recovered, which leads to a feeling of emptiness and of hopelessness about being able to experience life as meaningful. This part of Rosenfeld's description resembles the narcissistic depression of Kohut and Bleichmar, but with a different proposed underlying mechanism.

The empirical research literature provides some support for the idea that these two formulations capture different sub-types of depression, each one describing a group of depressed individuals with differing presentations and differing vulnerabilities, and with potentially differing responses to therapy. The work of Blatt (1998) outlines two empirically supported types of depression, distinguished not on the basis of manifest symptoms but, rather, on the individual's unconscious conflicts, defences, and fundamental character structure. Blatt calls these "introjective" depression and "anaclitic" depression.

Introjective (self-critical) depression is characterized in Blatt's account by a marked vulnerability to disruptions of an effective and positive sense of self and is expressed in feelings of worthlessness, guilt, failure, and a sense of loss of autonomy or control. In this type of depression, concerns are primarily about disruptions in self-definition and self-esteem leading to feelings of guilt, emptiness, and self-criticism, and a sense of lack in both autonomy and self-worth. These individuals have a powerful longing for perfection but are vulnerable to criticism both from others and from themselves. Research suggests that such individuals may have histories of parental rejection and excessive authoritarian control early in life (Soenens et al., 2008). They may often be ambitious and very successful individuals who are plagued by intense self-doubt and criticism, and this group are at considerable risk for serious suicide attempts (Blatt, 1995). Previous studies of adult patients suggest that those with this type of depression are less responsive to short-term psychotherapy of any modality, but they do show some response to longer term, intensive psychodynamic psychotherapy (Blatt, 1998).

Anaclitic (dependent) depression, by contrast, is characterized by a marked vulnerability to disruptions of gratifying interpersonal relationships and is expressed primarily in feelings of loss, abandonment, and loneliness. Research suggests that such individuals may come from so-called enmeshed families and have histories of parental "psychological control", in which strivings for independence and separateness are limited (Soenens et al., 2008). In this type of depression, concerns about hurting or offending others lead to a fear of losing the gratification that dependent relationships can provide. Among this group, depression is often precipitated by object loss and is frequently expressed through somatic complaints. Such individuals seek out the care and concern of others, including mental health professionals. Previous studies of adult patients suggest that those with this type of depression are responsive to brief psychotherapy of various modalities (including CBT and psychodynamic psychotherapy), with the quality of the relationship to the therapist (therapeutic alliance) being the key predictor of successful outcome (Blatt, 1998). Narcissistic fragility would, of course, also ensue from identification with a damaged object, so these two "sub-types" are not necessarily mutually exclusive, as will be discussed later in this chapter.

Drawing on the various traditions within the psychoanalytic literature, Busch, Rudden, and Shapiro (2004) attempt to present an integrated psychodynamic formulation for depression which is based around five key areas. These key features are:

» narcissistic vulnerability – an insecurely founded sense of a separate self and heightened sensitivity to perceived or actual losses and rejections, leading to a lowering of self-esteem which in turn triggers depressive affects, existential angst, and rage in response to narcissistic injury;

» conflicted anger – anger, blame, and envy directed towards others, leading to disruptions in interpersonal relationships, confusion about what the individual is or is not responsible for, and self-directed anger and subsequent depressive affects;

» severe superego and experience of guilt and shame – feelings and wishes seen as bad and/or wrong, with doubt about whether love outweighs aggression, leading to negative self-perceptions and self-criticism and, in some cases, to confusion between reality and fantasy;

» idealized and devalued expectations of self or others – high self-expectations and/or idealization of others, often switching to sudden de-idealization and devaluation, leading to disappointment, anger at the self and others, and subsequent lowering of self-esteem;

» characteristic means of defending against painful affects – use of typical defences such as denial, projection, passive aggression, and reaction formations leading to increased depression (either the world is seen as hostile or the self is attacked); splitting is a characteristic defence against aggression, which is then not available to be integrated in the service of personality development.

Developmental considerations

Most of the psychoanalytic formulations outlined above derive from clinical work with depressed adult patients. While there are many areas of overlap between depression in young people and in adults, there are also significant differences, both in manifest symptoms and in the underlying psychodynamic processes. It is essential to take a developmental perspective when trying to understand disturbance (A. Freud, 1966; Harris, 1965). As Luyten, Blatt, and Corveleyn (2005) argue, in setting out their own "dynamic-interactionist model" of depression, "the classification, assessment and treatment of psychopathology should be linked to normal developmental processes and to disruptions in these processes" (p. 267).

In treatment and assessment for treatment, it is important to take into account the interaction of factors associated with the onset of depression with the developmental tasks of adolescence. Understanding this interaction permits the formulation of hypotheses concerning circumstances that might make a young person vulnerable to depression or, conversely, that could be protective and underpin resilience.

Vliegen, Meurs, and Cluckers (2005) have proposed an overview of the ways in which depression may manifest itself at different ages, focusing primarily on the presenting mood at each developmental age and on factors defined as concerning "activity" and "emotionality" (or, for pre-school children, "growth"; p. 167). According to their account, adolescents tend to present with sad mood; worrying activities include the inability to experience pleasure, withdrawal, boredom, weariness, and sleep disorder; while worrying emotions include feelings of guilt, low self-esteem, feeling uncomfortable in one's body or sexuality, and suicidal plans and/or attempts.

Identity, individuation, and adolescence

Psychoanalysts writing about adolescence have stressed its importance as the time during which the young person consolidates his or her own independent identity. Conversely, it is a time for facing a rather abstract but intense kind of loss: the loss of childhood (Mathes, 2013), sometimes experienced as the "total loss of a psychic 'home'" (Midgley, Cregeen, Hughes, & Rustin, 2013, p. 71). While authors such as Erikson (1950) and Blos (1967) have emphasized the achievement of autonomy, others such as Moses Laufer and Eglé Laufer (1975) have focused on the impact of developing a sexual body. This also involves the reappearance of oedipal anxiety and conflict from infancy (Klein, 1940; Waddell, 1998), as described further below, which can be extremely alarming for many adolescents, especially if they have limited or inflexible defences or their sense of self has not been firmly established. Although this offers the opportunity to establish a secure young-adult sexual identity, it can feel overwhelming or threatening. The anxiety aroused by this developmental challenge may lead to a state of retreat, or turning away, or to manic and promiscuous activity (Rustin, 2009a). The sense of hopelessness that so often characterizes depression also prevents the young person from utilizing the benefits of his or her peer group, creating a vicious circle. Adolescent depression can thus be viewed as a developmental crisis (Midgley et al., 2013).

Klein saw adolescence as another chance to work over fundamental issues of individuation that have been a feature of early childhood, though now with the additional urgency imparted by the surge of biological maturation and by the fact that the adolescent is physically able to enact sexual and aggressive impulses that would previously have been confined to the realm of phantasy (Waddell, 2000a). This points to the importance in adolescence, as well as in early childhood, of a secure setting that the child can feel supported by, as well as rebel against, and of caregivers with whom he or she can identify as role models.

Adolescence can therefore be a frightening time both for young people and for their parents, one in which creative developmental possibilities carry with them fears of loss, including the loss of the comparatively safe state of being a child. The peer group takes on a central importance, whether it is helpful developmentally as a way of exploring in others different potential aspects of the adolescent's own personality (Waddell, 2000a) or whether it takes on the quality of a potentially delinquent gang (Meltzer, 1973; Rosenfeld, 1971).

Adolescence thus understandably poses a particular challenge to young people at risk of depression. Blatt and Luyten (2009) suggest that this period is "a crucial time for a synthesis [between the developmental dimensions of relatedness and self-definition] that can result in the formation of a consolidated identity or the emergence of many forms of psychopathology" (p. 799). They argue that specific depressive dynamics may well underlie both the internalizing problems (including somatic problems) more typical of adolescent girls and the more externalizing problems (e.g., antisocial behaviour and aggression) more typical of adolescent boys. This would accord with the fact, emphasized in the NICE guidelines on childhood depression (NICE, 2005, 2015), that those in contact with the young people concerned often do not view their behaviour in terms of depression or, in consequence, take the necessary steps to get help for this. In addition, the hopeless withdrawal that is often characteristic of depression means that the young person cannot engage in the activities and relationships of his or her peers, so that a vicious circle may be set in motion.

Young people whose sense of self is fragile and insecurely founded might thus be expected to find the adolescent task of individuation extremely daunting and therefore to have an increased vulnerability to states of depression. Ways of coping that served reasonably well before the upheaval of puberty may no longer be adequate. Equally, the balance of vulnerable families may be threatened by the shifts entailed in the young person's move towards greater independence. This, in turn, can undermine the young person's developmental strivings by reinforcing a tendency to withdraw, or it can lead to a heightening of rebellious behaviour inspired by the hope of encountering helpful limits. More particularly, the task of consolidating a sexual identity inevitably confronts the young person with his or her phantasies concerning the parents' relationship, as well as with more realistically based feelings about it.

Oedipal anxieties and conflicts in adolescence

The adolescent developmental period and state of mind is one in which oedipal feelings, anxieties, and conflicts are re-encountered, re-worked, and re-negotiated. This process is related to how oedipal matters were experienced and managed in toddlerhood; now, in adolescence, there is a resonance with the curiosity and dynamics of those early years. The primary difference is that in adolescence, in the context of puberty and growing physical capacities, notably those that allow the individual to procreate, there is a developmental thrust towards genital sexuality, coupling, and the formation of a personal identity distinct from parents and family culture. The inevitable uncertainties and conflicts, advances and retreats, associated with this process not only require considerable psychic attention in the mind of the young person, but often bring interpersonal conflicts with parents, teachers, and friends. This can be a period of turmoil for families as intense emotions arrive suddenly and run high. As Waddell (2003) describes:

> The child's Oedipally freighted relationship with parents, with the actual parental couple and with its many internal versions, is diffused, displaced and distorted, first in the group-dominated

existence of early adolescence, and then, refocused and intensified, in the pairing relationships of the later adolescent years.
[p. 55]

Within a Kleinian framework, the young person's getting to grips
with, and working through, oedipal matters is, as with the experiences in toddlerhood, associated with movement between the paranoid-schizoid and depressive positions (Britton, 1995). This allows for
the creation of a "triangular space" which is "bounded by the three
persons of the oedipal situation and all their potential relationships"
(Britton, 1989, p. 86). The individual's capacity to be in the "third
position" (p. 87) allows for "seeing ourselves in interaction with others and for entertaining another point of view whilst retaining our
own, for reflecting on ourselves whilst being ourselves" (p. 87). This
oedipal development is intrinsically associated with a depressive-
position state of mind:

> If the link between the parents perceived in love and hate can be
> tolerated in the child's mind, it provides him with a prototype for
> an object relationship of a third kind in which he is a witness and
> not a participant. [Britton, 1989, p. 87]

Given favourable circumstances, the hard-won achievement of
increased depressive-position functioning is linked to the young person being able to bring together in his mind, in an alive and reality-
based way, a picture of a parental couple upon whom he depends
for his existence, but from whom he is now impelled to make moves
away in order to establish himself more independently in the world,
identify with his peer groupings, and seek to create his own couple
relationship. This brings with it new ways of viewing and relating to
parents and to internal parental objects. Alongside the move away
from a child-based dependence upon the parents, and a need to
develop a more separate identity, the young person is reliant upon
identifications with internal parental figures and couplings as a basis
for his own efforts at coupling with another.

The young person's movement away from interest and belonging
in the family to peer relationships, the possibilities for sexual experimentation, and encounters with previously unknown ideas and ways
of living in the wider world may be supported by parents or create
familial fear and conflict. Often it can be both in a rapidly oscillating

dynamic. For the young person, in addition to the pleasures of new discoveries, there can also be loneliness and pining for that which is being lost, most notably his or her loved, immature, position in relation to the parental couple, and the centrality of the parental couple in his or her psychic world. This inevitably brings uncertainty, which is sometimes retreated from through a reluctance or fear to seek out or embrace new experiences. This can include a turning away from, or disabling under-confidence in, the growth of unfamiliar sexual feelings, dreams, and desires. The sexual focus in the young person's internal world has moved from its previous location in the relationship with the parental couple to that of him/herself in relation to peers and possibilities outside the family.

For the young person's parents, there may be enjoyment of the new experience of space which can arise within their own couple relationship. This can be an opportunity for the couple to come closer together again, and can promote growth and the chance for more working through of their own oedipal experiences. It can also bring painful emotions, however, and some sense of regret for time passing, with recognition of what is now not so present in their relationship with their son or daughter. The parents of adolescents have to tolerate their comparative lack of knowledge of their adolescent child's feelings and thoughts and less familiarity with his or her friends and interests. Most challengingly, parents are required to find a way of managing the feelings engendered within them by the arrival of the new-found genital sexuality of their son or daughter and his or her choice of boyfriends and girlfriends.

For some parental couples, the young person's oedipal development, with sexual phantasies, feelings, anxieties, and experiences at the core, can generate a crisis. The parental couple may start to experience the ways in which they have grown apart from one another through the child-rearing years, including sexually. There may be a resurgence of adolescent sexual feelings and states of mind in one or both of the parents, as well as feelings of envy of their son or daughter's sexual potency and aliveness and jealousy of their sexual couplings which leave the parents on the outside. When things go well, however, the young person's renegotiation of oedipal matters within him/herself, and interpersonally with his or her parents, can bring a period of fertile growth for all.

Adolescents and the social world

In psychoanalytic work with adolescents in particular, it is important for the clinician to think about the young person's development as an individual within not only the family context but also that of their social and peer-group world (Meltzer, 1973; Meltzer & Harris, 2013; Waddell, 1998). Both in unconscious phantasy and external reality, the individual young person's relationship to and questions about his or her place within the social world expands exponentially. The internal pressure to make moves away from parental figures is intimately bound up with an equivalent pressure to move towards peer relationships and groupings. This can, very positively, lead to friendships with previously unknown levels of intimacy and intensity (both of affection and rivalry), the seeking out of sexual encounters and couplings, and the joining of groups and movements devoted to discrete activities (sports, music, arts, politics, science, and much more). The coming together in groups provides a social crucible within which new ideas and ways of conceiving of oneself can be encountered, identified with, and assessed by the individual. Groups provide an alternative social structure to the family, in which adolescents may seek to define or re-define themselves.

The young person's interest in a particular group's life and activity, and his or her identification with the ambitions, values, and ethics that are operational within that specific group, may be short-lived or turn out to be lifelong. At their best, these activities and groupings allow experimentation and growth of the young person's sense of having some freedom of mind to make choices about what sort of young adult he or she might be becoming, in ways that may have both similarities to and differences from their parents and siblings. Group life provides a social structure and set of relationships that can be employed by each individual within it for the purposes of projection, introjection, and identification. Dynamically, what once was primarily within the domain of the family is now manifested more actively within the peer group. Coming together with passion, and falling away from one another in disillusionment, is a common feature of such adolescent groupings.

With regard to a young person's engagement in STPP, we have to bear in mind that they may be both suspicious of our thinking and methods and attracted to them in an idealizing way. Group life is highly active (whether enjoyed or feared) for adolescents, not only in external life but also within their minds. Psychotherapy may be approached by some adolescents as if it were a system of magical beliefs, either seductive or sinister, or perhaps a political structure designed to liberate or tyrannize. If the treatment and therapist are related to with this sort of social idea residing within the patient's mind, it could be thought of as a form of "basic assumption" (Bion, 1961), not subject to reality-testing. For adolescents in particular, in addition to the parental transferences, the psychoanalytic clinician may be viewed as representing the ideas, values, and politics of a discrete psychosocial grouping in relation to which the adolescent as a patient needs to locate him/herself. If so, this will inevitably inform the transference and needs to be borne in mind and worked with.

In the psychotherapy relationship, the young person's preoccupation with his or her place in a social grouping, particularly with respect to being inside or outside the circle, needs to be taken account of when considering interpretation. If the therapist simply takes this up as an aspect of the individual's dependent parental transference, for example, this may lead to the young person feeling that the therapist has failed to realize the psychic reality of the young person's emotional preoccupation with his or her peers as being in at least equal measure to his or her interest in the relationship to his or her parents. The two are, of course, intimately connected, especially with regard to oedipal concerns and dynamics, but it can also be a rich experience to identify and work with the transferences associated with siblings and peer-group relationships, which are differently nuanced from those relating to parental figures.

Parental mental health, intergenerational loss, and parent–infant relationships

Where parents or carers have serious problems of their own, this can interfere with their ability to support their children and can make it difficult for each generation to achieve a developmentally appropriate relationship with the other. If there is a deficit in the parent's or carer's capacity to contain the young person's emotional communications or to "mentalize" (Fonagy, Fearon, Steele, & Steele, 1998), this can lead to confusions between bodily and mental experience, to somatic symptoms, and to the experience of being invaded by frightening thoughts.

Parental mental illness, such as depression, is known to be linked to childhood depression and functional impairment (Kovaks & Sherill, 2001; Todd et al., 1996). While the interaction of genetic and environmental factors is complex, there is some support for a "diathesis-stress" model whereby genetic predisposing factors interact with environmental stressors to produce a mood disorder (Carr, 2007). Particular stressors are parental psychopathology, conflict, stressful divorce, domestic violence, and child maltreatment (Shortt & Spence, 2006). Such factors may also have adverse impacts on children's emotional development (Garoff, Heinonen, Pesonen, & Almqvist, 2011, p. 227).

People who have had significant histories of problems in the parent–infant or early parent–child relationship, particularly with closeness or enmeshment, are also more likely to experience depression in adulthood (Bifulco, Brown, & Harris, 1987) or adolescence (Mikulincer & Shaver, 2012). Equally, for adolescents whose early relationships were very distant, promiscuous sexual behaviour may be more likely, along with other risk-taking such as drug or alcohol abuse (Carol Hughes, unpublished data). Such young people may conflate and confuse emotional intimacy with sexuality and be driven by fantasies of all their emotional needs being met. Where unreasonable expectations lead, as they often do, to relationship breakdown, this constitutes a further loss and generates feelings of abandonment. This may precipitate a suicide attempt.

Midgley et al. (2013) describe such a case, where the young person desperately sought a relationship of total, yet fragile, intimacy:

> At the age of 14 ["Josie"] developed an intense relationship with a boy who lived nearby, in which the two of them "felt like we were one person, we always knew what the other one was thinking". The breakup of this relationship clearly precipitated her depression, although it was only with a second loss (when her sister left the family home) that Josie broke down more overtly. . . . Once Josie's mood lifted she described how being depressed had felt as if she were liquid: "I felt sorta like water, liquid, just draining away. In fact, I wanted to soak away, just not to be anymore. Now I am not depressed I feel kind of solid. The wind can blow, I am solid – I am here." [pp. 70–71]

Some young people, faced with such a sense of loss or abandonment, experience it as an unconscious realization of the fragility of their internal and external relationships or "core self"—a common feature of depression in adolescence (Gretton, 2011). They may experience profound anxiety about annihilation, as though they believe themselves to be living in a "black hole" and to lack the right to exist (Rhode, 2011).

Towards a psychoanalytic formulation of depression for adolescents

Trowell and Dowling (2011) offer reflections on a psychoanalytic conception of childhood depression, based on the clinical experience gained from a study of childhood depression (Trowell et al., 2007). Trowell and Dowling describe the children and young adolescents in their study, aged from 9 to 15 years, as largely "opt[ing] out" of the developmental changes of adolescence described above: "emotionally they were still functioning as younger children" (2011, p. 248). These patients exhibited a "stuck" quality, with concrete thinking and without the vocabulary or awareness to describe states of feeling. Many seemed to present as though traumatized or abused. Trowell and Dowling observe: "there was often a sense that they were children and young people struggling with the very basic question of whether they had a right to exist" (p. 249). They also describe the families of these young patients as struggling with serious problems of their own, including depression in the parents, leading to a lack of emotional resources to sustain the children and help them grow up. Many of the parents had little support from their own families of origin or extended families and came from emotionally deprived backgrounds (Miles, 2011, p. 116). Trowell and Dowling (2011) conclude:

> These were emotional and social environments where depression and isolation seemed to be the norm. . . . It is difficult to separate out the genetic from the psychosocial factors here. However, what became clear is that these young people were stuck, caught in a web of complex family dynamics; for some, it seemed that the world outside was a dangerous place. [pp. 249–250]

These observations offer a model of childhood and adolescent depression that is broadly consistent with the wider psychoanalytic literature on depression while also rooted in a psychoanalytic understanding of development, including considerations of intergenerational trauma.

The model of adolescent depression upon which the present manual is based is well described in the observations above (Trowell & Dowling, 2011) and can be summarized as based on the following psychodynamic, developmental, and environmental factors:

» unconscious conflict, especially in relation to anger and aggression;
» existential anxiety;
» narcissistic difficulties and loss of identity;
» the severity of the superego, involving very painful feelings of guilt and/or shame;
» idealization and denigration of self and others;
» the impact of early relationships, loss, and relational trauma;
» the impact of parental mental health and intergenerational loss and/or trauma;
» the re-emergence of oedipal conflict and emerging sexuality during adolescence.

As can be seen, the theoretical underpinning of this manual therefore draws on the wider psychoanalytic literature on depression, but also pays particular attention to the developmental tasks and context of adolescence.

CHAPTER TWO

Psychoanalytic child psychotherapy: principles and evidence

Short-term Psychoanalytic Psychotherapy is rooted in psychoanalytic child psychotherapy, a well-established specialist treatment for emotional and developmental difficulties in childhood and adolescence. The intellectual background of psychoanalytic child psychotherapy lies in psychoanalysis, drawing particularly on the classic contributions of Melanie Klein, Anna Freud, and D. W. Winnicott, and also in the study of child development. This includes both the more academic and empirical research domain (e.g., Murray, Sinclair, & Cooper, 2001; Stern, 1985) and work in the tradition of psychoanalytically informed naturalistic observation of babies and young children (Bick, 1968, 1986; A. Freud, 1953). More recently it has also been influenced by the development of family therapy, attachment theory, and the field of developmental psychopathology. In its application to depression in children and young people, it is underpinned by an understanding of depression based on the psychoanalytic models of depression outlined in the previous chapter.

There has been a considerable growth in the literature on psychoanalytic child psychotherapy over the last 40 years, represented in a wide range of influential publications (e.g., Alvarez, 1992a; Tustin, 1986; Waddell, 1998; Williams, 1997a). There has also been a surge in research activity in this field (e.g., Midgley, Anderson, Grainger,

Nesic-Vuckovic, & Urwin, 2009; Midgley & Kennedy, 2011), and child psychotherapists have been actively engaged in the development of evidence-based practice. In the UK, this has been linked both to the development of opportunities for doctoral-level research to be conducted as part of child psychotherapy training and to the increasing recognition of the importance of adding to the evidence base for child psychotherapy as a clinical treatment.

Psychoanalytic psychotherapy with children and young people

Basic principles of psychoanalytic child psychotherapy

Child psychotherapy focuses on understanding unconscious communication, including the ways in which it is conveyed through the transference made by the child to the therapist. Its techniques are based on close and detailed observation of the relationship the child or young person makes with his or her therapist and on the theoretical assumption that the child or young person's free play, drawings, and conversation can be seen as equivalent to the psychoanalytic principle of "free association" (Klein, 1929; Rustin, 2012). A central aspect of the work is the attention the child psychotherapist pays to striking the right balance, for the particular child or young person, between interpretation of the transference, containment of the child's conscious and unconscious anxieties, and other techniques in the work, each aspect being underpinned and facilitated by the therapist's understanding of the transference–countertransference experience.

A suitable playroom with toys is required for younger children (Joseph, 1998) or a simple consulting room for adolescents. Sessions take place in this same room and at the same time each week for ongoing therapy. The therapist introduces the context to the child or young person as one for understanding feelings and difficulties in his or her life. Undirected play and talking are the fundamental sources of the relevant "clinical facts" (O'Shaughnessy, 1994).

The therapist's stance is non-judgemental and enquiring and conveys the value of words: even with young children, the aim is to put into words the therapist's understanding of what the child communicates through play, behaviour, and verbal expression. This will include conscious and unconscious thoughts and feelings. The therapist attempts to convey an openness to all forms of psychic experience – current preoccupations, memories, daydreams, fantasies, and dreams – but will be attuned specifically to evidence of unconscious phantasies that underlie the child or young person's relationship to self and others. This attentiveness to unconscious phenomena is specific to psychoanalytic psychotherapy, and to what is known as the "analytic attitude", and is related to the theoretical importance attributed to these deep layers of the mind. This attitude or stance has been described as involving "evenly suspended attention" (Freud, 1909b) and as "active receptivity" (Bott Spillius, 1988) or a state of "reverie" (Bion, 1962a, 1962b). The psychoanalyst Bion invoked Keats's concept of "negative capability" (Keats, 1817, p. 43) to describe a state of "reverie" (Bion, 1962b) or being "without memory or desire" (Bion, 1967). In order for the psychotherapist to achieve and maintain such an attitude, there is a clear requirement for careful personal attention to his or her own state of mind, as this is understood to be the most important factor in the therapeutic provision to the patient.

These principles underlie the focus on the transference relationship made to the therapist, which is central to psychoanalytic psychotherapy—that is, the relationship made not in response to "real" aspects of the therapist's person and behaviour but to those arising from characteristics of the figures of the child or young person's internal world. These are believed by the child to be present in the therapist, as a consequence of the externalization of the child's picture of the world. Systematic observation of these transference elements allows for clarification of the child or young person's fundamental assumptions about the external world (which are also related to Ainsworth's and Bowlby's concept of "internal working models" of attachment; Bretherton, 1992).

Underlying these beliefs, the child or young person is likely to have a number of anxieties about him/herself or the world, including the "nameless dread" (discussed in the previous chapter) which so often seems to underlie severe depression. The child or young person is likely to protect him/herself from the impact of such anxieties by using a range of defences; the interpretation of such defences (discussed further below) is a key aspect of the psychoanalytic technique. Once the underlying anxieties can be analysed and discussed, the child or young person is able to begin to differentiate psychic from external reality and, as a result, to test out reality and establish a fruitful relationship to it.

Also important as a source of information for the therapist are the emotional responses evoked in the therapist by the child or young person. These are broadly referred to as countertransference phenomena (Tsiantis, Sandler, Anastasopoulos, & Martindale, 1996). They can include personal factors that intrude upon and distort the therapist's capacity for objective understanding, but they may frequently be responses to being the recipient of primitive non-verbal forms of communication (projective identifications: Klein, 1952; Spillius & O'Shaughnessy, 2012), of which the therapist becomes aware. These are somewhat similar to the ways in which infants can communicate to their caretakers prior to the development of language, and they depend on emotional availability and space for "reverie" (Bion, 1962b) in the therapist. These primitive modes of relationship can, however, be used to control anxiety by ridding oneself of it and pushing it elsewhere, rather than for communicative purposes. The distinction between benign (communicative) forms of projection and malign (destructive) forms (e.g., to cause confusion) is vital in clinical work.

Working with parents, carers, and the wider network

The psychoanalytic work in the playroom or consulting room is only possible if the psychotherapist has established a relationship of trust with the parents or carers of the child or young person and can also depend on support from multidisciplinary-team colleagues who can attend to the support of the family (Rustin, 2009b) and the wider community setting of the child or young person's life, particularly the school. Unless child-protection or safeguarding issues are raised, the details of the session material remain confidential, as is discussed at the outset. Working with the multidisciplinary team and the wider network around the child is discussed below (see "Case management, collaborative working, and psychiatric issues" in chapter 3).

Work with parents or carers has two distinct forms: liaison to support the child's therapy, and support for the parents. The latter is usually referred to as "parent work", and the parent worker will usually also hold the function of liaising with the child's therapist to review progress. Liaison with the parent(s) or carers can usually be achieved by a thorough initial meeting or meetings, followed by regular review meetings involving the parent(s) and the child's therapist, whereas parent work is usually undertaken in parallel by another professional, ideally another child psychotherapist or a multidisciplinary colleague able to work in a psychoanalytically informed way. Parent work has a range of functions, including but not limited to supporting the child's therapy, and these range from supporting parental function and reflecting on the child's concerns through to psychotherapy for the parent or parents in their own right. Working with parents in STPP is discussed in chapter 5.

The training of psychoanalytic child psychotherapists

Psychoanalytic child psychotherapists in the UK undertake a doctoral-level, four-to-five-year postgraduate professional training. Entrance to the training is open to people with an honours degree; substantial professional experience of work with children of different ages; and a pre-clinical Masters-level course of theoretical and practical study, including training in infant and young child observation. (Training is offered by four training schools under the auspices of the Association of Child Psychotherapists [ACP: www.childpsychotherapy.org. uk].) Concurrent personal analysis is a requirement of the training and, alongside the intensive supervision and tutorial support offered within training schools, provides an opportunity for individual vulnerabilities and personal problems to be explored and understood. It is vital that professionals working with seriously troubled young people have the intellectual and emotional resources to sustain relationships with their patients, whose behaviour will at times be very disturbing.

The development of STPP

STPP builds on well-established practice within multidisciplinary clinics in the UK, where a substantial amount of once-weekly therapy with adolescents has long been a key part of what is provided.

Adolescents tend not to remain in therapy for extended periods, as befits their developmental trajectory, so the model of work being limited to less than a year's duration is well known. Child psychotherapists have also been committed to and are experienced in a range of explicitly brief interventions with adolescents (Briggs, Maxwell, & Keenan, 2015; Copley, 1993; Edwards & Maltby, 1998; Joffe, 1991; Salzberger-Wittenberg, 1977) and younger children (Edwards & Maltby, 1998; Emanuel & Bradley, 2008; Schmidt Neven, 2014).

A study of time-limited psychoanalytic psychotherapy for depressed young adolescents (Trowell et al., 2003, 2007) laid the groundwork for this approach to helping particularly severely impaired young people. This RCT compared Focused Individual Psychoanalytic Psychotherapy (FIPP) to systemic family therapy, for children and younger adolescents aged between 9 and 15 years. In the FIPP arms of the study, up to 30 sessions were offered to the children and adolescents, with the parents receiving up to 15 sessions, one for every two sessions with the child. FIPP was developed from the model of Malan (1976; Malan & Osimo, 1992) and Davanloo (1978), focusing on interpersonal relationships, life stresses, and dysfunctional attachments (Trowell et al., 2007). This 30-session model was previously studied in an RCT of psychoanalytic child psychotherapy for children who had been sexually abused (Trowell et al., 2002).

The model of STPP in the present manual was based on the FIPP model used by Trowell and colleagues, but with some adaptations reflecting the older age group of the patients with whom it was used in the IMPACT trial (Goodyer et al., 2011). The frequency of parent work was also different in the IMPACT trial, with one parent session being offered for every four of the young person's sessions, as described in this manual. The study by Trowell and colleagues is described further below, after a brief overview of the evidence base for psychoanalytic psychotherapy with children and young people.

The evidence for psychoanalytic psychotherapy
with children and young people

The empirical evidence supporting STPP for depressed children and young people may be drawn from the following key areas:

» the evidence base for psychodynamic psychotherapy for adults with depression;

» the evidence base for child and adolescent psychodynamic psychotherapy;

» the evidence base for STPP for children and adolescents with depression.

We now outline each of these in turn and then give a brief overview of the evidence for specific suitability criteria, both empirical and based on clinical experience.

The evidence base for psychodynamic psychotherapy for adults with depression

The evidence for both long-term and short-term psychodynamic psychotherapy in the treatment of adults has been mounting during the last decade (Leichsenring, Rabung, & Leibing, 2004; Leichsenring, 2005; Abbass, Hancock, Henderson, & Kisely, 2006; Leichsenring & Rabung, 2008; de Maat, de Jonghe, Schoevers, & Dekker, 2009; Shedler, 2010). A recent set of clinical practice guidelines for the treatment of depression in adults (Malhi et al., 2009, p. 17) identified short-term psychodynamic psychotherapy as having evidence at Level II status for its effectiveness (i.e., based on at least one properly designed RCT), with comparable effectiveness to other psychological therapies (Cuijpers, van Straten, Andersson, & van Oppen, 2008) and medication (Salminen et al., 2008). There are some indications that for major depression, combined treatment (psychodynamic psychotherapy and medication) is more effective than either one alone (de Maat et al., 2008).

Driessen and colleagues (2010) conducted a systematic review and meta-analysis of short-term psychodynamic psychotherapy for adults with depression, including 23 studies with a total of 1,365 subjects. Of these, 13 studies were RCTs, 4 studies used a non-random comparative design, and 6 studies used a naturalistic design without a control group. They found that short-term psychodynamic psychotherapy had a large and significant effect on depression (with a statistically significant large effect size) at the end of treatment. When compared to control conditions ("treatment as usual" and being on a waiting-list), short-term psychodynamic psychotherapy was much more effective (again with a large effect size). When comparing it to a range of psychological therapies, the alternative therapies demonstrated a small but statistically significant superiority in outcome at the end of treatment, but at longer term follow-up, there was no statistically significant difference between them, indicating that short-term psychodynamic psychotherapy was equivalent in outcome to the other therapies at follow-up.

The authors concluded that there is clear evidence for short-term psychodynamic psychotherapy being effective for depression, superior to having treatment as usual or being on a waiting-list, and comparable to other therapies at follow-up. There was some evidence that on some outcome measures, short-term psychodynamic psychotherapy was *less* effective immediately after treatment, but in these cases it was equally effective by follow-up at 3 and 12 months after treatment. The authors concluded that more higher quality studies of short-term psychodynamic psychotherapy are needed. Despite this, they challenged the earlier contention of Connolly Gibbons, Crits-Christoph, and Hearon (2008) that short-term psychodynamic psychotherapy for depression does not meet criteria for an empirically supported treatment. These criteria stipulate that two independent research teams must have demonstrated the intervention's superiority over placebo, no-treatment control, or alternative treatment, or its equal efficacy to an alternative evidence-based treatment (Chambless & Hollon, 1998). Driessen and colleagues (2010) argued that, on the basis of the evidence in their review, short-term psychodynamic psychotherapy may be considered to be an empirically validated treatment for depression. They also examined evidence of differences between more "expressive" (interpretive) and more "supportive" short-term psychodynamic psychotherapy and found no significant differences in outcome.

The effectiveness of short-term psychodynamic psychotherapy for adults with both depressive disorders and personality disorders was considered in another systematic review and meta-analysis (Abbass, Town, & Driessen, 2011), which included eight RCTs. This found that the majority of the patients showed clinically significant change on all the self-report measures. The authors concluded that short-term psychodynamic psychotherapy warrants consideration as a first-line treatment for combined personality disorder and depression.

More recently, the Tavistock Adult Depression Study (TADS; Fonagy et al., 2015), a pragmatic RCT, compared "long-term" psychoanalytic psychotherapy comprising weekly sessions for 18 months to treatment-as-usual (which could include referral for psychological therapy if indicated) for adults with severe and chronic "treatment-resistant" depression. The patients in this study were followed up until 42 months from the time they were recruited into the study (2 years after the end of treatment). Complete remission of the depression was not common in either group, at the end of treatment or at final follow-up. At the end of treatment, partial remission was not significantly more likely in the psychotherapy group than in the control group, but at follow-up it was, with the psychotherapy group more likely to maintain the gains made whereas the group receiving treatment-as-usual were more likely to relapse. This statistically significant difference between the two groups increased with longer follow-up: at 42 months, 30% of the psychotherapy group were in partial remission compared to only 4.4% of the treatment-as-usual group.

The evidence base for child and adolescent psychodynamic psychotherapy

A systematic review of the evidence base for child and adolescent psychodynamic psychotherapy (Midgley & Kennedy, 2011) identified 34 distinct research studies, including 9 RCTs. Almost half of these (15 studies) had been reported on between 2004 and 2011, suggesting that there had been an exponential increase in research into the effectiveness of psychodynamic therapy with children in that period. While many of the studies had small sample sizes, and the lack of control groups also limited the robustness of the evidence, the review indicated that there was increasing evidence suggesting the effectiveness of child and adolescent psychotherapy. The authors noted that the majority of the studies had been based in clinics using "clinically referred cases with considerable severity of disturbance" and were of children presenting with a range of difficulties rather than particular diagnoses (p. 6). This would indicate that the findings are likely to have relevance to the "real-world" clinical setting. This is significant because many studies cited to support "evidence-based" interventions involve recruited samples, with patients selected because they fit a particular diagnosis. Children with complex problems or co-morbid presentations are often excluded from such studies, yet these are precisely the kind of children increasingly seen in public child mental health services and referred to child psychotherapists. Unusually, many of the studies reviewed by Midgley and Kennedy included a long-term follow-up, with seven following participants for 18 months, seven following them for 2 years, and six studies having follow-up periods of at least 4 years (one including their outcomes in adulthood; Schachter & Target, 2009).

Overall, Midgley and Kennedy (2011) found that psychodynamic treatment of children and adolescents appeared to be as effective as comparison treatments. They noted a particularly strong evidence base emerging for the treatment of children and young people with depression (Horn et al., 2005; Target & Fonagy, 1994a, 1994b; Trowell et al., 2007). There were some indications that the pattern of effect might be different from other treatments, with improvement during treatment being slower than in some other psychological therapies but continuing beyond the end of treatment (Midgley & Kennedy, 2011, p. 248; Muratori, Picchi, Bruni, Patarnello, & Romagnoli, 2003; Muratori et al., 2005; see also below for discussion of Trowell et al., 2007): a "sleeper" effect (Kolvin, Macmillan, Nicol, & Wrate, 1988).

These findings were largely supported by a systematic review and meta-analysis of short-term psychodynamic psychotherapy for children and adolescents (Abbass, Rabung, Leichsenring, Refseth, & Midgley, 2013). Using narrower inclusion criteria to identify high-quality studies, this review found 11 studies, with a total of 655 patients, covering a broad range of conditions including depression and anxiety. They found evidence to support the idea that short-term psychodynamic psychotherapy is effective across the range of common mental disorders and that its effects tend to increase beyond the end of treatment. They found less evidence to distinguish short-term psychodynamic psychotherapy in effectiveness from other psychological therapies. They also noted that the data need to be interpreted with caution due to the heterogeneity of the studies and analyses and the relatively small number of studies on which the conclusions were based.

The evidence base for STPP for children and adolescents with depression

The systematic reviews described above included a study of STPP for children and adolescents with depression by Trowell and colleagues (2003, 2007). This RCT was conducted across three treatment centres in London (Tavistock Centre), Helsinki (Children's Hospital), and Athens (Aghia Sophia Children's Hospital) and included 72 children aged between 9 and 15 years meeting the criteria for major depression and/or dysthymia. The patients were randomly allocated within each centre to receive either STPP (in this study, FIPP), as described above, or systemic family therapy. FIPP closely resembled the approach described in this manual, with a total maximum number of thirty 50-minute sessions and fifteen parent sessions (one for every two child sessions). In the family therapy arm of the trial, up to fourteen 90-minute sessions were offered. At the end of the treatment, there was a significant reduction in depression in both arms of the trial: 74.3% of STPP cases and 75.7% of family therapy cases no longer met the criteria for depression (including dysthymia and "double depression"). At follow-up, 6 months after the end of treatment, 100% of the STPP cases were no longer clinically depressed – again suggesting a "sleeper effect" for STPP – whereas this was only the case for 81% of the family therapy patients (although this difference was only statistically significant when four family therapy cases who had been lost to follow-up were excluded).

On the basis of this study, the researchers also offered a number of treatment recommendations for those working with depressed young people: to look out for behaviour and symptoms masking underlying depression; to involve the family in the treatment plan and promote communication in the family; to invest time and energy in connecting with the professional networks; to enable the involvement of the school; and to be aware of the emotional impact of the work on the clinician (Trowell & Dowling, 2011, p. 252).

STPP as described in the current manual is currently the subject of two clinical trials. The first is the largest RCT of psychodynamic therapy for young people to date, the IMPACT trial (Goodyer et al., 2011). This multi-centre, pragmatic effectiveness superiority trial included 480 patients with moderate to severe depression, aged 11 to 17 years (inclusive), in three regions: North London, East Anglia, and

North West England. At each centre, the patients were randomized between STPP, CBT (consisting of 20 sessions over 30 weeks), and Specialist Clinical Care (12 sessions over 30 weeks). The patients were assessed at baseline and at 6, 12, 36, 52, and 86 weeks. The treatments were conducted in ordinary clinical settings by staff with training and expertise appropriate to each treatment.

A sub-sample of 77 young people who were taking part in the clinical trial, along with their parents and therapists, were also interviewed in-depth as part of a qualitative, longitudinal study, IMPACT–My Experience (IMPACT–ME; Midgley, Ansaldo, & Target, 2014). The young people's feelings about depression were investigated before the start of treatment, and five themes were identified in how they described it: "misery, despair and tears"; "anger and violence towards self and others"; "a bleak view of everything"; "isolation and cutting off from the world"; and "the impact on education" (Midgley et al., 2015). Asked about their hopes and expectations for therapy before it began, the young people expressed views that could be grouped into five themes: "the difficulty of imagining what will happen in therapy"; "the 'talking cure'"; "the therapist as doctor"; "therapy as a relationship"; and "regaining the old self or developing new capacities" (Midgley et al., 2014). Five therapists were also interviewed about their views of working with parents' childhood experiences within psychoanalytic parent work in parallel to the young person's therapy, and they emphasized the need to negotiate permission to work in this way along with the differences between such work and individual adult therapy (Whitefield & Midgley, 2015). Psychotherapists involved in the development of the trial from the start were also interviewed about their experiences; they emphasized the process of acclimatizing to being part of a research study and their increased confidence and open-mindedness about this (Henton & Midgley, 2012).

The second study currently evaluating the effectiveness of STPP is being carried out in Norway: the First Experimental Study of Transference work–In Teenagers (FEST-IT; Ulberg, Hersoug, & Høglend, 2012). This is a "dismantling study", in which the effectiveness of STPP for depressed adolescents is compared with the same STPP treatment, but without the use of transference interpretations. (In the arm of the study without transference interpretations, therapists held the transference and countertransference in mind but did not make any explicit interpretations of it.) This follows a similar study carried out with adults in which both forms of STPP were found to be effective, but with differential effectiveness depending on certain key patient characteristics (Høglend et al., 2008).

Although the findings of the IMPACT and FEST-IT studies have yet to be published, there is nevertheless a small, but growing, body of evidence in support of the effectiveness of psychodynamic child psychotherapy, with encouraging indications that STPP specifically may be effective in the treatment of child and adolescent depression (Trowell et al., 2007). It was on the basis of this evidence as it developed that the UK's national guideline on the treatment of child and adolescent depression recommended "psychodynamic psychotherapy that runs for at least 3 months" (NICE, 2015, 1.6.1.2) and "individual child psychotherapy (approximately 30 weekly sessions)" (1.6.3.3).

Suitability for psychodynamic psychotherapy: the evidence

In their systematic review of psychodynamic psychotherapy for children and young people, Midgley and Kennedy (2011) note that there is some evidence to suggest that children with emotional or internalizing disorders respond better than those with disruptive or externalizing disorders (p. 248) but that where those with disruptive disorders have engaged in treatment, it can be effective (p. 249). The American Academy of Child & Adolescent Psychiatry (AACAP) notes that psychodynamic psychotherapy "has been used effectively for internalizing disorders, externalizing disorders in the mild to moderate spectrum of severity, developmental character difficulties and maladaptive, internal responses to life events" and that it is "helpful in complex cases because it addresses the underlying psychological functions" (AACAP, 2012, p. 547). AACAP also notes that the child's "ability to work with the therapist towards self-understanding" (p. 547) must be considered.

The literature on suitability for psychodynamic therapy with adults is similarly inconclusive. There has been some suggestion that the patient's "object-related functioning, motivation and 'psychological mindedness' appear to have a low-to-moderate influence on the outcome of psychodynamic therapy" (de Jonge, Van, & Peen, 2013, p. 35), but psychological mindedness was not found to be linked to outcome in a study of psychodynamic therapy for panic disorder (Busch, Milrod, & Slinger, 1999). Svanborg, Gustavsson, and Weinryb (1999) studied the characteristics considered by therapists to be important for psychodynamic psychotherapy, finding that therapists were more likely to recommend it for patients who were healthier and mostly characterized by predominantly neurotic personality organization. Driessen and colleagues (2010) found in their meta-analysis of short-term psychodynamic psychotherapy for adults with depression that there were no differences in effectiveness based on age group (adults or older adults), different levels of severity of depression, or gender.

Busch and colleagues have argued that positive indications for psychodynamic therapy for adults with depression may be the ability to think psychologically and reflect on complex relationships, and the motivation to understand the roots of their symptoms, whereas marked difficulties in forming an alliance or the inability to tolerate frustration are among the contra-indications (Busch, Rudden, & Shapiro, 2004, p. 6); they also note severe depression as a contra-indication. They add, however, that patients without these characteristics are also able to make good use of psychodynamic therapy (Busch, Milrod, & Slinger, 1999) and suggest that more short-term, structured psychodynamic therapy may be suitable for a wider range of patients.

By contrast, however, the Tavistock study (TADS; Fonagy et al., 2015), described above, demonstrated the effectiveness of psychoanalytic psychotherapy for adults with severe, treatment-resistant depression. The patients in this study had suffered from depression for around 20 years on average and had experienced around four previous failed treatment attempts.

The view that emerges from most of this literature – for which empirical evidence is patchy at best – is broadly that psychodynamic psychotherapy may be most suitable for psychologically minded individuals who are able to form a treatment relationship readily and who are more likely to have an internalizing disorder. This view, however, is mostly based on research into psychotherapy with adults and is not a view recognized by most practitioners of psychoanalytic child psychotherapy, who are used to working with children and young people who do not readily express themselves verbally (for instance, working through play or through interpretation of unconscious communication) and with those whose behaviour is extremely disturbed or whose distress severe. Many child psychotherapists draw on the work of Bion (1957, 1959), Winnicott (1958), or Anna Freud (1966), who in different ways all describe working psychoanalytically with patients whose ego function is disturbed or who have an impoverished ego (see also Williams, 1997a).

In fact, audits of psychoanalytic child psychotherapy cases in the NHS have suggested that psychodynamic therapy tends to be used as a "last resort" (i.e., when other, shorter term interventions have been unsuccessful) or for the most complex of cases (Kam & Midgley, 2006; Rance, 2003). Child psychotherapy is conducted with children with learning disabilities (Sinason, 1986), who do not fit the profile of a "psychologically minded" patient, and with children disturbed by early neglect and abuse whose behaviour may be extremely disturbed and disturbing (Boston & Szur, 1983; Canham, 2004; Cregeen, 2009; Rustin, 2001). This contrasts with, for instance, Interpersonal Therapy with Adolescents (IPT-A), in which it is regarded as essential that the patient is not actively suicidal and has no psychotic symptoms (Mufson, Dorta, Moreau, & Weissman, 1993, p. 36). It is also regarded as important in evidence-based practice to consider the patient's choice. This necessitates providing a range of approaches, in order to meet the needs of people who want an approach in which their experience can be thought about and explored in a relatively open way, with a focus on the meaning of their experience. Suggestions that psychodynamic treatment is not suitable for the most severely depressed are also clearly not borne out by the Tavistock study (TADS; Fonagy et al., 2015), by Trowell and colleagues' (2007) study of childhood depression, or by clinical experience gained through the IMPACT trial (Goodyer et al., 2011). We discuss this further below in relation to STPP (see "Referral for STPP" in chapter 3).

Short-Term Psychoanalytic Psychotherapy for adolescent depression: framework and process

Short-Term Psychoanalytic Psychotherapy for young people with depression is a time-limited treatment that addresses their difficulties in the context of the developmental tasks of the adolescent years. Giving meaning to the varieties of emotional experience is central, both in the work with the young person and in the parallel work with parents or carers which is integral to the model. STPP draws extensively in terms of overarching principles upon longer term psychoanalytic psychotherapy; Trowell and colleagues' work (2007); and also, to a degree, the work of Busch, Rudden, and Shapiro (2004). STPP is also consistent with the AACAP (2012) "practice parameter" for psychodynamic work with children.

Principles, aims, and techniques of STPP

STPP is a time-limited model of psychoanalytic psychotherapy in which sessions are offered on a weekly basis for 28 weeks, with up to seven parallel sessions (i.e., one for every four patient sessions) being offered to the parents or carers (described in chapter 5). As with longer-term psychoanalytic psychotherapy, the predictability and reliability of the setting are essential if deep-seated fears are to be dealt with, including fears of abandonment and fears of the young person's own destructiveness. Breaks in the therapy are carefully handled, with prior notice being given of holiday breaks. Except in unavoidable circumstances, sessions therefore take place as they would in longer term work: at regular intervals; on the same day of the week; at the same time of day; and in the same room, which provides a protected, private setting.

Individual psychoanalytic psychotherapy of this duration is a substantial intervention. Nonetheless, for some very troubled young people, the assessing or treating therapist may feel that it will not be enough. The time-limited nature of STPP can feel to some therapists, particularly if they are more familiar with open-ended psychotherapy, like a cruel imposition on both patient and therapist, especially when working with adolescents with particularly severe depression or with long histories of loss and abandonment (important countertransference issues are raised, which will be discussed here in due course). In fact, we know that therapists tend to underrate the potential value of time-limited therapy (Cassidy, 2011; Molnos, 1995), as was found anecdotally in the IMPACT trial. Where such concerns arise, it may be worthwhile offering STPP while holding in mind that, for particular young people, more may be required at some point.

Young people themselves, however, particularly when they have not previously experienced therapy, tend not to see STPP as a short-term matter: 28 sessions can seem like quite a lot to many of them. It lasts the equivalent of most of a school year and will usually include at least two holiday breaks. The young people often convey that they find the time-frame manageable: it enables them to commit themselves to an experience which then provides a substantial opportunity for work on crucial issues of separation and the management of aggression. Many young people, in fact, can be fearful of being trapped in a long-term commitment. The time-limited contract allows them to have a solid experience of what therapy can offer, without arousing too great fears of dependence or too much claustrophobia. Briggs, Maxwell, and Keenan (2015), in fact, argue that young people offered time-limited treatment may react in either of two opposing ways: "for some adolescents, even a short-term therapy can be experienced as entrapping, whilst for others, any hint of a thought of an ending can be experienced as an abandonment or an affront to the developing adult ego" (pp. 315–316).

In time-limited psychoanalytic psychotherapy, the therapist needs to bear in mind Winnicott's suggestion that one may not be asking "how *much* can one be allowed to do?", but rather "how *little* need be done?" (Winnicott, 1962, p. 166, emphasis in original). Both therapist and young person need to be wary of the omnipotent fantasy of the total cure and be able to work towards a more realistic sense of a "good-enough" ending (Lanyado, 1999a).

In STPP, as in longer-term psychoanalytic treatment of children and young people, individual therapy with the patient is ideally accompanied by parent work conducted in parallel, and supported by psychoanalytic supervision. These are discussed in detail in chapters 5 and 6, respectively. In the remainder of this section, we first briefly touch on the broad principles of liaison with parents and others in the network of the young person's external environment which the child psychotherapist must undertake, before focusing on the individual work with the young person—its aims and the range of techniques used in STPP.

Liaison with parents, carers, and school

Liaison with parents or carers is essential to sustain a collaborative approach to STPP and has the aim of helping them to support their adolescent child's therapy and of enabling the therapist and parent(s) to discuss any significant ongoing developments. Where the young person is looked after by the state, this principle of liaising with carers may need to be extended to a relevant social worker, residential unit manager, and/or key worker, and this will be based on consideration of who is legally responsible for the young person and who is responsible for his or her emotional well-being and development, as well as the young person's own preference.

It is often helpful, when meeting with the young person for the first time, to make the distinction between confidentiality and secrecy. This indicates that if the young person wants to discuss the therapy he or she is free to do so with parents or anyone else (it is not a secret), although parents are encouraged not to press their child to do so if the young person does not wish to, or to be too intrusive in their questioning. The therapist, however, will treat session material as confidential, discussing with the young person first if or when the therapist is going to talk to others about any aspect of what has emerged in a session. An exception to the rules of confidentiality can arise when there are child-protection (or "safeguarding") concerns. With adolescents, this often involves risk to them from their own behaviour, as well as risks posed from outside. The child psychotherapist undertakes to discuss with the patient any need to involve anyone else (such as parents, carers, or social services) prior to such action being taken.

As with any clinic-based therapeutic work, there is also a necessity to communicate with the young person's school or college, provided that the young person and the parents consent to this; it can also be a challenge to work out how much information it is helpful to give. A young person may feel relieved to know that the teachers or tutors have been given at least some indication of what he or she is experiencing. The degree of depression that the young person is suffering will have a bearing on how much is said to school or college staff, but it is helpful to elicit the school's or college's support for the young person's attendance of therapy, as well as their sensitivity to his or her needs, and there may be important implications for what the young person is able to achieve academically or for peer relationships within the school or college.

The aims of STPP for young people with depression

STPP for young people with depression aims to focus not only on "symptom relief" (although this is, of course, important) but also on addressing some of the underlying vulnerabilities to depression, in order to try and create increased resilience and foster a capacity in the young person to manage difficult feelings and experiences. In the STPP model, the young person's symptoms are understood as directly related to the underlying dynamics. The fostering of increased resilience is achieved by means of its focus on the central personality organization that may have contributed to the young person's depression. The main features of these central depressive dynamics are described in chapter 1. When they are addressed successfully, outcomes of the treatment may include the following (adapted from Busch, Rudden, & Shapiro, 2004):

» the young person can manage depressive feelings and aggression better;

» the young person is less prone to guilt and self-devaluation;

» the young person can make more realistic assessments of his or her own behaviour and motivation and that of others;

» the young person has a better developed sense of agency;

» the young person has a better capacity to be thoughtful rather than to express his or her emotions through action ("act out");

» the young person has a more realistic view of what he or she is responsible for and of the difference between internal and external phantasy and reality;

» the young person is less vulnerable to depression in the face of loss, disappointment, and criticism;

» the young person has developed a sense of his or her own identity.

The principles and techniques of treatment set out below are followed in order to maximize the opportunities for young people to achieve these outcomes—in particular, to manage current depressive feelings better (symptomatic improvement) and to become less vulnerable to depression (enhancing resilience).

Transference, unconscious communication, and the therapeutic relationship

Transference and unconscious communication

The transference relationship is central to STPP, as it is to all forms of psychotherapy that pay attention to unconscious mental life. It may become manifest through verbal communication, but it may also take the form of placing the therapist in the position of experiencing some of the patient's problematic feelings, in the hope that these feelings may prove to be manageable. (This may be the result of projective identification, as discussed above.) For example, some young people may ask the therapist, implicitly or explicitly, to fulfil various roles in a drama, such as the role of being excluded, and to express appropriate emotions about this. This can be a useful form of communication, but the therapist may also have to consider whether it is being used to control him or her or the scope of the work if it becomes habitual. (See Boston & Szur, 1983; Sandler, 1976.)

Such aspects of the relationship constitute an important part of the therapeutic experience, since it is hypothesized that the therapist's ability to deal with difficult experiences will be internalized and henceforward will become part of the young person's own equipment (Bion, 1962a). These internalized qualities are applicable beyond any specific insight that may have been achieved, so that the therapeutic experience becomes generalizable rather than being confined to solving specific problems. This is very important in understanding why time-limited work with a specific focus (such as arising from a depression diagnosis) can have a much wider impact on the young person's functioning.

Working directly with the negative transference is also extremely important. The capacity to acknowledge all the young person's negative feelings – pain, rage, destructiveness, hostility, self-destructiveness – and to put them into words and be able to tolerate them without the need to "look on the bright side" is crucial. Being able to allow and tolerate the young person's negative feelings and thoughts in relation to the person of the therapist are important aspects of the STPP process, although from the outside they may appear to indicate a breakdown in the "therapeutic alliance". The development of such negative feelings during the course of the work is especially important in the context of depression, where idealization and denigration, self-hatred, and guilt are likely to be central issues (Emanuel, Miller, & Rustin, 2002; Rhode, 2011; Trowell & Dowling, 2011).

The techniques of interpretation are central aspects of psychoanalytic work, and these are described below ("Varieties of interpretation"). The concept of the "mutative interpretation" originates with Strachey (1934), who argued that interpretation within the transference relationship had the power to bring about profound change by encouraging the patient to recognize his or her unconscious instincts, particularly aggressive ones.

The therapeutic alliance

The concept of the "therapeutic alliance", "treatment alliance", or "working alliance" is now widely used in all types of therapy, and research consistently indicates that establishing such an alliance in the early stages of treatment is a predictor of good outcome (Martin, Garske, & Davis, 2000; Norcross, 2011). (It is also sometimes referred to as the "therapeutic relationship", although it is more helpful to reserve this term for the relationship in its broadest sense.) The concept was first developed within the psychoanalytic tradition (Zetzel, 1956), with clear roots in Freud's concept of the positive transference which he described not only as "unobjectionable" but also as "the vehicle of success" (1912b, p. 105). Freud also described the patient as a "collaborator" with the doctor (Freud, 1895d) and the analytic situation as a "pact . . . to give [the patient's] ego back its mastery over lost provinces of his mental life" (1940a, p. 173).

Greenson and Wexler (Greenson, 1967; Greenson & Wexler, 1969) delineated three aspects of the therapeutic relationship: the transference relationship; the "real relationship", based on the patient's accurate observation of the therapist and their relationship; and the "working alliance". They defined the working alliance as "the non-neurotic, rational, reasonable rapport which the patient has with his analyst and which enables him to work purposefully in the analytic situation despite his transference impulses" (Greenson & Wexler, 1969, p. 29), which might at any time "contain elements of the infantile neurosis which will eventually require analysis" (Greenson, 1967, p. 193). Luborsky (1976), also working in the psychodynamic tradition, distinguished between the therapeutic alliance in the early stages of treatment and that in the later stages. In the early stages, the alliance is characterized by the patient's perception of the support and help of the therapist; in the latter stages, by the feeling of joint work towards overcoming the patient's distress. More recently, Nuttall (2000) has drawn on the concept of containment (Bion, 1962a) to define the therapeutic alliance as "the dependable and understanding container in which [therapeutic change] can take place" (p. 23). In psychoanalytic child psychotherapy practice, the conceptualization of the alliance as a container may be based on the idea of "gathering the transference" (Meltzer, 1967) and the patient's anxieties within the relationship to the therapist, which will necessarily include both positive and negative elements.

Conceptualizations such as Greenson's leave space for the separate consideration of transference and therapeutic alliance, while acknowledging their dynamic interaction. It should be borne in mind that both "resistance" and "negative transference" are key elements of STPP and should not be considered as contrary to a good therapeutic alliance; indeed, working through these elements may be seen as taking place within the broad framework of a therapeutic alliance and should thus be seen as a central aspect of it. (This is further elaborated as part of the middle stage of STPP under "Deepening of the transference relationship" in chapter 4.)

The development of the therapeutic alliance concept in other models of psychotherapy has somewhat changed the original meaning of the term, especially within the humanistic tradition, where the emphasis has been on the therapist's empathy and warmth. Several empirical measures of the therapeutic alliance have drawn upon Bordin's (1979) distinction between three different components: agreement on tasks, agreement on goals, and the bond between patient and therapist. Terms such as "tasks" and "goals" are not ones that are fully consistent with the therapeutic method of STPP, although the idea of treatment "goals" can be more helpfully reframed as one of overarching "aims", in a way that is consistent with psychoanalytic practice (Emanuel, Catty, Anscombe, Cantle, & Muller, 2014; Meltzer, 1969), and operationalized helpfully as "hopes and expectations" (Urwin, 2009). (Using aims- or goals-based measures in the context of routine outcome monitoring is discussed under "Setting-up, reviews, collaboration, and routine outcome monitoring" in chapter 5.)

The therapeutic alliance has been the subject of a vast amount of empirical research (Martin, Garske, & Davis, 2000; Norcross, 2011) which has far outweighed discussions of it in the clinical literature (Wynn Parry & Birkett, 1996; Catty, 2006). The empirical research has established strong associations between the therapeutic alliance and therapeutic outcome, although it may have misleadingly implied that the alliance is curative in itself (Catty, 2006), in contrast to clinical psychoanalytic perspectives on the alliance that see it as "a necessary, but not a sufficient, condition of therapeutic change" (Hanley, 1994, p. 457).

Therapeutic alliance research over the last decade has increasingly paid attention to the role of fluctuations in the alliance, or "ruptures" and "repairs" (Safran, Muran, & Eubanks-Carter, 2011). There have been some indications that in a successful treatment there is a pattern of the therapeutic alliance being good at the start of treatment, then appearing to get "worse" or suffering a "rupture", which if worked on or "repaired" leads to improvement in the alliance before the end of treatment (Safran, Muran, & Eubanks-Carter, 2011). This would seem to provide empirical support for the emphasis of psychoanalytic psychotherapy on working with the negative as well as positive transference. Indeed, Long and Trowell (2001) found in a study of sexually abused girls that those who did well had therapists who were able to address the negative transference, particularly in the ending stage (as well as having parents who engaged in the treatment).

Techniques

While working in the transference and interpreting unconscious material are the key principles of psychoanalytic technique in STPP, as they are in longer term psychoanalytic psychotherapy, it is also useful to deploy a range of other interventions; the key task is to achieve a balance between these elements. Both interpretations and other, non-interpretive interventions may make use of four modes of intervention (AACAP, 2012, p. 554):

» direct – the therapist refers directly to the child or young person's immediate appearance or behaviour (description);

» therapist-related mode – the therapist refers to the child or young person's perceptions in terms of the transference (how the therapist is seen at this moment);

» indirect – the therapist refers to the child's or young person's behaviour through the metaphors of play or other people (see "Interpretations in displacement" below);

» therapist's perspective – the therapist comments on his or her own thoughts, encouraging the patient to take these into account.

Reflection on the most useful technique to use with a particular patient is a focus of the ongoing supervision necessary to support effective time-limited work and should be linked to the case formulation that emerges from the assessment period. Supervision is especially important to clarify the nature of the transference and to help in formulating what can be offered in interpretation.

Varieties of interpretation

An interpretation is any intervention in which the therapist makes explicit latent aspects of the material, particularly with reference to unconscious processes. Interpretation will be informed by the therapist's overall formulation of the young person's anxieties and defences and exploration of aspects of the total pattern of unconscious phantasy (Joseph, 1985). Interpretation is central to psychoanalytic technique and may take several forms, as detailed below.

Transference interpretations

Appropriate transference interpretations will, for many young people, be crucial to the degree to which the therapy becomes a lasting internal resource. All the issues that arise will have some bearing on the developing transference and countertransference and will need, at least to some extent, to be addressed as related to the young person's feelings towards their therapist (Alvarez, 2012; Mitrani, 2001; Roth, 2001). It is important to get the balance and timing right in dealing with the transference, on the one hand, and in making links with current and past external experiences, on the other. It is the opportunity offered by the therapeutic relationship to learn new ways of relating that will be the agent of change (Fonagy, 1999; Rustin, 1999), and, because of this, work in the transference is essential. Adolescents can be particularly vulnerable to feeling trapped, however, and care must be taken to acknowledge the importance of the experience outside the therapy, as brought to the sessions – for example, in peer relationships, including relationships with boyfriends or girlfriends, and with siblings – and to use all these elements as building blocks for exploration of the transference. Elements of transference are likely to be present in any of the other varieties of interpretation described here.

Interpretations in displacement

Interpretations in displacement (A. Freud, 1966; Hurry, 1998) are widely used in psychoanalytic child and adolescent psychotherapy. With some children who are particularly frightened of a direct relationship with the therapist, the technique of ascribing feelings to characters in their play, without immediately relating them to the child and the therapist, can be particularly useful. For example, with a younger child, the therapist might comment, "the baby bear seems to be so angry that the mummy bear has gone away". An extension of this technique also relevant to older adolescents relates to describing feelings in the room without immediately attempting to locate them in either the patient or the therapist ("It feels as though finishing for today is really difficult").

Patient- and therapist-centred interpretations

Steiner (1993) has discussed criteria for choosing a "patient-centred" or an "analyst-centred" interpretation in terms of how much of his own experience a patient is equipped to own at a given time:

> Some analysts, in these circumstances [where the patient experiences interpretations as having something he or she cannot cope with being pushed back at him or her], tend to phrase their interpretations in a form which recognizes that the patient is more interested in what is going on in the *analyst's* mind than in his own. . . . I think of such interpretations as *analyst-centred* and differentiate them from *patient-centred* interpretations, which are of the classical kind in which something the patient is doing, thinking, or wishing is interpreted. . . . In general, patient-centred interpretations are more concerned with conveying understanding, whereas analyst-centred interpretations are more likely to give the patient a sense of being understood. [p. 133, emphasis in original]

One might say, for example, to a very withdrawn young person who cannot feel any curiosity about his or her emotions, "Perhaps I am to know something of how frightening it is to be aware of any feelings". Casaula, Coloma, Colzani, and Jordan (1997) have usefully distinguished the mental work necessary for the formulation of an interpretation from the choice of appropriate means for communicating it to the patient.

Process interpretations

Process interpretations are those that focus on the therapist's observation of the nature of the process in a session rather than the content of what is being said. For instance, the therapist might say, around the middle of a session that has been filled with a great deal of anxiously imparted detail from the young person, "There has been a lot to tell me about today, so much so that I've noticed that I haven't said a great deal. I wonder whether it's hard for you to believe that I might want to help you with these upsetting events that have been going on."

"Feeling" interpretations

A feeling interpretation makes explicit and names a feeling that may have been unconscious. This signals the value of verbal thought, which is fundamental to psychoanalytic psychotherapy. The therapist might say, for instance, "Although you have been talking about how annoying people have been to you at school recently, I have noticed that you don't sound annoyed about it; in fact, you sound really sad."

Defence interpretations

Defence interpretations focus on the means by which the young person attempts to manage or protect him/herself from the perceived danger of an impulse, feeling, or thought. Recognizing the importance of such defences may be a first step in allowing them to be considered and possibly modified. The therapist might say, for instance: "You seem to be telling me that you understand how low your friend is and how that makes her behave in a really demanding way towards you. I wonder whether you also feel quite angry with her about that – but maybe you really don't want her to know that or to risk having an argument with her." Here the therapist would have in mind the need to link the young girl's defence with her anxiety (Segal, 1973, pp. 117–124): that she is defending against her anger with her friend because of her anxiety about upsetting her, and that this may be an indication of a much more profound worry about whether those she cares about can tolerate or withstand her emotions.

Basic clinical techniques

Description/clarification

A descriptive commentary on the young person's narrative, along with basic clarification about the young person's communications, serves the essential function of making the young person realize that he or she is being attended to and thought about. Bibring (1954),described the process of clarification as follows:

> Clarification . . . does . . . not refer to unconscious (repressed or otherwise warded off) material but to conscious and/or preconscious processes, of which the patient is not sufficiently aware, which escape his attention but which he recognises more or less readily when they are clearly presented to him. [p. 755]

A simple reflection of the events and feelings the young person is describing can also provide a validation of his or her viewpoint, emotions, and indeed identity. These techniques can usefully support the process of containment, which Sorenson (1997) emphasizes is performed by "an active and responsive mind which is performing certain actions" (p. 118).

Validation

Validation is an intervention that conveys to the young person that his or her feelings have been understood, or that his or her circumstances are really seen to be as he or she described them, as far as the therapist knows. It conveys that the patient's feelings and thoughts have worth. For instance, the therapist might acknowledge the degree of pressure being put on the patient by the demand to sit school or public examinations. This type of intervention may be particularly relevant to young people who have been substantially projected into, or with those with a more borderline grasp on reality which frightens them. With the latter, the therapist might, for instance, agree with the patient that a sound heard during the session is coming from outside the room (rather than from inside the young person's mind). Particular tact may be required in the use of validating interventions where the delicate area of family relationships is concerned. The therapist may, for instance, wish to validate the patient's painful experience of living with a parent with a mental health problem of his or her own, while taking care not to be misinterpreted as blaming the parent; careful attention to the countertransference is likely to be required here.

Mirroring

Mirroring is a process of reflecting on or acknowledging the young person's feelings which may focus on what is being communicated emotionally (e.g., "It really hurts") or on how it is being conveyed in his or her behaviour (e.g., to a young person very bent over so as to hide his or her face, "What we've been talking about seems to feel really private"). Alternatively, this can be done in displacement, so that, for instance, the young person's feelings might be attributed by the therapist to a character in a story that the young person has told, or to a character in the play of younger patients. Mirroring interventions are especially important for young people who lack a coherent sense of identity, as is frequently the case for those suffering from depression. It is therefore essential that the interpretation of unconscious conflict with this patient group be underpinned by this sort of mirroring work, which conveys that the therapist has noticed something important.

Questioning

Although discussion is led by the young person, the therapist may use questions both to help the young person elaborate what he or she is saying and to clarify aspects of what he or she is describing. With very silent young people, the therapist also needs to make particular use of close observation and attention to countertransference reactions (as described in chapter 7).

Confrontation

Confrontation is a technique that is fundamental to psychoanalytic psychotherapy. Busch, Rudden, and Shapiro (2004) describe it as:

> a thoughtful, empathic, but strongly worded statement about a patient's self-destructive or aggressive behaviour. . . . Phrases often used to point out such behaviours include: "Have you

noticed that you are . . . ?" and "It may have slipped by you, but each time I have suggested x, you have tended to . . . ". [p. 59]

It is essential that the therapist bring a sense of curiosity, or an enquiring attitude, to such an intervention, to help mitigate any possibility of the patient feeling criticized.

Working with dreams

Dream work is likely to arise more with young people at the older end of the age range, though some younger adolescents and indeed children also bring dreams (Rustin, 2009a). The therapist will help the young person to explore his or her private associations to the elements of the dream, in order to gain a greater understanding of the latent content as well as the immediately apparent manifest content (Freud, 1900a). This can provide a window onto important unconscious processes in a way that carries conviction to the young person, to whom the experience of a dream may feel profoundly real. It can also indicate both a growing ability to distinguish between inner reality and external happenings and an enrichment of contact with inner experience. It is helpful to mention the usefulness of dreams in psychotherapy during the assessment or initial sessions.

Delivering interpretations and other interventions

The phrasing of interpretations is frequently a major technical challenge. Some young people with variable ability to be clear about what they are and are not responsible for can feel threatened by interpretations of fears and wishes unless these are very carefully phrased. They can, for example, misinterpret the formulation of a fear as a description of reality (Alvarez, 1992a). Without providing reassurance, it may be helpful to rephrase a potential interpretation that the patient may hear as a threat and feel trapped by. Alvarez (1992a) describes a little girl with borderline psychosis:

> Although she panicked at every parting, however brief, I could never, in the early years, say that she imagined something terrible might happen to one of us during a weekend break: I had to turn the idea around, and talk to her about her difficulty in believing

that both of us might make it through and meet again on Monday. [p. 115]

Similarly, Alvarez emphasizes the importance, with severely depressed young people, of not undermining the beginnings of potency and hope by interpreting them as omnipotent or manic defences: "The distinction between manic states which are a denial of depression and states which signal a recovery from depression is absolutely vital, and if the therapist confuses the two she may really succeed in killing hope for her depressed patients" (p. 132).

Holding projections depends on working in the countertransference towards the containment of psychic pain. Therapists working with severely depressed adolescents, like those working with severely deprived children (Boston & Szur, 1983), need to be able to manage communications of despair, worthlessness, exclusion, and so on. Very often a comment such as, "Perhaps I need to understand what it feels like to be completely useless/helpless/no good" can be particularly helpful and will need to precede any kind of implication that the feeling in question actually belongs to the young person. When this kind of attribution is made prematurely, the young person may misinterpret the therapist's comment as though the therapist were attempting to fix him or her in an unendurable position and may react by becoming manic, destructive, or impervious. Mitrani (2001) argues that the process of establishing a containing object in the patient's mind depends crucially on different aspects of the therapist's containing function, which, developing Bion's ideas, she delineates as reverie (or "taking the transference"), transformation, and publication (or interpretation).

With young people who are particularly frightened of their own aggression or anxious about their developing sexuality, as very depressed young people often are, the negative transference during treatment will need tactful handling. This emphasis comes from the psychoanalytic theoretical model of depression, according to which problems in managing aggression in interpersonal contexts can lead to aggression being turned against the self (see chapter 1). This can often be achieved by a description of what kind of qualities the young people feel the therapist would need to have in order for them to feel safe. This implicitly recognizes their fear that the therapist might not have such qualities. At the same time, it demonstrates the therapist's understanding of their needs and fears. For example, if a young person describes an uncaring teacher who does not like children, it might feel insensitive and invalidating for the therapist not to acknowledge the emotional reality of this experience before making a transference interpretation.

Transference interpretations often need to start with clarification of the young person's feelings towards the therapist, in general or at that moment; for instance, in the previous example, the therapist might say, "I wonder whether it feels like I don't really care about what you're going through either". For a young person who is especially vulnerable, this may be the full extent of the transference interpretation that can be made at this point. With another young person, the therapist might choose to make a further link between the patient's feelings about the teacher and therapist and the young person's more deep-seated feelings about the most significant figures in his or her life, such as, "perhaps this is making you feel that nobody really understands what you're going through, not your mother, nor your teacher, nor me". Avoidance of speaking about the direct relationship with the therapist can compound the young person's sense of fragility if he or she fears that the therapist is avoiding difficult matters. Roth (2001) argues that transference interpretations may be at different "levels": from interpretations that link current issues in the therapy to events in the patient's history, through those that link events in the patient's external world to his or her phantasies about the analyst or analysis, to those that foreground the patient's use of the analyst to enact unconscious phantasy.

Some young people may be very disturbed and/or very wary of involvement with the therapist or others. Such young people often have insufficient symbolic capacity to make use of the kind of verbal interpretations that would be helpful with other young people. This lack of symbolic capacity means that they often have difficulty in sustaining the "pretend" element of transference work, so that a clumsily phrased transference interpretation can feel to them as though they were being asked to take responsibility for everything that had gone wrong in their lives. In thinking about technique with these young people, Bion's (1962a) work on containment and Alvarez's (1992a) work in relation to children who have been traumatized or abused, or who suffer from psychosis or borderline psychosis, are particularly helpful.

This is not to say that transference interpretations should be avoided with such young people. Indeed, they are often the essential currency of the therapy. There must, however, be careful and tactful attention paid to timing, "dose" (the amount of transference material named and its emotional intensity), and phrasing; also, due acknowledgement must be made of actual external circumstances; furthermore, the ground must be prepared through the use of the other techniques already mentioned (Rhode, 1997; see also Hurry, 1998; Meltzer, 1976). This kind of tact may, of course, also be needed in relation to other techniques—perhaps, in particular, questioning or confrontation. Some very depressed young people may find even mirroring interventions difficult if these feel (to them, by their very nature) intrusive. Such young people, particularly if they find it difficult to speak freely to the therapist and are rather silent, may be especially "attuned to the non-verbal aspects of [the] relationship, such as the tone of [the therapist's] voice" (Magagna, 2012, p. 103).

Technique with younger adolescents

Working with patients at the younger end of the adolescent age range, such as younger teenagers, may have important implications for technique. This is likely to depend more on the young person's stage of emotional development than on their chronological age. Young patients are more likely to need their parents or carers to participate in parent work as part of the STPP model; conversely, much older adolescents may not wish their parents to be involved.

Some younger adolescent patients may find it helpful for art or play materials to be provided. These may be made available from the beginning of the treatment or offered after the therapy has started. What is offered, how such materials are introduced to the patient, how they are kept private and safe, and what happens to them at the end of the therapy are matters for the individual clinician's judgement. The provision of art or play materials may be of particular help for young people who present with emotional immaturity or who have difficulty in talking about their feelings and anxieties. Such patients may, through the manipulation of concrete materials, be able to generate and communicate meaning in symbolic form that can become shared and further elaborated with the therapist. Art and play materials may also be of use with some younger adolescents who feel easily persecuted and intruded upon. For them, the possibility of using such materials will allow the development of curiosity and thereby facilitate the investigation of their internal world by themselves and their therapist. [See also Joseph's (1998) discussion of the setting and Rustin's (1971, 2009a) accounts of adolescents' use of writing in sessions.]

The following vignette shows how a younger adolescent, "Jacob", was helped to engage in his therapy by the provision of play material.

Jacob, aged 12, was a middle child in a single-parent family where there were five siblings. The mother's current partner was the father of the youngest sibling, while Jacob and the other children all had different fathers who were not actively involved in their lives. Jacob was considerably smaller than his peers, and it was hard to believe that he was of secondary-school age. He was also socially immature and often got into fights with other boys. He had difficulty in maintaining concentration in his lessons. His referral to the multidisciplinary clinic was for behavioural reasons, but on assessment this presentation was found to mask moderate to severe depression.

Before meeting with Jacob, the therapist met with his mother and her partner to give them an opportunity to tell her about their concerns. They described Jacob as having always been quite sensitive and not someone who would readily talk about his worries or feelings. They also described him as being rather inhibited with adults; the therapist wondered whether he was a boy who could easily feel intruded upon. He liked to draw, however, and to play like a younger child. With this in mind, the therapist prepared a therapy box for him that contained play materials for him to use in his sessions. The simple selection of coloured felt pens, paper, three small pots of playdough, string, sellotape, glue, pencil, eraser, and foam tennis-sized ball were chosen with a view to encouraging creativity without suggesting any particular form of play. There was also the hope that the play materials might reduce the intensity of the one-to-one encounter with the therapist, as directly talking about anxieties might feel too difficult.

On meeting Jacob, he appeared much younger than his age. He was tiny in stature, and his school uniform seemed to swamp him. He seemed uncomfortable with the therapist at first. She introduced the work and the setting by explaining that she was someone who was there to help him with his worries. They would meet weekly in the same room and at the same time for 50 minutes each time, for 28 sessions. His box and his folder (for drawings to be kept in) were for him to use and would be kept solely for his use. The therapist would look after them for him between the sessions. Just as she would keep his materials safe, so she would also keep a place for him in her mind, even when it was not a day for him to come to the clinic. Jacob took to this idea straight away; nodding, he wrote his name on his folder and silently examined the contents of his box. Symbolically, he seemed to be claiming his thinking space.

The themes of being noticed and remembered became a significant theme in the work. By the thirteenth session, Jacob had really caught on to the idea that his play, his words, and even his demeanour could have meaning in the context of his therapy, and he delighted in anticipating the sort of interpretations his therapist might be expected to make. The following is an account of part of a session that took place shortly before Christmas, when he and his therapist had just been discussing the forthcoming break from their work. The therapist had made him a calendar to show him graphically when the break would be and, crucially, when the therapy would start again.

Jacob took out the red playdough and carefully gathered up tiny fragments of dough as he emptied the pot onto the table ready for moulding. The therapist talked about him wanting to gather up the pieces of playdough which might be easily overlooked. Perhaps, she added, he felt a bit like the tiny bits of dough. Jacob confirmed this: "Left out", he commented with a nod. The therapist acknowledged that he had told her about his worry about possible family tensions at Christmas, but that he also had hope that she could keep him in her mind and think about him, keeping his box and folder safe until they met again in January. Jacob responded by making a playdough ring for his finger, and they spoke about how he might be thinking about his link with his therapy and his link with the therapist. He glanced at the therapist very briefly and then began flattening the playdough, using a felt pen as a rolling-pin, and using the dough pot as a template to cut out circles of dough, telling her that he was making "mince pies". He used his circles to make "pastry" lids for the empty pots, reinforcing them with a sausage-shaped piece of dough. He curved the dough carefully round the edges of the pastry lids as he told the therapist that this was the "crust, to make them stronger".

The therapist spoke about the pie standing for the therapy as something that helped Jacob to feel strengthened. To her surprise, Jacob showed her that he understood this metaphor and volunteered that his feelings could be the "meat" in the pie. They spent a few more minutes thinking about the changes in him since he had started to come to therapy, the importance for him of feeling valued, and that although it was hard to have a break, he really felt that there was a place here for his feelings. The therapist added that, in the long run, there was a hope that he would learn better ways to manage his feelings for himself.

Jacob nodded and carried on with his play, silently and thoughtfully, until the therapist told him that they had just five more minutes until it would be time to go. Jacob glanced at the clock, displaying only the smallest signs of disappointment, but in a stabbing gesture and with clenched teeth, he punctured several holes in his pastry lid, telling the therapist that they were "to let off steam". The therapist responded by making links to his really angry feelings about both the Christmas break and the end of the session, but she reminded him that the therapy was a place where he could safely let off steam. She also reminded him that there were three more sessions before the Christmas break, so they would have more time to think about it.

In this session, we can see how Jacob was able to use the play materials to express himself in ways he could not readily express through verbal language alone. His enjoyment of possibilities for expressing himself through the metaphor of play were a revelation for a boy whose depression was in large part an expression of despair about his capacity to communicate and to have his thoughts and feelings understood.

Case management, collaborative working, and psychiatric issues

The child psychotherapist offering STPP will also need to liaise with members of the multidisciplinary team when this is needed to support the therapy, manage risk, or review overall progress. This will include the consideration and management of medication such as antidepressants, where the degree of depression warrants discussion of risk, concerns about self-harm, psychotic thinking, or any sudden increase in depressive symptom severity.

In the multidisciplinary clinic context, it is usual clinical practice for the young person undergoing STPP to have a case manager (sometimes called a "lead practitioner", "case holder", or "care coordinator") with overall responsibility for holding oversight in relation to the various aspects of the clinic's involvement with the young person, family, and network. Who holds this position will vary according to local clinic or service cultures, resources, and contexts, and from case to case, depending on clinical need, risk, and so on. In STPP work, the young person's therapist may also be the case manager. This role could, however, equally well be held by the STPP parent worker, or perhaps a third member of the multidisciplinary team (e.g., a child and adolescent psychiatrist). Whoever carries these responsibilities, it is important that the framework of the young person's treatment be respected and maintained, given the nature of the psychoanalytic approach. This includes all involved clinicians maintaining a distinct boundary around the young person's STPP treatment and for communications between clinicians, young person, parents/carers, and those in the network (e.g., school, college, or social worker) to be mindful of this. This is also necessary given the developmental tasks and anxieties of adolescence, where there is a need for the young person to experience some separation and privacy from his or her parents (and other adults) while also being dependent upon the non-intrusive presence and availability of parental figures. The young person in STPP treatment is likely to need to know that the familial or professional network exists and is alert to his or her difficulties and needs; the young person also needs to know that the network is able to contain its own anxieties about him or her and thus allow a protected emotional space and individual therapeutic relationship within the therapy to develop in its own right.

In the context of the structure outlined above, the clinicians will need to agree prior to the start of the treatment the arrangements required in relation to this particular patient or family regarding communication between themselves. The function, form, and frequency of meetings between the clinicians involved will all need to be considered. As with all clinical work within a multidisciplinary service, this is a dynamic situation and the arrangements agreed initially may need reviewing as the STPP treatment proceeds and the clinical knowledge of the young person and family develops. For instance, specific concerns regarding risk or safeguarding will necessitate close cooperation, communication, and sharing of clinical tasks. Other issues, however, will also bear upon the clinicians involved with the young person and the family: for instance, there may be familial dynamics that, in an unconscious or subtle way, impact on the functioning of the clinical team, leading to widely differing clinical views or conflicts between colleagues. In some cases, these may have emotional resonances with the family functioning, or they may be understood as arising from the different relationships with the various family members being experienced by the various clinicians. When there is a larger network of professionals involved, the potential for differences of view (sometimes helpful, sometimes not) increases. The case manager is the person who is responsible for keeping a watchful eye on the overall clinical situation and for ensuring that there is a helpful framework for communication within the clinic, between the clinic and the family, and between the clinic and the wider network.

Concurrent psychiatric treatment and use of medication

There may be times when greater medical involvement, including the supplementary use of medication, proves necessary. This may be indicated by the degree of severity and persistence of the young person's depression, indications of psychotic symptoms, or other presentations of concern such as panic attacks or physical symptoms.

Any decision to prescribe medication naturally needs to be made by psychiatric colleagues, whose responsibility it will be, but it is helpful to collaborate in sharing information and clinical understanding that will inform the decision to prescribe, involving the parent worker if parallel parent work is taking place. The multidisciplinary team will be guided in the UK by the NICE guideline on depression in children and young people (NICE, 2015), which recommends that combined therapy of fluoxetine and a psychological therapy should be considered for initial treatment of moderate to severe depression (2.2.10.4), with fluoxetine offered if the depression is unresponsive after four to six sessions (2.2.10.7). The guideline is clear that antidepressant medication should not be used without a concurrent psychological therapy (2.2.10.9).

Even if parents or carers are not engaged in parent work, their collaboration in supporting the decision-making process is valuable in supporting and monitoring the young person's medication. It is interesting to note that in the IMPACT trial, the young people offered STPP were mostly not receiving medication; requests for medication were often explored within therapy sessions and did not then lead to medication being prescribed. The issue of psychotic symptoms is discussed further below (see "Psychotic symptoms" in chapter 7).

It is important to distinguish between situations in which medication, or another medical intervention, is necessary or even essential alongside therapy, and others in which the request for it may primarily be an expression of the high levels of anxiety that can be a feature of work with seriously depressed young people. One possibility is that the young person and/or the parents may get in touch with the psychiatrist (if already known to them) or the case manager in order to request medication or, indeed, to convey their anxiety or dissatisfaction. This may be an appropriate request, but it may also be an expression of their lack of confidence in the therapy at this point. (This is discussed further in chapter 7.) Where the latter is the case, it will be particularly important for it to be made clear that the treatment team will together formulate their response. This is important because it is a common behaviour pattern in adolescence to play parents off against each other, a pattern that can be replicated in the treatment setting. Many young people with moderate to severe depression have parents who are separated or whose relationship is conflictual (Trowell et al., 2003, 2007). In such situations, it is particularly helpful for professionals to model cooperative relationships.

Suicidality, self-harm, and risk assessment

Anderson (2008) locates the suicidal behaviour in young people in relation to the developmental demands of adolescence:

> The adolescent has to move from everything being orientated upwards towards the parents and the adult world, to becoming an adult who is capable of being a parent. This means that all the more disturbed parts of the personality have to be helped into the new situation. In those vulnerable adolescents the violent and murderous version of human relations which exists in all of us breaks out from its place of residence in the mind and can be played out in reality. [p. 71]

Anderson relates suicidal behaviour to Bion's (1957) concept of the psychotic part of the personality which develops "when the degree of violent explosiveness is not contained for the baby" and is "dominated by a preference for projection and evacuation" (Anderson, 2008, pp. 66, 67). In understanding such behaviour, Bell (2008) argues that "suicide attempts never take place for the stated reason" (p. 48) and are often motivated by an unconscious desire to inflict pain on the parents or carers (p. 50).

Today's young people are often keenly aware of the reality of mental illness, including among their peers. Suicidal thoughts are likely to occur in the treatment of many, particularly among older adolescents. It will be important for the therapist to be aware of this and to enquire specifically whether the young person is thinking about suicide if the material suggests this and if the young person does not mention it him/herself. The fact that the therapist can entertain the possibility of suicidal thoughts or actions can in itself provide substantial steadying. This may not be sufficient, however, even when the associated emotional constellations can be accurately assessed and interpreted, to ensure the patient's safety. The therapist will in this case need to make clear to the young person that he or she (the therapist) has the obligation to consult other professionals, and possibly to inform the parents, in the interests of the young person's safety, which *in extremis* takes precedence over the duty of confidentiality.

The professional network here would include the parent worker, the case manager, and the supervisor. There will also be instances where a psychiatric assessment is necessary and where the use of medication or hospitalization may need to be considered. This will be with the aim of keeping the young person safe in the immediate term, and this needs to be made explicit. In many cases, the knowledge that professionals are working together to respond to a communication that is taken seriously will in itself have a stabilizing effect. It is also important for the clinic team to establish good communication with the young person's physician or GP from the start. Holidays may be a time in which suicidal impulses are exacerbated, and it needs to be made clear, both to the young person and to the parents, what cover arrangements are in place. The young person may also convey intense anxiety about suicidality to his or her parents, siblings, or friends. Families, and sometimes the school, will require support in managing these communications and in responding appropriately.

Apart from such crises, it is anticipated that a routine risk assessment in line with clinical governance requirements will be carried out once a term, in the context of preparing termly summaries. It is essential that any material suggesting suicidal ideation should be communicated to the case manager and recorded in the file. Cases where inpatient admission or day hospital treatment are indicated are discussed in chapter 7.

Referral for STPP

How young people are referred to STPP will vary depending on the individual clinic's usual practice in managing referrals. Here, we make a distinction between a young person being referred for STPP within the clinic, which will include some consideration of his or her suitability, and conducting a psychoanalytic psychotherapy assessment, which will focus particularly on the young person's openness to thinking about him/herself and coming to a formulation of his or her difficulties. Deciding to make a referral might be done by members of the multidisciplinary team based on information received from the GP and an initial generic appointment or appointments, followed perhaps by consultation with the psychotherapist who might be able to offer STPP. We suggest that this should be informed by the guidance given in this chapter, which draws on our discussion of the evidence (both empirical and clinical) on suitability under "Suitability for psychodynamic psychotherapy: the evidence" in chapter 2.

By contrast, a psychoanalytic psychotherapy assessment would be conducted by a child psychotherapist; this might be done as a free-standing assessment (of three or four sessions, depending on the therapist's usual practice within the clinic) or as part of the early stages of STPP treatment. On occasion, where it is done as a free-standing assessment, the assessing psychotherapist might not be the one to conduct the STPP treatment but might, instead, refer on to a colleague (e.g., if the assessing therapist refers the young person for STPP to a colleague, including a trainee psychotherapist).

The referral process

Referral for STPP in a clinic context has to be embedded in the established care pathway and the pattern of first response to referrals. While this is not uniform either nationally or internationally, it is clear that the trend is towards the initial contact being generic across cases and that it is increasingly likely to include some routine screening tools and to be undertaken by staff with varying levels of skill and diverse therapeutic expectations.

To link the clinic's usual assessment processes to the referral for STPP, the clinic would need to be committed to the idea of routine thinking about what cases should go where. Some clinics, for instance, may consider having a direct pathway from the initial contact to referral for STPP assessment for severely depressed young people, bypassing the brief interventions that are routinely offered in some settings. The first contact would then have to include whatever routine tools or screening processes are in place in the service, together with an explanation that an assessment for STPP is an option, if the clinician judges that the referral information and the first contact suggest that course of action. (Routine outcome monitoring in relation to STPP is discussed in "Setting-up, reviews, collaboration, and routine outcome monitoring" in chapter 5.)

If agreement on a pathway can be achieved, an exploration of the suitability of STPP for the young person can then follow. As indicated above, this will involve exploration with the family about their capacity to support the young person's therapy and to attend regularly themselves (depending on the age of the young person).

In the first consultation, important questions would be: "Does the young person respond with interest to the idea of being seen on his or her own?" and "Are the parents or carers interested in the idea that consultations for them would be part of the package?" The age of the young person referred is also very significant in determining what STPP would entail. Younger adolescents (between age 11 and 14 years) need the support of family and school in accessing treatment; for them, parent work is vital. Older adolescents, especially those over 16 years, are likely to be taking responsibility for their attendance, and their individual motivation is thus a central issue. (This would also be relevant for the young adults aged 18 to 24 years for whom services are being developed and for whom we anticipate STPP will be appropriate.)

If there is a high level of risk, such as suicidal behaviour, a clear team structure around the case needs to be established before therapy begins, and this would also apply if the treatment plan was for immediate referral to STPP with a period of assessment in the early weeks. This might involve a preliminary psychiatric consultation for the patient, if this had not already taken place. Similar requirements arise if the case involves medication or is likely to do so, and if there are active child-safeguarding issues that need to be tackled at the outset.

Time-limited therapy requires careful placement in the calendar year. It is not helpful to start very close to a holiday break, and it is vital to have the parent work ready to start at more or less the same time as the young person's therapy. If a gap is thus necessary between the completion of the referral process (such as an initial meeting) and the start of therapy, a plan for careful case management during this gap is likely to be required.

Considerations in referral for STPP

As described in chapter 2 (under "Suitability for psychodynamic psychotherapy: the evidence"), there is little empirical evidence to guide decision-making about the personal qualities of a young person that make him or her more or less suitable for psychoanalytic work, while received wisdom from work with adults (such as the idea of "psychological-mindedness") does not match the clinical experience of child psychotherapists in general or those experienced in using STPP. In referring for STPP, multidisciplinary colleagues would therefore most helpfully consider the type of problem and the context.

The type of problem

STPP may be indicated where the young person is diagnosed with moderate to severe depression, including the more treatment-resistant "double depression", and for those with co-morbidities (Trowell et al., 2007). Depression may not be identified by the young person, his or her parents, or the network as the only reason or even as the primary reason for referral, but it may be part of a wider range of difficulties. STPP may be particularly indicated for young people with more long-standing and complex relational difficulties (AACAP, 2012), within which the depression is situated. Where transgenerational difficulties are apparent, such as a history of mental health problems in one or other parent or in the wider family, STPP may be particularly helpful, given its strong developmental, familial, and relational framework for understanding the young person's depression, and its commitment to parent work in parallel to the young person's therapy.

There may be some caution about the suitability of STPP for young people with severe behavioural problems or conduct disorder. While there is no evidence that STPP is contraindicated for this group, they are likely to be more difficult to engage.

Characteristics of the context

When young people engage in STPP, it is important that their external world is able to provide them with a sufficient "holding" environment (Winnicott, 1974), including relationships with adults able to provide some "containment" (Bion, 1962a) to help support them with the experience of the psychotherapy and the emotions it may generate. While it is not helpful or necessary to restrict STPP to young people in stable home environments – indeed, difficulties in relationships at home and/or at school are to be expected given the nature of the young people's difficulties – a judgement has to be made about the capacity of the environment and the network to support the young person and his or her therapy. Where the external environment is very unstable – for instance, where there are serious problems with housing or involvement with the youth justice system – the young person may be difficult to engage in STPP. The young person will also need a degree of support in the practical aspects of attendance and engagement from his or her parents or carers, depending on his or her age. Regardless of age, the broad support of the parents or carers for the treatment is extremely helpful, and to some extent this is represented by the parents or carers being prepared to attend parent work as part of the STPP model, as discussed in chapter 5.

Anna: a composite case study

A composite case study of 15-year-old "Anna" is used here and in subsequent chapters to exemplify the stages of STPP as it develops. Anna's referral is illustrative of the typical process of referral for depressed young people, along with the usual generic assessment process within her multidisciplinary clinic which led to the referral for STPP.

Anna: referral

Fifteen-year-old Anna was referred by her GP for persistent low mood at the start of the school summer holiday. She received an initial generic assessment in her local multidisciplinary clinic which indicated that this low mood began after the death of a trusted family friend the previous year. The clinician noted that much of Anna's emotional turmoil and distress seemed to be hidden "proficiently" behind a façade of coping and competently getting on with her education. (Later, in the middle stage of STPP, Anna was to remember the clinician's use of the word "proficiently" and find it helpful in thinking about her need for emotional defences.)

Anna, who identified as black British, lived with her mother, stepfather, 4-year-old half-sister, and baby half-brother. Anna had never known her father, who had split up with her mother after a brief relationship before Anna's birth. Anna's mother had met her stepfather when Anna was about 10 years old. Anna's aunt, the elder sister of her mother, who had played a major role in her early years, had died around the same time, although this did not come out until the early STPP sessions.

At the point of referral, Anna was due to begin her final year of compulsory education and wanted to leave school and go to a further education college for vocational training, which was also causing tension within the family. The initial clinic assessment showed that Anna was suffering long-standing struggles with low mood. Anna described crumpling into tears, struggling with intense headaches which she described as "melt-downs", and feeling that her world was falling apart. The clinician suggested that an assessment for STPP might be appropriate. Consistent with usual practice in this clinic, it was agreed that there would be an initial meeting between the psychotherapist, the parent worker, Anna, and Anna's mother and stepfather, and that this would be followed by a series of three individual sessions for Anna as a psychoanalytic assessment for STPP. If this assessment led to an agreement to proceed, she and her therapist would continue to the end of the 28-week treatment.

CHAPTER FOUR

The stages of treatment in Short-Term Psychoanalytic Psychotherapy

Although STPP is not a structured treatment in which formal "stages" of treatment are explicitly delineated, it is helpful to distinguish some of the tasks and techniques appropriate to its early, middle, and late stages. This chapter outlines some of the main features of the different stages of treatment in STPP. The composite case study of Anna, introduced at the end of the last chapter, is used to illustrate the clinical processes as they unfold through the course of STPP treatment. The case study is also used to demonstrate the writing of two clinical formulation reports: one during the beginning stage, the other at the end of the treatment. The kind of parent work that might typically be conducted for such a case is described in chapter 5, in an illustrative case study of the work conducted with the mother and stepfather of Anna, while some of its implications for supervision are described in chapter 6. Key characteristics and clinical dilemmas are also noted as they are likely to arise during the process of STPP, some of which are explored further in chapter 7.

We begin with an account of the first consultation between Anna, her mother, and the therapist offering STPP.

Anna: initial meeting

Because of a combination of the family's and the professionals' summer holidays, the initial meeting took place in early September. It provided an opportunity for the therapist and the parent worker to introduce the idea of both individual psychotherapy and the parent work element of the STPP treatment model. Both Anna and her mother were receptive and open to embarking on psychotherapy; her stepfather did not attend the initial meeting, but Anna's mother agreed to discuss with him the idea of coming to further sessions with her in the clinic. The only uncertainty was about how they could establish a weekly time slot at a stage when Anna was in a significant school year, with public exams due the following summer. A time was agreed upon, and it was decided that the STPP treatment would begin in October, with the first three sessions or so to be regarded as an assessment, at which point Anna and her therapist would explicitly discuss whether or not to proceed.

The therapist was struck by their all being engaged in an amiable, compliant discussion about practical arrangements. There was little overt expression of anxiety and no apparent concern about Anna's emotional struggles, either from Anna or her mother. This contrasted with the sense of crisis in the GP's referral letter and the initial clinic assessment. Anna's low mood and struggles with bereavement seemed obscured behind a proficient engagement with information delivery and agreement about practical arrangements. It was as if the difficulties had been smoothed over.

It was established that, if they went ahead, the sessions would be weekly, with an acknowledgement that there would be a session during the half-term school break. There would be breaks over the Christmas and Easter period, and these would be clarified well in advance. The parent worker would meet with Anna's mother once a month, who was also encouraged to bring her partner. Despite the enthusiasm with which these arrangements seemed to be met, Anna's therapist wondered whether they would take up the treatment.

The early stages of STPP

As explained above, the psychoanalytic assessment for STPP may be conducted as a free-standing assessment (usually of three or four individual sessions) or within the 28-week STPP contract (for instance, as its first three sessions, followed by an agreement to proceed). In the latter case, it is important that the assessment end with a clear agreement being made between the therapist and the young person as to whether or not the treatment will proceed; the support of parents for continuing with parent work for the duration of the treatment will also need to be established. This chapter is written on the assumption that the assessment is conducted as the first three or four sessions of STPP. Where a psychoanalytic assessment has already been conducted before the start of STPP treatment, some of what is described below will already have been achieved.

A psychoanalytic assessment for STPP within the early stages of the treatment will include the following elements:

» establishing the framework and setting for assessment and treatment;

» balancing information-gathering with reflection on internal experience;

» examining transferential elements and monitoring countertransference;

» exploring the young person's capacity for curiosity and reflection;

» confirming the appropriateness and scope of time-limited work;

» establishing the therapeutic alliance;

» articulating the therapist's understanding of the nature of the young person's difficulties (the psychoanalytic formulation).

These early sessions also provide a vital opportunity to experience or explore the young person's feelings about entering into a therapeutic relationship, which will inform the rest of the therapy. In STPP, as in longer term psychoanalytic psychotherapy, the young person's motivation or willingness to engage in the treatment may be indicated not by anything as tangible as articulating his or her feelings or thoughts, but simply by turning up to the sessions: indeed, this is sometimes a powerful indication of the degree of hope, however tiny, that keeps the young person coming in the face of high levels of despair. With less verbal young people, their participation in the work may be indicated by the subtlest of gestures, such as a fleeting look of relief, or momentarily making eye contact, in response to an interpretation or the naming of a feeling they are unable to put into words. (Working with silent patients is described in more detail in chapter 7.) Conversely, a young person presenting with rather manic or alarming behaviour, or with a hostile or dismissive attitude to therapy or to any treatment, may nevertheless be able to engage in STPP once he or she experiences the impact of the therapist's response (the commitment to understanding his or her behaviour or aggression). (See also "Acting out and acting in" in chapter 7.) The therapist will be looking out for what may be needed technically to elicit meaningful emotional engagement from the young person.

Establishing the framework and setting

In the initial meeting to set up the therapy, it is vital to make the number of sessions clear from the beginning, both the 28-week structure of STPP and the point at which an agreement about proceeding with the treatment will be reached. It is also important to explain that the sessions will take place, wherever possible, at a regular time and in the same room. Hartnup (1999) suggests that in establishing a therapeutic setting for psychodynamic treatment, particular attention needs to be paid to the practicalities; the room; consent, trust, and confidentiality; and beginnings, endings, and breaks.

A clear description of the structure of STPP is therefore vital—not only the number but also the frequency and length of sessions; holiday breaks; agreeing a regular time for the sessions; starting dates; arrangements about cancellations; and perhaps also clarity about roughly when the therapy will end, such as the likely month. This will establish the idea of a consistent setting (the same room and the same time each week, except when a change is unavoidable), so that disruptions can be kept to a minimum. It is also essential to explain that missed sessions will be counted towards the total unless the cancellation is by the therapist. Exceptions to this can arise, for public exams or pre-booked family holidays. The therapist will establish arrangements for contact between sessions which may be needed from time to time – for example, for either therapist or patient to communicate about illness or other problems about regular attendance – within the parameters of whatever is acceptable to the clinic. Many adolescents use text or mobile messages to communicate about arrangements, as letters feel outdated to them. The parallel work with the parent(s) needs to be discussed, as an integral part of the treatment.

It is also important to establish clarity around issues of confidentiality. This would usually involve explaining about the confidential nature of what is said, but also outlining the rare circumstances in which the therapist would need to share information with other adults, such as when there are concerns about the young person's safety. This may be especially important for young people with a history of suicidal attempts and deliberate self-harm, or where there have been concerns about physical, sexual, or emotional abuse. It can be helpful to explain how such situations would be handled if and when they arise, with an emphasis on including the young person in decision-making as much as possible.

The principle of holding review meetings with the family or carers also needs to be explained. This usually involves the young person's parents or carers, and for this reason it is discussed in chapter 5, under "Setting-up, reviews, communication, and routine outcome monitoring".

In establishing the practical framework for therapy from the outset in this way, the therapist has the opportunity to convey to the young person the way in which the therapeutic setting can be reliable and constant, a place in which things can be thought about and explored in a non-judgemental way. Many depressed adolescents will have had experiences of significant loss, so the therapist will be implicitly communicating an understanding of the importance of presences and absences. This framework:

> provides parameters within which the patient can relate and the therapist work. . . . A key part of the therapist's work is the recognition and understanding of the patient's reactions to the breaks, gaps, limitations and frustrations inherent in the therapeutic encounter. [Taylor & Richardson, 2005, p. 132]

As Wilson (1991) has written:

> The primary task of a psychotherapist [early on in treatment] is to ensure conditions of work that facilitate communication, and enable both psychotherapist and patient to observe and think about what is happening within and between them. The concept of a therapeutic setting refers to everything that forms the background in which psychotherapy takes place. [pp. 450–451]

Balancing information-gathering with reflection
on internal experience

In the early sessions, the therapist must strike a balance between allowing the young person to take a lead if he or she is able to do so and making sure that certain areas have been covered. The therapist has to combine important information-gathering about the young person's external life context (home, school, friendships, and so on) with offering a space in which he or she is invited to focus on internal experience: whatever comes to mind in the session, dreams and fantasies, hopes, fears, and feelings of all sorts. The psychotherapist should try to establish a sense of space to explore the young person's own concerns.

Not offering a structured set of questions and explanations is itself part of establishing the therapeutic frame for STPP, in which the content of the sessions is largely led by the young person. Unlike more structured approaches to psychotherapy, the initial sessions of STPP should be more like a "process" than a "procedure" (Waddell, 2000b, p. 146): one in which a space is created for "examining the anxiety and ambivalence which usually accompany a request for help [in order to determine] whether the fear of change is greater than the bid for relief and for emotional freedom" (Waddell, 2000b, p. 146). It has to be borne in mind that very depressed young people may not be able to say very much spontaneously and that such patients will need help through interpretation to find ways of expressing themselves. (This is discussed further in chapter 7.)

While STPP is not a symptom-focused form of treatment, the young person's particular symptoms of depression need also to be kept in mind. Busch, Rudden, and Shapiro (2004) suggest that what is most important from the very start is that the patient is "introduced to the idea that symptoms have meaning and are triggered by events in the present that evoke unpleasant affective experiences and the fantasies linked with them in the past" (p. 39). During the assessment phase, the therapist attempts to convey to the young person that the method of work involves developing an understanding of the meaning of all communications between them and trying to make connections between depressive symptoms and conscious and unconscious thoughts and feelings. What is said is only one part of the communication: all the external factors that enter the therapy will also be considered in this way, including missed sessions, reluctance to come, or reluctance to leave. In this way, the therapeutic setting is being drawn on all the time, providing a boundary around all aspects of the therapeutic work. Over time, the therapist will try to help the young person to see the deeper unconscious meaning of all his or her communications, verbal and non-verbal, and the links between this and past and present areas of conflict and difficulty.

Examining transferential elements and monitoring countertransference

During the assessment or early sessions, transferential elements can be observed as they emerge and the therapist's countertransference monitored closely, with the support of supervision. In combination with what emerges in the discourse as led by the young person, this allows for a psychoanalytic understanding of the young person's state of mind to take shape in the therapist's mind and a picture to form of the dynamic of current internal object relationships.

Exploring the young person's capacity for curiosity and reflection

These early sessions also provide an opportunity to explore the young person's capacity for curiosity about him/herself, openness to linking comments, and responses to being understood. It is also important to assess the degree to which the young person may feel a desire for change rather than an investment in things staying as they are. Whether there are developmental difficulties or deficits, cognitive or other, which might significantly affect the appropriateness of psychotherapy, is also essential to assess.

Confirming the scope of time-limited work

It is important to explore and take seriously what precipitated the referral: what was the particular issue, and why did the referral come now? It is also important not to imply that all problems, conflicts, or concerns can be resolved during STPP. This is relatively short-term work, and the therapist being clear in his or her own mind about the aims of the work will help to set realistic expectations for the treatment. In such time-limited work, we do not expect that every aspect of the young person's life will be changed, but the treatment does aim to address troubling symptoms and to begin to do some work on the underlying vulnerabilities so that the young person will have increased resilience in regard to depression in the future and some grasp of his or her characteristic anxieties and defences.

Identifying barriers to engagement in treatment

There are a number of reasons why depressed young people may struggle to engage with therapy, and it is important that these are identified either in an assessment or early in treatment, in order to try to prevent premature ending. A number of issues are pertinent to young people with depression, including (adapted from Busch, Rudden, & Shapiro, 2004, pp. 48–51):

» excessive shame and fear of exposure;
» oppressive, conscious guilt, and fear of its exposure;
» family views on depression or aggression;
» overvalued explanations for depression which the treatment may challenge – including the fixed idea of a physiological basis for the depressed mood and, in consequence, an inflexible desire for medication.

Another important issue is hopelessness, with regard to circumstances both in the young person's external life and in his or her private experience which he or she may feel are not open to change. This situation is often linked to fears concerning aggression, whether the young person's own or the hostility and condemnation he or she may expect from another person, which make it difficult to engage in an emotionally important relationship. The therapist providing STPP must remain especially alert for indications of this in the negative transference and be prepared to interpret this when it has the potential to interfere with engaging in treatment. Such interpretation might take the form of a "therapist-centred" comment (Steiner, 1993), which locates the problem in the therapist's mind, in order to contain feelings that the patient cannot yet own, such as, "Perhaps you feel that I am very doubtful about whether I can help you."

Anna: initial assessment sessions

Anna's psychoanalytic assessment was conducted within the time-frame of the STPP treatment, with a clear agreement that it would comprise the first 3 sessions of the potential 28-session contract.

> On the day of her first individual session, a few weeks after the shared initial appointment with her mother, Anna sent a text message to cancel the session. The therapist replied by text message, acknowledging the missed session, and confirmed the next week's appointment. Anna arrived independently to her second session, explaining that as she had so much to attend to she had forgotten about coming last week until it was too late to get there. She talked about how busy she had been in starting the new academic year. There was a surface confidence and competence to Anna's accounts that left her therapist wondering where the struggle or uncertainty might be. Something was missing, much like in the initial session with Anna and her mother together.

> As if Anna gauged what her therapist was thinking, she went on to talk about how she often felt low and that this was linked to a "crisis" in her family. The words tumbled forth in a confused jumble. Anna said that her problems started after the death a few months previously of a close family friend, a childhood friend of her mother's. Her mother had been very upset at this untimely death and had taken to her bed for a while, leaving Anna looking after her 4-year-old sister and baby brother along with her stepfather. This had caused tension, and a row ensued in which her mother had accused Anna of not caring enough about the death. In fact, Anna had been very upset too, as she had been close to her mother's friend. Her stepfather had been drawn into the row between mother and daughter, in which Anna's actual feelings about the death seemed to have been lost.

> Anna's description of this conflict and its significance became increasingly tangled, as she gave a long narrative about the relationship between her mother and her friend in their childhood, different life

events that had affected them, and the reactions of the family friend's children to their own mother's death. The overall impression was of a 15-year-old feeling unjustly blamed for creating a conflict within a complex, yet close-knit circuit of families, in which she lost track of her own deeper feelings. The generational divide seemed blurred as Anna described her mother's childhood relationships and her own attempts to care for her younger half-siblings, and it seemed as though parental function was fluidly taken up by various adults.

The therapist experienced her mind being filled with a crowd of people whose family position, relationships, and functions were muddled. She resisted the temptation to ask questions that would clarify and order Anna's narrative. Instead, she reflected on how dramatic the crisis seemed to have been and how it must have left Anna feeling in a spin, not knowing which way to turn and who might be able to help her. Anna nodded, saying that she often got headaches, and then she talked about suffering from pains in her stomach. Pain and sadness infused the session, contrasting with the initial speedy and energetic communications. Forlorn, Anna quietly explained that her aunt had died when she was 10 years old. Her aunt had looked after her a great deal until then. Indeed, Anna had felt as though she had two mothers. After a moment's pause, she said that somehow it had always felt as though her aunt were her "real" mother and her mother an elder sister.

Anna explained that when her aunt died, the family had a "melt-down" (unwittingly using the same word she used about her own headaches). The therapist described how Anna had begun to let her know about important things such as the recent crisis and another important family experience when she was much younger. The therapist talked about how Anna might have felt that she had to manage these difficult circumstances independently, especially now that she was much older and getting ready for adulthood. It might feel as though it were best to get on without asking for help, especially when there might be a worry that nobody could be of real help; perhaps when help *was* available, it could easily be forgotten like the missed session last week. Anna's therapist added that despite this, there were these big important things on Anna's mind that hurt and that needed time to think about. Anna listened quietly and seemed thoughtful. The therapist explained that there would be time over the 26 sessions that now remained to begin to make some sense of the painful experiences that Anna had been telling her about. Anna nodded, yet appeared more vulnerable and lost.

Anna missed her next session without sending a message. It felt as if she had disappeared. When she arrived for the following session, she apologised for not having been in touch. She explained that it had been a difficult time because it had been the anniversary of her aunt's death. She had also lost her mobile phone. In addition to this, she had had to do a lot of babysitting for her baby brother and household chores to earn enough to pay for a replacement phone. Her therapist commented that as texting had been Anna's preferred line of communication, it had been difficult to know how best to get in touch when there had been no response. Anna nodded, saying that she had received her therapist's letter but then lost it, and so she was unable to ring.

Anna conveyed how hard it might be to hold the beginning of a link with her psychotherapy in the face of different kinds of losses: the death of her aunt and the loss of her phone as past and present bereavements. There was also the dynamic of Anna feeling that she had to take on the responsibility of looking after others. The intense activity that Anna described seemed to function as a defence against the pain and vulnerability that had been glimpsed towards the end of the first session. It felt as though it would be premature and undermining to describe this dynamic to Anna at this point, or to describe the transferential dynamic of Anna feeling that therapy was yet another demand or chore that she had to attend to, to meet another's needs rather than her own (that she was resisting being "proficient"). Instead, her therapist reflected on how Anna had made it here today even though things had been so busy and difficult. Anna nodded and turned to describing how much she was enjoying school. Yet she went on to describe friction in her friendship groups, with conflicting loyalty and scapegoating. This resonated in her therapist's mind with the family "crisis" that Anna had described in her first session. The therapist found herself thinking about an underlying dynamic of insecurity and unpredictability.

Anna then explained that she was unsure whether the session time was possible for her any more because she wanted to attend a course in peer mentoring that was taking place after school. The therapist experienced this announcement like a very real attack: a jolt to a fragile house of cards. The therapist reflected on how Anna had to manage so much and asked Anna whether she felt there was anyone who could support her. Anna explained that when arguments happened in the family, people would take sides; her mother would snap because she was tired looking after the baby; and then her mother would shut herself away and Anna would feel she had no one to talk to. Anna explained that her little sister would get really cross when her baby brother cried, and Anna would try to keep the peace. When her therapist commented on how hard this might be, Anna said that she did often feel like she was falling to pieces. She described experiences of forgetting things and intense headaches, again referred to as "melt-downs".

Anna began to talk about her experiences of bereavements, including the protracted illness of her mother's friend and how this fitted in with events in the friend's immediate family. Anna's therapist experienced an undigested mass of communications as the session drew to a close. She commented on the concentration of difficult experiences in a short amount of time. This seemed linked to painful loss when Anna was much younger. Anna's therapist reflected on there being time to think about this: it was really important to try to make sense of it because of the headaches, pain, and stress Anna was experiencing. Anna smiled and seemed to value the idea of "time to think".

Aware that they were now at the end of the assessment phase of the work (and having inwardly decided to articulate this here despite the two missed sessions), the therapist took this opportunity to ask Anna directly whether she felt she could agree to proceed with STPP, which she thought might be helpful to Anna. Anna nodded and said she agreed, and her therapist reminded her of what this would entail, including the parallel work with her mother and stepfather. The therapist said that she would keep the time that they had agreed for the next week and they could think together about different arrangements if this became necessary.

In supervision, Anna's therapist was struck by how hard it was to describe Anna's appearance, her descriptions falling into a rather vague sketch of a young girl with a pleasant demeanour. She did not particularly stand out. Some thinking about how easily Anna could disappear from people's minds was helpful in deciding to conserve a steadiness around the agreed frame for attendance. The supervision group discussed the significance of early experiences and how this might inform Anna's internal object relations, particularly maternal objects and oedipal dynamics. That Anna was at the threshold between adolescence and adulthood seemed to be a particularly important developmental context for her.

Establishing the therapeutic alliance

As discussed in chapter 3, building up trust in the therapist is essential and depends on the therapist being reliable and consistent; without that, it is very difficult to establish the sense of safety that is vital for the therapeutic work. The establishment of a "secure base" or a "therapeutic alliance" is one of the aims of the early stages of treatment and is one of the greatest challenges when working with depressed young people. As Busch, Rudden, and Shapiro (2004) put it:

> As the therapist is seen as caring but dispassionate and dedicated to understanding the meaning of the patient's difficulties without "taking sides" or being judgmental or invasive, a relationship evolves in which the patient learns to trust the therapist with the most intimate fears and sadness. This is crucial because only in the context of a trusting relationship can a patient feel truly comfortable exposing areas of shame and vulnerability in order to do the necessary therapeutic work. [p. 44]

Anna: establishing the therapeutic alliance

Anna's next session, the first after the agreement to proceed, also came after a joint review in which progress so far and the decision to proceed were discussed with the parent worker and Anna's mother (see "Anna: first review meeting" in chapter 5,). This was not an easy meeting for Anna, and her therapist wondered whether she would return for her next session, despite the sense of their having made genuine emotional contact. Anna, however, did attend her next session promptly and, in fact, missed no further sessions until much later in the year, when the end of the therapy, and her public exams, were in sight.

Anna continued to talk about the "melt-downs" and dramas taking place at home. Although her therapist continued to feel a pressure to sift through a huge mass of complicated material, as though Anna were the one to manage it "proficiently", she (the therapist) struggled to take it all in. It also gradually became possible to think together about the difference in ethnic background between the therapist, who was white, and her young patient. Anna was at first reluctant to think that this might be relevant; like the generational difference between them, it seemed to be something to be ignored, with the differences collapsed. Yet her therapist naming this as something to think about seemed to occasion some sense of relief in Anna – perhaps an impression that how Anna regarded her therapist was something that her therapist could bear.

At her next supervision, Anna's therapist spoke about this much more regular attendance. She described Anna's distinctive short, dyed hair (a bright, striking appearance at odds with her sad presentation) and how astonished she felt at not having noticed this before. They discussed how the therapist could now map out in an initial report, which would draw on the transference experience in these early sessions of STPP (see below), some of the key internal dynamics contributing to Anna's struggles.

Assessment report

A summary of the assessment process should be included in the young person's notes after the assessment phase, in consultation with the clinical supervisor, in addition to any information gathered from the initial sessions with the young person and his or her parents or carers. This assessment can draw upon family information derived from the parent worker and from any earlier meetings with multidisciplinary clinicians prior to allocation to STPP.

This summary would usually include the following information:

» reasons for referral, and current difficulties, including some assessment of the severity and complexity of the young person's depression and a statement regarding any psychiatric diagnosis;

» a brief statement about family history, developmental history, and current care or family set-up and dynamics;

» a brief account of the assessment sessions that indicates the evidence for the therapist's conclusions;

» an assessment of risk, including potential risk to self (including self-harm and suicidality), risk to others (including violence), and any potential protective factors, including a risk assessment plan, in line with standard clinical practice;

» a statement of possible aetiology, including evidence of resilience and protective factors;

» a statement outlining the therapist's initial formulation and hypotheses about central psychodynamic features and how they link with the young person's depression (see below).

Psychoanalytic formulation: developing a picture of the young person's mind

One of the key tasks of these early sessions is to reach some assessment of the central dynamic processes that appear to be underlying and maintaining the young person's depression (often referred to in other treatment modalities as a "case formulation"). While STPP does not make use of explicitly sharing such an assessment with the young person, an indication of it at the point of agreeing to proceed is essential, to help the young person to feel understood and to feel engaged with the idea of STPP treatment. This is also a good opportunity to consider the explicit aims of the treatment or to review any aims identified during the young person's first contact with the clinic. (These may be returned to during meetings to review the therapy: see "Setting-up, reviews, communication, and routine outcome monitoring" in chapter 5.)

To come to such a formulation, both external reality and internal reality need to be taken into consideration. Where, as so often happens, there have been major life events, these are likely to be significant, so it can be helpful to explore these in some detail. Some of the young people may have considerable problems with interpersonal relationships. There may be difficulties with expressing feelings, initiating and/or maintaining relationships, and communication. Exploring these difficulties and promoting a capacity to relate to others, which is such a key aspect of adolescence, requires careful and sensitive work. The assessment should also take into account the particular ways in which depression may manifest itself during adolescence.

While hearing and understanding the conflicts that the young person reports in his or her external world, it is important for the therapist to help the patient to think about the links with earlier conflicts and to try to sort out a sense of what belongs to external reality and what is internal, deriving from the here-and-now or from earlier experience. The therapist should work with the young person to try to help him or her to recognize some of the key processes that make him or her vulnerable to depression (such as excessive guilt or narcissistic vulnerability).

In writing about this initial formulation in the assessment report, the therapist may wish to pay particular attention to the following areas and develop some working hypothesis on how each of these areas, where relevant, may be contributing to the young person's depression:

» unconscious conflict, including in relation to anger and aggression;

» existential anxiety (Rhode, 2011);

» narcissistic difficulties and loss of identity – this may range from the ordinary narcissistic sensitivity and preoccupation that is part of the adolescent developmental process to deeper emergent narcissistic personality states;

» idealization and denigration of self and others – this makes for a cycle of repeated disappointment and loss of hope, potentially leading to despair;

» the impact of early relationships, loss, and relational trauma;

» the severity of the superego – involving very painful feelings of guilt and/or shame, this frequently underlies adolescent depression;

» the impact of parental mental health and intergenerational loss and/or trauma;

» the re-emergence of oedipal conflict and emerging sexuality during adolescence – this reawakens oedipal issues in an often intense form, which can make for great difficulty in both family and peer relationships and can often evoke a sense of loneliness and failure;

» defences against all these sources of psychic pain – these may further intensify depressive states.

The therapist should continue to develop ongoing "working hypotheses" throughout the treatment, which can refine the picture achieved during the early stages. This will draw on all the aspects of the assessment described above.

Anna: the assessment report

Below is the assessment report written by Anna's therapist for her GP and the clinical team, which includes the beginning of a psychoanalytic hypothesis of Anna's depressive and developmental struggles. It includes a psychoanalytic formulation that deliberately avoids professional jargon. It draws on parent work with Anna's mother and stepfather described more fully in chapter 5.

Referral and current difficulties

Anna was referred by her GP. She was described as experiencing persistent low mood for approximately a year. The death of a close family friend last year was felt to be a trigger. Anna was seen by a practitioner in the clinic who assessed that Anna was suffering from persistent low mood and referred her for STPP with a child psychotherapist, with a different child psychotherapist colleague offering parallel parent work. Both mother and daughter conveyed their motivation to commit to this intervention, which involves 28 sessions of once-weekly psychoanalytic psychotherapy for Anna and seven parent sessions for her mother and stepfather. It was agreed that this work would begin in September with the first three sessions being regarded as an assessment. Anna then agreed to proceed with the treatment after this initial taste.

Anna is due to take public exams in her mainstream school. She then wishes to leave school and progress to college for training in care work. This is causing some tension at home as her parents would prefer her to stay at school for further academic study. She also described struggles with peer relationships, where she often feels antagonized or ostracized from various peer groups.

Family and developmental history and current family set-up

Anna is the eldest child in her family. She has never met her father and lives with her mother and stepfather. She has a half-sister aged 4 years and a half-brother aged 6 months.

During her assessment sessions, Anna explained that she was primarily looked after by her mother's elder sister until she was 10 years old. Anna described how, as she grew up, she never quite felt like her own mother's daughter, and the death of her aunt in middle age was a devastating loss. Anna conveys experiences of internal representations where relationships are confused. There are perceptions of blurred generations, where adults fluidly take up parental roles and where Anna co-opts the parental mantle. This creates confusion in her mind about where she fits in terms of her identity and her developmental transition between childhood and adulthood, and has impeded her capacity to make sense of and mourn the death of central parental figures in her life.

Anna's mother, Ms A, and Anna's stepfather attended some initial sessions while Anna's assessment was taking place and express commitment to continuing to engage in parent work. They are clearly aware of and concerned about the possible impact of Ms A's own mental health difficulties on Anna.

Experience of the early sessions

Anna found the sessions challenging. She initially struggled to commit to regular attendance. It was as if she experienced her sessions as an additional demand or expectation rather than something that had been arranged to offer help. It was hard for her to understand and take up the offer of help from an adult figure and how to understand this as different from, for example, a peer relationship. There was an outward communication of capability and activity that belied the concerns about depression and struggles with bereavement. This carapace provided some protection from the underlying complex and confusing emotions that Anna can push out of her awareness. Yet, with some space to explore this, Anna described her frustration and distress about rifts in her family and the fracturing impact of family bereavements. The death of her mother's friend last year was terribly upsetting, particularly as it also re-ignited unresolved loss from when Anna's aunt died. Anna expressed an experience of being left to fend for herself while also somehow having to take on the role of a matriarch in the family.

In her initial sessions, Anna's hurt and confusion were palpable, but there was also a subtle quality of a critical judgement of others and a feeling that she could look after herself better than the parental figures around her. This dynamic was played out in the immediacy of the therapeutic relationship. There were contrasting experiences of Anna negating the need for another while also being hard to hold in mind.

There was a dual impression both of psychotherapy being unnecessary, as Anna was managing well, and Anna seeming lost and without support. Similarly, the difficulty in her peer relationships seems to be about what position Anna takes in her friendships. Is it as a critical authority figure or as an adolescent peer who is exploring tasks of individuation and separation from parental figures? It is not clear what sort of mentor she can turn to among her peers.

Risk and protective factors

Exam pressures are likely to cause additional anxiety and emotional strain for Anna. At times, she can present as outwardly competent and self-sufficient. Beneath this, however, she has communicated an ongoing experience of low mood, emotional turmoil, and confusion that leaves her vulnerable to sinking deeper into a depression that may risk her education and engagement with peer and family relationships. Protective factors are that Anna has not self-harmed and does not describe any suicidal ideation. She is engaging in psychotherapy, attending school, and is able to let key people know about her distress.

Psychoanalytic formulation

Anna's description of the confusion and conflict within her family appear to mirror an internal relational muddle that leaves Anna struggling to orientate herself and to feel coherent in her developing sense of self. This is impacting on a significant threshold of emotional and psychological development as Anna faces the demands of her last year of school and putting strain on her family relationships. Anna conveys a sense of not being able to access solid-enough internalized parental figures from which she can then confidently address the tasks of individuation and separation. There seems to be profound confusion generated by the loss or absence of supportive internal figures (e.g., aunt, father) and also of not needing them because she is already in a parental role. It is significant to note that Anna has experienced her mother's pregnancy and the arrival of a sibling on the cusp of her own adolescence. During these initial sessions, it has been difficult to locate Anna's aggression, as she can present as amenable and compliant. Her aggression seemed subtly present in her initial struggle to engage in STPP; however, there was a quality of self-sufficiency and criticism which protected her from feeling dependent on another person.

There may also be an internalization of aggression that is contributing to Anna's experience of headaches (which Anna describes as "melt-downs") and possible psychosomatic pain.

The middle stages of STPP

During the early stages of STPP, the primary focus is on establishing the therapeutic frame or setting, building the therapeutic alliance, and identifying the barriers to engagement in treatment and the central depressive dynamics. It is hoped that this will have enabled a therapeutic relationship to begin to develop, and that the young person will have begun to get a sense that his or her symptoms have meaning connected to his or her underlying thoughts and feelings. In some cases, this may lead to some level of symptomatic improvement, which in turn will generate a level of hope that things may improve and that treatment may be of help.

These processes continue to be a focus of work throughout the course of the treatment. Unlike some more structured treatments, there is no clear-cut distinction between the early and later stages of STPP, although there may well be a shift of emphasis. During the middle stages of treatment, the earlier work is thus both continued and developed further. Its main features are (Busch, Rudden, & Shapiro, 2004):

» building increased trust in the therapist;
» a deepening of the transference relationship;
» the emergence of a greater capacity in the young person to confront problematic areas in the self and his or her relationships.

These processes will be supported by the therapist's main tasks of:

» enabling the young person to express him/herself, whether by means of words, play, drawings, or actions within the therapeutic setting;
» finding a way to give meaning to the young person's communication and to express this in a way that makes sense to the young person;

» observing and reflecting on his or her own reactions to the young person and striving to be aware of the transference and counter-transference;

» selecting from the mass of verbal, non-verbal, and unconscious communication those areas that can be most helpfully addressed.

During this period of treatment, a high proportion of the therapist's interventions will probably consist of verbal description aimed at reflecting back the young person's experience, clarifying the emotions in play for younger adolescents, and making links with other relevant experiences. Some of the young people may speak about their dreams, and this can facilitate a powerful focus on the evolving transference relationship. Enabling these processes to develop will thus involve – perhaps even more than in the early stages – drawing on the range of interpretive techniques described in the previous chapter.

This stage of treatment spans the period in which the time remaining in the therapy becomes less than the time already spent in therapy. Although the therapy will continue to be patient-led and to proceed at the patient's own pace, the therapist needs to be aware of its time-limited nature and to keep in mind the need to address issues that are being avoided or denied when the young person's behaviour indicates this to be appropriate. This can be particularly difficult, for the therapist as well as the young person, when important areas are being worked on. While there may be an experience of the patient–therapist relationship developing and deepening during this middle stage, there may also be a growing awareness, in parallel, of the limitations of the relationship, linked to the known time limit. This makes it significantly different from open-ended treatment. Experiences of loss, conflicts around separation, and difficulties with mourning are likely to be prominent in this patient group. The time-limited framework provides an opportunity to tackle these issues.

Increased trust in the therapist

The aim of STPP is that the young person's trust in the therapist and in the treatment should increase through the repeated experience that the therapist can understand and tolerate the young person's feelings – both good and bad – and can respond with continuing interest and concern and convey a sense of meaningfulness. Although in reality this may not always happen, it is important to be aware of how the therapist can work to give the best opportunity for the young person's trust to increase.

The therapist aims to do this by working on the topics raised by the young person, particularly focusing on what happens in the room and on the relationship with the therapist, making links with material identified in earlier sessions. The evolution of the relationship with the therapist is key, as is the therapist's capacity to face negative feelings, both within the young person and in the young person's attitude to the therapist.

One aspect of the development of this greater degree of trust is based on the experience of separating from the therapist for holiday breaks from which the therapist returns. It is important to prepare the young person carefully for these holiday separations, both in terms of giving adequate notice and in terms of addressing the break's emotional meaning. Some young people feel abandoned and uncared for, while others may find it difficult to consider the emotional significance of breaks in the therapy, or convey to the therapist their sense of being insignificant and forgotten. In each case, it is important to address the difficulty of imagining that any therapeutic relationship, particularly a relatively brief one, could make a difference, or that the therapist could be a reliable source of support.

Holiday breaks present an invaluable opportunity to address the young person's experience of the therapist in a way that feels meaningful and natural (Trowell et al., 2003). The therapist's return after a break demonstrates to the young person that the therapist has not been damaged by difficult interactions in the therapy or by the young person's negative feelings towards the therapist. Increased trust can also be supported by the ability of the therapist to cooperate with other professionals in the young person's interest. It can be particularly important for the young person to know that the therapist cannot be separated from the parent worker (where there is one) or from other professionals (such as the psychiatrist with medical responsibility), but also that the therapist has a particular role and task and will remain loyal to that and not be drawn into other kinds of intervention.

While attention to the impact of separations is significant in time-limited work such as STPP, there are many other opportunities to make use of transference phenomena. Anxieties about intimacy and the sexual transference may be a prominent feature, for instance, given the dominance of these dynamics in adolescence. It is both possible and useful to pick this up in a straightforward and clear way. Supervision helps the clinician to think about how to do this, particularly if there are concerns about addressing it in a time-limited treatment. Clinical experience suggests that engaging with this sexual transference reduces primitive oedipal anxieties and is experienced as containing, opening up exploration and analysis of key relationships in the young person's external and internal world.

Anna: increased trust in therapy

As Anna progressed into the middle stages of her STPP sessions, an eagerness to attend her sessions regularly developed and she often arrived early. This contrasted with the stop-start experience at the beginning.

Anna talked about rows with her mother. She also started to talk much more about relationships with her friends and her anxieties about being included or excluded by them, or judged by them. In one session, she talked about her anxiety about whether a small group of friends would come to a gathering she wanted to arrange. Anna's therapist picked this up in relation to the initial uncertainty that she had about whether *she* was going to come to her therapy. Anna agreed, explaining that it had made sense to postpone the peer-mentoring course she had wanted to pursue. Anna said that she felt bad about missing those sessions, and her therapist reflected on how hard it might feel that she needed some help or "mentoring" herself, rather than her being the one to take on the care-taking role. The therapist reflected that perhaps it was even quite difficult for Anna to feel sure what the therapy would be like that would be different from having support from a "peer". Anna agreed with this. The supervision group later picked up, however, that there also seemed to be a deeper communication going on about competition or rivalry with an internal maternal figure that Anna might unconsciously feel she was triumphing over (relegating her from mother to peer, if not to child), as well as a fear that her development might elicit an envious or judgemental reaction. In the countertransference, her therapist felt at once as though she were an old woman somehow needing a younger person to enliven or humour an otherwise drab or lifeless existence, and also as a young person herself, rather incompetently trying to offer help where none was needed.

Deepening of the transference relationship, including resistance and negative transference

Increased trust brings with it a deepening of the transference relationship. This involves both a greater appreciation of the treatment alliance and a heightened capacity to bear aspects of the treatment that are frustrating. It will help the therapist, in working out the most relevant material to bring to the patient's attention, to scrutinize his or her own countertransference responses, as well as the overall clinical picture.

As the relationship deepens, negative aspects of the transference may emerge more clearly. The therapist is likely to be tested as to his or her capacity to bear the patient's doubts about the therapy being helpful, for example; if so, the therapist's willingness to face profound despair will be vital. Anna's therapist certainly felt some of this doubt and anxiety in her early sessions with Anna, particularly in relation to the missed or cancelled sessions early on and, more subtly, in relation to the pervasive dynamic in which Anna seemed not to need the help of a parental figure. From the perspective of the therapist delivering STPP, the emergence of the negative transference is a hopeful sign, in that it indicates sufficient trust in the therapist's capacity to work with these difficult feelings. It also brings aggressive impulses and phantasies into the work, allowing links between aggression, depressive anxieties, and feelings to be thought about within the therapeutic relationship.

If young people or their families say that things are getting worse and the therapy is not helping, this may be a realistic assessment and needs to be taken seriously, but it may also be an important stage that has to be tolerated. When anxiety is high and cannot be managed within the individual work with the young person and his or her parents, there needs to be the opportunity for a professionals' meeting to evaluate the situation. The therapist's supervisor may be an important member of such a meeting. (Such communications may involve queries about introducing medication, and this is discussed in chapter 7.)

Anna: deepening of the transference relationship

In another session during this middle stage, Anna explained that she liked keeping busy with schoolwork and extracurricular activities. It meant that she did not have to look after the baby or do chores around the house. The therapist started to wonder about Anna's ambivalence about taking on adult roles so "proficiently" and commented on how hard it had been for Anna to feel that she needed to take charge of things, and yet to feel quite sad or even angry about it. Anna then explained in more detail about how she had never known her father and how she had been looked after such a lot by her aunt. She recalled that when her aunt died, she began to have terrible tantrums and would not do as she was told. Not long after this, her stepfather moved in with them. This caused conflict, as Anna struggled to deal both with a new person entering the family while she was still mourning her aunt and, in particular, with uncertain expectations as to what a father might be like. Things at home had been difficult for a time, and she had found her mother's friend helpful as a source of comfort, perhaps a substitute, to some extent, for her lost aunt. Scarcely pausing for breath, she spoke about the funeral of this family friend. It was as if the two deaths had happened in close succession rather than four years apart.

Anna's therapist reflected on Anna's experience of people leaving her or a relationship that did not feel quite right, like with her mother or her stepfather. Maybe her struggle in attending her sessions at the beginning might have been to do with a feeling that the same would happen in her therapy – that it would not feel right with her therapist and that it would suddenly end. Anna looked thoughtful, as though her therapist's reflection were resonating in her mind.

Anna became more reflective and began to talk about different family members who suffered from depression, including her mother and aunt. Anna thought that her aunt used to "cheer up" her mother, but she sounded uncertain about how successful this had been and then, quietly, talked about how she had had to look after her mother when she felt very low, even before her aunt died. Anna described often feeling older than her age and said she thought that this used to create problems in her friendships as a little girl. Even now, she felt older than she was. Anna's therapist wondered whether this would also cause problems in Anna's current friendships. Anna was thoughtful as the transgenerational aspects of her distress came into view, and her depression seemed more accessible to exploration.

Greater capacity to confront problematic areas

The experience of the therapist as an adult with emotional resilience should ideally contribute to the young person developing the capacity to try out new modes of relating, where possible. Although the therapist will not suggest specific problem-solving techniques or make suggestions, support can be given to the young person in thinking through the issues raised by asking questions, commenting on outcomes or reactions that the young person may be concerned about, highlighting inhibitions, and so on.

The process of delineating the young person's experience of the therapist and his or her expectations both of the therapist and of other significant people can help in the process of distinguishing phantasy from reality and can therefore support the young person to achieve a more realistic picture of what he or she is (or is not) responsible for. With this can come a lessening of the inhibitions stemming from anxieties about expressing aggression and, therefore, an increased sense of agency. Equally, for those young people with a pronounced narcissistic vulnerability, the sense of self and, through this, the sense of agency, can be strengthened through the experience of having their emotional experience recognized. Very small steps to move out of depressive apathy, for example, need to be noted and described; young people in the grip of passive hopelessness will be helped by very close observation of any change in their level of vitality and exploration of such changes.

The young person's depressive symptoms must be continually monitored, and the therapist must remain aware that crises may occur. Depression or anger may escalate. It is important to anticipate these crises where possible and to be able to think about them and put them into words. This will help the young person consider more realistically what might be the consequences of a suicide attempt or other serious acting out. If a crisis occurs, it must be taken seriously; the therapist may need to discuss this with the young person and consider the need for other adults (such as the parents or psychiatrist) to be consulted. The young person may need to realize that in an extreme situation, the therapist has a duty as a responsible clinician to protect the patient in consultation with others. (Such situations are discussed in chapter 7.)

Anna: confronting problematic areas

As the middle sessions of STPP unfolded, Anna's therapist talked about the ending of their work and how this would be carefully thought about and was still several months away. Before then, there would be a break over the Christmas holiday period. Anna accepted this in a realistic way, as if the finite period of her psychotherapy could be trusted and could be used. She reliably attended her sessions, even before and after the break. At times, she seemed authentically cheerful, describing enjoyable times with her mother. She explained in one session during this period that it was hard to see the point of coming to her sessions when she had had a good week.

In Session 16 (several weeks after the Christmas break), Anna linked her feelings of happiness to a feeling that her stepfather was spending more time outside the home, either working late or socializing with friends. Anna described cooking and eating a meal with her mother while the younger children slept and her stepfather was out until late. In her account, it sounded like rather an intimate scene, from which the other family members were excluded, but one in which there was no clear generational divide (both mother and daughter cooking and eating together like friends). While appropriate to Anna's chronological age, it seemed to have a deeper significance. The idea of interpreting this dynamic at this moment made Anna's therapist feel concerned about being violently intrusive, bursting the bubble of cosiness and comfort that seemed so hard-won and precious. Anna's story shifted gear as she began to talk about how much shopping, dog-walking, and babysitting she had done of late. She did not mind this because she wanted to help her mother, but her brother was sometimes really difficult to look after and once kicked her and bruised her leg.

Anna's therapist reflected aloud on the contrast between the two accounts of family life: between the lovely cosiness of being with her mother with no stepfather or siblings to complicate things and then the annoyance of ending up having to do a lot for the family. It was as if Anna were being thrust forward to be in charge like a partner or father. There did not seem to be the possibility of a balance between the two. Anna did not seem to take up her therapist's thoughts, instead continuing with another description of being expected to look after her brother too much. The therapist suggested that perhaps Anna felt that she was not really listening to how hard it was for Anna when everything landed on her shoulders and it could feel like Anna was the only one who was doing all the hard work. Anna nodded. They were then able to think together about how complicated it was to experience work being done together as a joint endeavour: work that it was not possible to do single-handedly. Anna found herself at times feeling either that she was having to do everything or that she wanted to be looked after and held in mind completely, a little like a mother would care for her baby. The descriptions of her baby brother kicking also provided an opportunity to think about these aggressive and protesting parts of Anna. In supervision, it became possible to think about how the idea of a father and the need for a paternal function was beginning to emerge, in a way that had felt quite obscured in the work up to that point.

The ending stages of STPP

> Since beginnings and endings are so intrinsically linked in all life experience, the care taken during the initial consultations in setting treatment up is ideally counterbalanced by a similarly painstaking process at the point of considering entering the last phase of therapy.
>
> Lanyado, 1999b, p. 364

As STPP is a time-limited form of treatment, the young person will be aware throughout of the length of the treatment and the reality of an ending after the planned 28 sessions. As the treatment begins to move closer to the end, however, the awareness of an ending is likely to become increasingly central. As with all forms of psychotherapy, most endings are less than ideal, but a "good-enough" ending in STPP allows enough time for the following to take place:

» review of the progress to date and any changes;
» some thought about how to identify symptoms that may be heralding a return of depression in the future (warning signs);
» eliciting feelings about ending treatment and working through reactions to ending;
» considering the need for any treatment in the future.

The ending stages of STPP may also raise specific countertransference issues for the therapist. This is discussed at greater length below, as are issues of "premature" requests to end treatment and the question of post-treatment contact with the therapist.

A review of events and changes during therapy and identification of warning signs

During the ending stage, reviewing the course of treatment (using, for example, the metaphor of the photo album as described by Wittenberg, 1999):

> enables reflection on the experience [of therapy] and offers a third position. When the work is ongoing the experience is from inside. But when the work is ended the experience is from the outside. [Ryz & Wilson, 1999, p. 399]

A kind of speeded-up reworking of all the major themes of therapy often occurs in the last stage, although how much of this will be a conscious verbal exchange will vary greatly. This may give rise to a flare-up of the original problems. The therapist will need to assess whether this is a communication about the difficulty of ending, or whether it needs to be addressed by realistic measures. Consultation with the parent worker and other colleagues will be important in coming to a conclusion about this. While the therapist's role will involve the interpretation of the young person's experience of ending, specifically in terms of the kind of person the therapist is felt to be in that context, the parent worker may, for example, need to alert the network that the young person may require extra vigilance and attention for a time.

Eliciting feelings about ending treatment and working through reactions to ending

> The termination of an analysis stirs up painful feelings and revives early anxieties in the patient.
>
> Quagliata, 1999, p. 411

In this stage, the fact of the approaching ending becomes the central focus, though not, of course, to the exclusion of important issues in the young person's life. In addition to the aims previously discussed, the therapist will strive to help the young person to be fully aware both of the changes that have been achieved during the course of the therapy and of his or her frustration and feelings of disappointment at what it has not been possible to achieve. This may take the form of reproaches against the therapist for not extending the treatment, for leaving the young person with unresolved problems, for being uncaring, and so on. The therapist can often feel extremely guilty, which is complicated by the fact that the therapist's own wish may be to continue treatment and that he or she may feel unfairly blamed for something that is not his or her choice. Additional complications can come about if the parents express similar feelings towards the parent worker, leaving both workers with the fear of having been useless.

It is important to address such feelings as fully as possible and for the therapist not to confine herself to pointing out the progress that has been made in the attempt to part on a good note or to defend herself from the pain of these accusations. The therapist should beware of avoiding hostility in this way. Some young people will also avoid expressing negative feelings or hostility for fear that expressing any disappointment or resentment will leave them with a sense of the good aspects of the therapy being irreparably spoilt. In this case, it is essential for the therapist not to give in to the temptation to go along with this. It can be particularly hard not to do so in cases that have gone well and where the therapist feels that precious gains may be lost. As mentioned previously, however, having a good outcome at follow-up may be associated with the therapist confronting hostility during the ending stage of the treatment (Long & Trowell, 2001). On the other hand, the therapist's conviction of good progress made by the young person may represent a projection into the therapist either of more hopeful feelings of the young person's or of a stronger part of him/herself (or "ego strength"); careful attention to this process can enable the young person to own his or her hopefulness and recognize new-found strength or resilience.

One useful way of approaching this can be to explore the possibility that young people's complaints may be justified. In view of their difficulties and the many issues they could profitably address, it is reasonable for them to feel that they should have had more help, and for them to harbour feelings of disappointment, resentment, and even hatred. When these negative feelings are taken seriously, patients are generally able to recognize that they also feel lasting appreciation of the therapeutic opportunity; thus, loving and hating feelings may become better balanced.

Confronting the negative feelings strengthens the young person's sense of inner security, which is based on hope that his or her good feelings outweigh his or her aggression, and that both can be recognized and accepted. As Wittenberg (1999) puts it:

> the [therapist] is seen to survive attacks and continues to care, and is seen to be attentive and loving in spite of the patient's disappointments, accusations of abandonment, betrayal and disloyalty; the analyst goes on being concerned and understanding even if the patient temporarily turns away in anger; is able to bear and share the grief at losing what is valued. [p. 355]

This very difficult work is therefore essential to the patient's later capacity to draw on the internalized experience of the therapy:

> The work of learning to let go of having an analysis can . . . be of great value as a preparation for later experiences of loss and relinquishment. [Wittenberg, 1999, p. 355]

Some young people put the therapist in the position of being the one who is left behind – the one who would like to continue working with a patient who, on the contrary, is looking forward to a new life in which the therapist has no part to play. This can be acted out by non-attendance of the final sessions. This may sometimes be understood as age-appropriate in part, but it can also contain an element of role-reversal and revenge for the pain of dependence. Whichever form it takes, the work of the last stage places considerable emotional burdens on the therapist and parent worker, and support from team meetings and from supervision is essential.

In one sense, the ending stage may be considered to start whenever thoughts of ending are raised and discussed as a realistic possibility by the therapist or the young person. Some patients are so anxious about having to stop before they are ready that they cannot get started at all until their fears about premature loss of the therapist have been analysed.

Issues of separation and loss are likely to have been central for young people with moderate to severe depression, given the links between depression, mourning, separation, and loss. The ending stage provides the opportunity to work on this in the here-and-now, as this is a planned ending. Reflecting on the process of the treatment will be helpful, as will reviewing what has been worked on and achieved. The stage of ending is likely to encourage thoughts about the future, of what may come next, and also encourage the patient to think about what kind of person he or she might develop into.

As mentioned above, towards the end of STPP, the therapist may expect some reappearance of themes that have been worked on earlier in therapy, allowing a final working through and consolidation of internal changes. Certain feelings and behaviour are therefore common. These may include some of the following:

» return of symptoms, especially depressive symptoms, and pleas of helplessness (Wittenberg, 1999) – one needs to assess whether this is an attempt to hold on to dependency, a reworking of earlier stages of treatment as part of integration/working through, or a real setback;

» denial of dependency and dismissal of the need for the therapist;

» reactivation of "that part of their personality, which tries, through a phantasy of omnipotent possession, expressed through pathological projective identification, to obscure the reality of separateness and loss" (Quagliata, 1999, p. 412);

» enactments of rage about dependencies or unconscious enactments of feelings of rejection, including "acting out" and risk-taking behaviour;

» fear of the work done being lost;

» jealousy or envy of the fantasized new baby/patient (Wittenberg, 1999, p. 352);

» re-working of the young person's fundamental object-relationships in the context of facing loss.

Anna: the ending stages

The ending stages of Anna's therapy coincided with her public exams. Outwardly, Anna seemed quite unconcerned by the pressure of her exams. The structure of her studies was based around incremental assessment of course work, with which she had progressed steadily, much as she had engaged with her psychotherapy. Her course work results to date indicated that she would exceed the grades she needed to go to college. There was also another break in treatment for two weeks, over the Easter period. Soon after this, Anna had her sixteenth birthday. Anna talked about how neglectful her stepfather had been in marking her birthday. She was open about how hurt she felt. In another session, she described a state of acute anxiety at school, which she labelled as a "panic attack". She was able to get help from her teachers, yet described this experience as evidence of everything going back to the beginning. This felt like a powerful accusation of failure and of protest in the transference, which left Anna's therapist concerned that the ending was premature and somehow precipitous (despite having acknowledged the time limit sensitively throughout), rendering it inadequate and ineffective. (This also understandably generated anxiety in Anna's mother; see "Anna's parents: the ending stages of parent work" in chapter 5.)

Anna explained that she had to sleep with her mother because she felt so frightened of everything going wrong. Over the course of treatment, she had described how she often retreated to her mother's bed at night, which would result in her stepfather having to sleep in Anna's bed or on the sofa. A sense of looming disaster was tangible, and when this was named, Anna responded by saying that she had images in her mind of her mother dying and this made her question who she would then have to turn to. Anna's therapist talked about the sense of endings being sudden, painful, and shocking, like the experience of her aunt and the family friend dying. She also suggested that Anna might feel very angry about this, that too much was being expected of her too soon. The therapist expected Anna to block these interpretations by communicating something about how she could manage. Anna was thoughtful, however, and there was an emotional quality to her acknowledgement of the pain and seriousness of her circumstances that did not feel persecutory. Anna could allow her therapist to be alongside her. Indeed, her reliable and emotionally engaged attendance during this final stage was remarkable, with a passionate and open communication of conflicted states of mind that could be borne and processed. The sadness felt poignant and shared.

Countertransference issues for the therapist during the ending stages of STPP

> [The therapist] and patient alike will be beset by doubts: is this
> the right time to end? Is it too soon? Will the patient be able to
> manage to preserve what has been achieved? Will he manage
> without further help to face difficult times ahead?
>
> Wittenberg, 1999, p. 351

The ending of psychotherapy always raises specific countertransference issues, but this may be especially true with young people who have depression, where the developmental question of separation from or dependence on parents is fraught. Working with young people at risk of self-harm and suicide creates a number of specific countertransference anxieties for therapists.

As noted by Ryz and Wilson (1999), "endings, with their accompanying connotations of loss, separation, death, and bereavement, are a good illustration of experiences that can be felt as angular and nasty and can have a powerful impact on patient and worker alike" (p. 399). Especially in time-limited psychotherapy, such as STPP, the countertransference feeling associated with ending "can be one of cruelty and deprivation, leading to feelings of guilt and inadequacy" (p. 399). Wittenberg (1999) reminds us:

> Not only do we take on board the patient's pain, but it is essential
> that we are aware of our own feelings of loss at parting from a
> child/adult/patient in whom we have invested so much time,
> energy, thought, love and hope and who has stimulated our
> thinking, helped to increase our understanding and stretched our
> emotional capacity. . . . We may also miss being so needed, so
> much the focus of passionate feelings. [p. 353]

For Lanyado (1999b), the ending of therapy (perhaps especially with adolescents) is a "letting go", equivalent to the task that parents go through with their own children. This process of "letting go" is the counterpoint to the "holding" of the young person in mind that is central to the therapeutic task. In order truly to let go of the patient, the therapist needs to be aware of the whole range of "troublesome" countertransference feelings that she may experience, in order to help the young person to recognize and accept his or her own feelings about "moving on". From this perspective, the ending stage is better thought of as a transitional stage – not just an ending, but also a new beginning. The loss and pain of this process may be balanced by the excitement of wondering "what next?"; alternatively, the relief of ending the difficult work of therapy may be balanced by considerable anxiety about the future.

Anna: endings and losses

As the treatment progressed through the ending stages, it felt as though too many changes were coming at once: the end of school, end of therapy, and end of childhood. The feeling that fragile developments were being put at risk by a premature ending was worrying for Anna's therapist. The question of whether additional sessions might help to bridge the transition into college felt like a clinically appropriate consideration. This was discussed in supervision. The fantasy that the ending could feel like a sudden and cruel disaster was explored not only in terms of the external context but also in terms of Anna's internal object relations. The supervision group discussed a feeling that extending the work would create an incongruity that would enact something of Anna's central struggles about blurred boundaries. By staying within the framework of STPP, endings could be thought about as stepping-stones rather than as a catastrophic severance.

In the final sessions, Anna could cut a lonely figure. She often talked about her friends socializing without her or excluding her from communications. It was possible to think about the symbolism of these experiences in the aliveness of the therapeutic relationship because Anna attended regularly and communicated a need to want to think and make sense of them. Anna's therapist reflected on how Anna might feel as though her therapist were turning away from Anna during the break and at the end of her therapy to be with other people. Maybe Anna felt that her therapist was ending because Anna should be able to manage like an adult (now that she was 16) or because there were other younger patients who needed to be seen. It might be hard for Anna to trust that all the hard work of thinking and understanding that had gone on between them over those last few months would still be inside her. Could her therapy be a little like her experience of the learning she had done in this exam year: providing the foundation to college where she hoped to build upon her learning with the support of teachers, friends, and family? Her therapist reflected on it not being easy because it could feel as though nothing had been achieved and it could be hard to trust the work done in therapy. Anna seemed interested in these ideas.

In the last few sessions, Anna for the first time mentioned her burgeoning interest in a boy at school who was showing a romantic interest in her. Space opened up to think about partners and parental couples, including the possibility of her being in a couple herself. Anna talked about what it felt like not to know her father, wondering whether she looked more like him than like her mother. Access to an internal creative, caring parental couple seemed more explicitly available, as did the idea that there could be time to work things through and to plan, and time for significant life events to take place and be processed, rather than happening out of the blue. The concept of being recognized and recognizable felt significant, as there was a quality of Anna becoming more coherent and recognizable to herself, rather than feeling that psychic experience was catastrophic or disastrous.

Consideration of the future, including the possible need for further treatment

Sometimes the clinical team may feel that the young person is in need of prolonged work. It is preferable not to raise the possibility of this in definite terms during the ending stage, since this can otherwise serve to gloss over the experience of ending. The follow-up review provides an opportunity to reassess the situation (see below, "Post-treatment contact").

Young people's ambivalent feelings about the end of the therapy may be expressed particularly in relation to the idea of further sessions. For example, a girl in her last session of psychoanalytic psychotherapy during Trowell and colleagues' (2003) study of adolescent depression said that she hoped that when she had stopped, all the progress would not get lost; but she would not want further treatment if it were available because she had a lot to do at school. She then went on to describe a good time she had had with friends, and how sad it had been coming back to a darkened house; her mother was probably depressed and in bed. The therapist took up how important it was for this girl to feel that the therapist was prepared to let her go;

however, on reflection, the therapist thought that it would have been useful to link the girl's fear of losing the improvements she had made with the fear that these left her mother and therapist in the depressed state she herself had been in previously, which would not feel like a secure foundation to build on.

Anna: looking beyond the therapy

Anna and her therapist discussed the availability of review appointments at the end of treatment that Anna could ask for on her own terms. This was contrasted with the reality of the actual ending of regular contact. In her final session, Anna talked about feeling more confident but not being sure if this feeling would last. She described how the prospect of not coming for her sessions felt "weird". She repeated this word several times, and when her therapist asked if she could explain a little more what she meant, Anna said, "I think I'm ready". Some exploration of Anna's resilience followed and how even through the recent intense struggles, Anna could talk and think about them without it feeling like her world was falling apart so completely. They talked about how understandable it was for this to feel strange, yet they noticed that somehow this did not feel as dangerous as a few weeks previously, when Anna had described her panic and sense of foreboding.

Anna: summary report

Anna's therapist also wrote a final summary report for her GP about Anna's progress. This report was designed to be read in addition to and in conjunction with the initial report written during the beginning stage of treatment.

The unfolding experience of Anna over the course of STPP

Anna established a regular rhythm of weekly attendance. She only missed a further two sessions after the assessment. One occurred at the time of her public exams and one also related to Anna engaging with processes of separation at the end of treatment. Anna significantly invested in STPP, and this was most vividly evidenced in her capacity to explore complex and unsettling feelings of frustration, criticism, and the painfulness of loss. These conflicts underpinned Anna's experiences of low mood and feeling that her world was falling to pieces, as she had experienced over the previous year.

Underlying dynamics of Anna's experiences of low mood

At the point of Anna's referral to our clinic, she was assessed as suffering from long-standing low mood, which had most likely been triggered by the death of a loved family friend. Her emotional struggles were often hidden behind a façade of coping and competence and her tendency to step into relationships as the caregiver or as a parental authority. Anna also described experiences of intense headaches or bodily pain (such as stomach aches) that seemed psychosomatic in nature. Anna was able to feel contained by the development of a therapeutic relationship over regular and reliable weekly contact. The possibility of exploring Anna's states of mind and patterns of relating as they were played out in the therapy sessions enabled an exploration of some of the deeper hidden dynamics contributing to Anna's experiences of low mood. These dynamics fell into the following key areas:

Struggles with individuation and separation in adolescence: The level of confusion and blurring of internal representations of parental figures has been significant and long-standing. This is likely to have been influenced by Anna's experience of an absent father and by her experience of a dearly loved aunt who played a significant role in her young life and died when she was 10 years old. During psychotherapy, it became possible to understand that Anna was struggling to find a position in her current relationships because of an unconscious, confused relational configuration. An example of this was of an internal maternal figure that was quickly interchangeable with a sister or child figure. This seems to have pushed Anna into the position of carer in her close-knit extended family. The death of her aunt remains keenly felt. It seems that Anna's perception of the family tumult and conflict that followed this bereavement came to the fore when a beloved family friend died more recently. This also coincided with the complex developmental tasks of adolescence.

At the time of her aunt's death, Anna described being out of control much like a toddler having tantrums. Her stepfather joined the family around this time, and she found this series of events difficult to manage, which created tension within the family. Her mother and stepfather

have confirmed that this was a difficult time for the family, and Ms
A has explained the significance of the loss for her too, as this was
a dearly loved elder sister who brought her up after their mother's
untimely death. It seems that the understandable distress and protest
that generated these intense behavioural outbursts were in due course
gathered into a persona of a competent and pseudo-adult little girl who
entered into puberty and early adolescence in a state of strong identification with a confident and in-control parental figure. This emotional
defence seems to have crumbled at the point when she was faced with
negotiating the transition into adulthood, with school education ending,
and with the death of Anna's mother's friend. This has generated an
emotionally disorientating crisis where Anna's unconscious positioning
as a capable moral authority could no longer defend her from feelings
of falling apart, uncontrollable crying, and psychosomatic pains (e.g.,
intense headaches and stomach pains). It has been possible for some
of these unconscious dynamics to come into view and to be thought
about in her therapy. Anna has been curious and engaged in exploring
these dynamics and has expressed how helpful it has been to make
sense of her experiences. In turn, it has become possible for Anna to
feel more balanced and to consider her struggles while keeping in sight
her emotional and educational strengths.

Mourning: Over the course of treatment, the underlying dynamics that
left Anna struggling to mourn and recover from the death of her aunt
and her mother's friend came to the fore. She particularly described
the visceral shock of her aunt's death and how this made her feel physically sick and led to powerful behavioural outbursts. It seems that she
has held on tightly to her relationship with her aunt by internalizing it
and installing it as a representational figure that is mature and able to
get things done in an organized and diligent manner. In some respects,
this has held Anna in good stead as she has progressed well through
school and managed the arrivals of her younger half-siblings during
her adolescence. Yet she has instinctively felt a pull towards acting as a
maternal figure to them (her mother has explained that she herself was
brought up by her elder sister), while also struggling with an underlying
resentment about this. While preoccupied by these issues, Anna has
avoided the usual tasks of separating and redefining her identity that
are characteristic of adolescence. This has put relationships with peers
under strain, as Anna often feels older and tends to feel critical of their
adolescent behaviour and has created a competitive relationship with

authority figures (particularly within the family). Anna has described feeling profoundly confused about where she fits into her life, making it hard to separate from family or to find herself a trusted peer group. The latter continues to be difficult, yet Anna has gained insight into the feelings underlying her perceptions and sometimes polarized relational experiences with key family members. She has been able to explore how she has been affected by experiences of both her aunt's and her mother's depression, and she has also been able to talk about how vulnerable and lost she felt as a little girl. This has offered relief from similar experiences in the present. As Anna's psychotherapy has progressed, she has become more able to notice her need for help and to access this from family, from school, and in her therapy. This seems to have increased her resilience in the face of acute distress and emotional states of fragmentation. Anna's experiences of somatic pain and headaches have significantly reduced.

Risk and protective factors

In my experience of Anna at the point of ending treatment, the risk of self-harm is very low. She is well prepared for college and excited at the prospect. She may be vulnerable to further depressive episodes, however, and it is significant to note that she described a family history of depression in her maternal aunt and mother. Anna is alert to the signs that might indicate a slip back into low mood, and she is aware of how to get help for this.

Post-treatment contact

Traditionally, many psychoanalytic psychotherapists have seen post-treatment contact between the therapist and their child or adolescent former patient as unhelpful, because it has been considered counterproductive with regard to the resolution of the transference. Yet if the therapeutic relationship is conceptualized more as a new attachment relationship (Lanyado, 1999b), or if the developmental aspect of the therapy is a strong element in the therapist's thinking, or if the patient's capacity to internalize needs ongoing support (Rustin, 2004), then the attitude to requests for post-treatment contact may be somewhat different. As Buxbaum (1950) put it many decades ago, when making the case for building in contact after the ending of therapy, "I think that such a procedure removes the traumatic effects of ending an analysis in an active way. The analyst himself refuses to let it be the threatening and sadistic 'never more'" (p. 190).

Child psychotherapists today usually offer follow-up appointments where this seems likely to be useful, which is particularly the case with young people for whom loss or fear of damage has been a particular focus. In STPP, a follow-up session somewhere around four to six months after the end of treatment can be offered, where indicated. This is an appropriate interval for this relatively short treatment, allowing time for both the gains and the limitations of the STPP therapy to become clear, without risking either an over-hasty offering of further treatment or losing the patient altogether through too lengthy a delay. The young person may not respond to this offer, and it is important that he or she is free to refuse. This underlines the reality of the therapist having to cope with letting go and often not knowing what the young person is making of the therapeutic work done.

Anna: follow-up session

Anna and her therapist had ended the therapy with the agreement that Anna might attend a follow-up session about four months later, which the therapist would offer but Anna would be under no obligation to accept. Her therapist duly offered this, and, after some delay in responding, Anna made contact to accept the offer. By the time the appointment had arrived, it was more than five months since they had finished the STPP treatment.

> Anna reported that she had now been at college for a term and that she was pleased that her mother and stepfather had allowed her to pursue her chosen course. At first, Anna delivered a wealth of material about her new life at college. This felt familiar feel to her therapist, giving her a sense of being overwhelmed with undigested information along with a feeling of being left out of an engaging young adult life. She reflected silently, however, that this material was significantly different from when she had first met Anna in its emphasis on appropriate

social activities with her peer group: these now seemed to be Anna's focus rather than a preoccupation with complex family affairs. As the session progressed, however, Anna did reflect on her current family life and reported a calmer atmosphere at home.

Anna had not experienced any relapse or return of depression since the end of her treatment. The therapist was struck by a certain vivacity about her descriptions of her life and wondered how she could have found this young woman so hard to call to mind in those initial weeks.

CHAPTER FIVE

Work with parents and carers

Principles of psychoanalytic work with parents and carers

> The parent worker stands, as it were, on the cusp between our concerns with the inner world of the child and the outer world of family, school, everyday events, and outer reality.
>
> Miles, 2011, p. 110

C hild psychotherapists engage with parents and carers in a range of ways to support the child or adolescent patient's therapy and emotional development. Parents' and carers' feelings about their child's difficulties, their child's psychotherapist, and the clinic team as a whole are a hugely important part of the picture. It is essential that these be addressed not only through a thorough process of setting-up, assessment, and review, but also through work with parents conducted separately from the young person's therapy, where this is desired by parent and child. The process of reviewing therapy is discussed briefly below, but the main focus of this chapter is on parent work conducted in parallel to the young person's psychotherapy, here called "parent work" but sometimes called "parental therapy" (Frick, 2000) or the "psychotherapy of parenthood" (Sutton & Hughes, 2005). While this is the model of parent work offered as part of STPP, other psychoanalytic writers have described parent work conducted where the young person is not having psychotherapy. Jarvis (2005) and Trevatt (2005), for instance, describe brief work usefully undertaken with parents on their own, where their adolescent child refuses to attend. Parents are also sometimes seen for group work (Rustin, 2009b). This chapter is written primarily with parents in mind, which might include adoptive parents. Much of it, however, is also applicable to other carers, such as foster carers, who have responsibility for providing the day-to-day parental function in relation to the young person; some specific attention to their differing situations and needs is given below ("Working with adopted and looked-after children and their carers").

Parents' relationship to therapist, service, and parent worker

Harris (1968) describes the importance of careful attention being paid to the feelings and phantasies of a child or adolescent patient's parents about the therapy and the therapist. She notes the unconscious anxiety and guilt so often felt by parents when their child comes for therapy:

> Somewhere in every parent still exist the little girl and boy who are convinced that they can never become a proper mother or father. When things go wrong, this little girl in the mother feels found out and projects upon the therapist her super-ego picture of her own internal mother who is going to blame her and take the child away because of her presumption and bad management. [p. 53]

Houzel (2000), with work with autistic children particularly in mind, argues that the therapeutic alliance with parents must be established during preliminary meetings, as "a true therapeutic alliance with the parents can be agreed upon once they themselves have witnessed attempts at understanding through interpretations and commentaries" (p. 122). This early alliance will be a "reference point" for the remainder of the therapy, when it will need to be sustained through regular review meetings. Review meetings allow the parents or carers direct (though limited) access to their child's therapist's views regarding the emotional life of their child, including what the young person may need from the parents, and about the progress of the work. Rustin (2009b) suggests that "at their best, such meetings can offer a real chance to integrate diverse perspectives and to enrich the understanding of both parents and therapist, but they can also be difficult occasions in which divergences in aim between therapist and parent may erupt" (p. 210). (Initial meetings and the review process for STPP are described below.)

Psychoanalytic parent work

Parallel work with parents alongside individual child and adolescent psychotherapy has long been regarded as an essential and integral part of the therapy (Klauber, 1998; Rustin, 1998a, 2009) which plays an essential part in successful treatment (Midgley & Kennedy, 2011; Novick & Novick, 2005; Szapocznik et al., 1989). While not all parents of adolescents engaged in STPP treatment may be seen, as discussed below, the importance of considering therapeutic work with parents should not be underestimated.

A major element of the process of parent work is well described by Hopkins (1999) in her discussion of work with families:

> As in individual therapy, the aim [of parent work] is to provide a safe and reliable setting with definite boundaries in which it is possible to feel increasingly secure. Within this setting, the therapist aims to provide what is termed "containment". This is a dual process in which the therapist has to tolerate and contain her own anxiety and frustration, as well as the family's, and to wait until she can see how to verbalise her experience of the family's conflict in ways that make them bearable to acknowledge and so to think about. As also happens in individual therapy, the therapist monitors the family's feelings about herself and the clinic, and may need to explore this aspect of the transference with them, especially if the family feels blamed or threatened. [p. 84]

The nature and scope of the work done within parent work carried out in parallel with the child or young person's therapy will vary depending on what is needed by the parents or carers and their child, and what is appropriate and manageable for them. Rustin (2000) delineates four main categories:

> At one end of the spectrum are cases where gaining the support of parents to protect and sustain the child's therapy is the prime

aim. The second group is where parents are looking for support in their parental functioning. . . . The third group is where the explicit aim of the work is change in family functioning, and this has been agreed by the parents as part of the work as a whole. . . . At the other end of the spectrum is individual psychotherapy for one or indeed both parents, to which they have committed themselves as patients in their own right. [pp. 3–4]

Rustin (2009b) illustrates the use of thoughtful observation and attunement to help understand aspects of the parents' personality and how these impact on their parenting of the child in treatment. She emphasizes the "continuity between the absolutely unavoidable everyday anxieties of being a parent and the extreme ones which bring families to the attention of child psychotherapists"; in attachment terms, "normal secure attachment is indeed the child's link to someone who is capable of being anxious about the child" (p. 209).

Drawing on Harris's (1975) emphasis on delineating the adult and infantile aspects of the parents' personalities to support improved parental functioning, Rustin (2009b, pp. 209–210) identifies four key areas, attention to which underlies all psychoanalytic parent work:

» the "distinction between infantile and adult states of mind" – helping parents to become aware of times when parental functioning becomes overwhelmed by infantile feelings and phantasies;

» the "characterisation of maternal and paternal aspects of personality and parental functioning" – "the balance of these within individuals and the way in which they are distributed in a parental couple is a fruitful vertex of development";

» "the Oedipus complex and its sequelae" – this may be particularly difficult when jealousies are aroused by new partners;

» "the experience of shame among parents who need help with their children".

Rustin (2009b) argues that the parent worker offers a model of response to emotional distress involving five core elements:

The first is attention to establishing and maintaining a reliable setting in which it is possible to talk about very upsetting things. . . . The second element is the co-creation of some shared language to describe painful emotional states. . . . Third is the valuing of boundaries and differentiation. . . . Fourth is an adequately complex understanding of human emotion and intimate relationships. . . . Lastly, and most important, there is the focus on giving meaning to behaviour. [pp. 213–214]

Sutton and Hughes (2005) have coined the term "psychotherapy of parenthood" for psychoanalytic parent work, to denote its status and importance and its focus on the parenting function (p. 171). They argue that this is analogous to "the focus in psychoanalytic work with couples on the relationship . . . rather than either partner being the 'identified patient' [Ruszczynski, 1992]" (p. 171). They discuss the parents' transference to the service, in particular the "grandparental transference as parents seek an adult to contain their anxieties" (p. 172) (see also Miller, 2001; Whitefield & Midgley, 2015). Sutton and Hughes (2005, pp. 173–174) offer a formulation of parent work comprising five areas of focus:

» "information exchange";
» "general 'child guidance' and specific communication about the child's therapy";
» "supportive examination of day-to-day parenting";
» "exploration of, and therapeutic interventions directed towards, family and other relationships";
» "exploration of, and therapeutic interventions directed towards, the current impact of parents' earlier relationship".

Frick (2000) describes the ambivalence produced in parents by the conflict between the wish for their child to be happy and the need to maintain their own defences: although this is true in individual psychotherapy, she argues, "if we regard a child's symptom as being part of the parents' own problems, motivation and resistance have been located in different people and are therefore more difficult to treat" (p. 67). She argues that such defences against their own traumas or difficulties, or powerful shame and guilt, may make it difficult for parents to engage in parent work or support their child's therapy (pp. 74–75). Understanding the origins and meaning of such difficulties is key. Klauber (1998) describes the strain on parents of living with a disturbed or troubled child – particularly where there has been medical intervention – and the need for sensitive work that understands the traumatic nature of this parental experience; this frequently requires a knowledge of post-traumatic phenomena. She emphasizes the importance of attending closely to the transference and countertransference, particularly when parents perceive the therapist or parent worker as a "prosecutor or persecutor" (p. 86):

> In the face of projected anxiety, hostility and despair, it is often difficult to hold onto one's own thoughts or to avoid being drawn into hasty and judgemental conclusions about who or what caused what, and to whom. There is also a need to be genuinely in tune with the lost parenting capacities of most parents of such children. [p. 86]

Klauber argues that the nature of the work can be deepened psychoanalytically "as the strength of the experience of being contained and understood builds greater trust and interest in understanding the unconscious meaning of experience" (p. 106).

As this indicates, building an alliance with parents or carers, analogous to the therapeutic or working alliance with the child or adolescent patient, is essential (Houzel, 2000; Miles, 2011) and is founded on a willingness to take seriously the depth of the parents' concerns about their child and, in many cases, the strain placed on them by their child's difficulties. Green (2000) argues that the forming of a working alliance with parents is often inspired by the parent's "*wish* to be a good-enough parent" (p. 26; author's emphasis), a "reparative hope" to parent better than they have themselves been parented. The extent to which parents or carers may be able to work on understanding their child in his or her own right may be gauged, Green argues, from the role the child plays within the family and the nature and weight of the projections he or she may be carrying for the parents:

> At one end of the continuum will be the parents who, for perhaps pathological reasons of their own . . ., find it very hard to view their child as separate from their own needs and desires. Somewhere else along the continuum might be the parents who struggle beyond their own anger, fear, hurt, or disappointment to understand their child but nonetheless find themselves constrained by their own histories, limitations, or conflicts. At the most hopeful end are those parents who are readily able to be emotionally aware of their child's feelings. [p. 29]

To sustain such an alliance during ongoing parent work, along with the parents' support for their child's therapy, it is often necessary to "contain those feelings of envy that may intervene in the progress of the child's therapy . . . [which] involves not only the parent's envy of the therapist and the fantasized perfect relationship between 'therapist-mother' and child, but also the parent's envy of the child's therapy" (Horne, 2000, p. 60).

The extent to which parent work may make explicit use of transference and countertransference depends on the nature of the agreement entered into by the parents or carers with the parent worker. Sutton and Hughes (2005, p. 173) argue that parent work in any of these areas may be conducted on either of two levels of work in the transference:

» "therapist's use of non-verbalised transference/countertransference understanding to inform and shape understanding to inform and shape responses";

» "therapist's use of explicit and verbalised use of transference/countertransference understanding".

They argue that "what varies is the nature of the transference, the extent to which it becomes an influence upon the course of the contact and its impact on the ability to attend to the primary tasks of assessment and treatment" (p. 172). They argue that, while it may not necessarily need to be verbalized by the therapist or parent worker, there are times when "speaking explicitly to the transference with a parent at the very first contact may be necessary to allow any chance of engagement" (p. 172). This may particularly be the case when feelings of shame or fear of authority so common in parents (Horne, 2000) are defended against by aggression or hostility (Sutton & Hughes, 2005, p. 172). By contrast, Horne (2000) argues that much of the work of parent work "takes place at the conscious or preconscious level, working with the functioning ego rather than the unconscious" (p. 63). She suggests that it may be that when the parent's material seems to come more from his or her unconscious, this may be an indicator of the need for separate work for the parent as a patient in his or her own right (p. 63). Whether such work should be conducted via a referral for individual psychotherapy with an adult practitioner is debateable, however; it may, for instance, be more helpful to the family that their diverse concerns and needs are contained by one service. Where parent work is conducted by a child psychotherapist, the extent to which there may be an explicit agreement to use transference interpretation has been debated (e.g., Rustin, 2009b; Whitefield & Midgley, 2015), although it is clear that the child psychotherapist parent worker will draw on his or her countertransference understanding in the service of both the parent in the room and the child in therapy.

Parent work in STPP

Psychoanalytic parent work in STPP, as with all psychoanalytic child psychotherapy, is clinical work conducted in parallel to the young person's own therapy, by a different therapist, with the aims of supporting the therapy, fostering the parents' or carers' understanding of their adolescent child's difficulties, and helping them with the inevitable anxieties aroused by their child suffering significant difficulties, such as depression. It is usually undertaken by a child psychotherapist, but it may be provided by a range of clinicians with a core training in another clinical discipline, who have also gained a significant degree of knowledge, skill, and experience in working with parents within a psychoanalytically informed framework. The STPP parent worker is often likely also to be the clinician responsible for the case management of the young person.

The task of working with parents and carers is multifaceted. It includes the engagement of the parents in the treatment process, thinking about the young person and his or her experience of the treatment, and considering issues connected to parenting. It also includes thinking about relational issues within the family; containment of parental anxieties aroused by the young person's depression; parents' own issues where these impinge on the young person (if they can be addressed within the time frame of STPP); and, where appropriate, addressing historical and transgenerational factors within the family.

Parent work in STPP is based on the principle that if parents' anxieties are sufficiently contained, then they are better placed to think about their experiences as parents. This includes the emotions and anxieties generated within them by their depressed adolescent child and how best to understand and support their child's development. If they are able to be more in touch with their child's depression, then they may be able to think better and act more effectively as parents. The parents may be enabled to relinquish some existing set notions of their relationship with their child, "dream" anew about their child, and conceive fresh thoughts about him or her. Changes in parent–child relating may begin to develop. This is in contrast to defensive ways of managing anxiety, such as rigidity, dissociation, acting out, splitting, or intrusive and controlling behaviour towards the young person.

Aims and objectives of STPP parent work

In order for a young person to make full use of STPP, the work with parents is of prime importance, as it is in longer term psychoanalytic psychotherapy. The parent worker's primary role is in helping parents keep the young person's welfare and psychological needs paramount. Nevertheless, many parents or carers may have had their own difficulties, including of a depressive nature, and it is important for the clinician to relate to them as people in their own right. If indicated, the worker may need to discuss with the parents other kinds of help they could consider for themselves towards the end of the work (as discussed further below). The nature of the parent work, and what it is possible to talk about with each parent or couple, is necessarily dependent upon their implicit or explicit consent regarding the range and depth of exploration and what can be tolerated emotionally.

The primary aims of STPP parent work are:

» to enable the young person to engage in and sustain his or her treatment;
» to enable the parents to be thoughtful in their understanding of their adolescent child's depression and their response to it;
» to observe, and to discuss if possible, the emotional aspects of the parents' states of mind, including experiences of depression or depressive anxieties and the functioning of the parental couple (where applicable), and to share such observations where possible;

» to facilitate discussion of parental experiences of their own adolescence and adolescent states of mind;

» to make informed links with other clinicians involved and also the young person's external world network, such as school or college, social services (where relevant), or the GP in relation to managing risk.

Some functions, such as managing risk or attending review meetings, may overlap with the case manager's role. In many clinics, responsibility for both may be held by a single practitioner.

Primary focus of STPP parent work

In STPP work with a parent or parental couple, it is necessary for the parent worker to be clear in his or her own mind, and in his or her framing of the work with the parents, that the focus is on the parents' adolescent child and on their parental thinking, experiences, and relating, rather than on the individual parent as a person or, for a parental couple, their relationship as an adult couple (Whitefield & Midgley, 2015). At the same time, in work with parental couples, the way in which their relationship is shaped and functions is an important matter to be considered in respect of their parenting and how their child experiences them as a couple (Harold & Conger, 1997; Rhoades, 2008). The primary aim of the parent work is likely to be "changing parental functioning" (Rustin, 2009b, p. 213). This may take a variety of forms, including:

> support for quite disturbed parents whose own mental state may impinge in damaging ways on their children, support for deprived and vulnerable parents (for example, bereaved families, mothers abandoned by their partners, refugee families), and work which attempts to explore ways in which parental functioning is disturbed by unconscious aspects of the parents' own way of seeing things. [Rustin, 2009b, p. 213]

In situations where one or both parents have significant emotional needs, or mental health problems of their own, this will involve considerable therapeutic tact (see also Bailey, 2006). The extent to which explicit psychoanalytic interpretations based on the transference and countertransference will be offered will depend on having the emotional consent of the parent or carer (Rustin, 2009b, p. 218) and on the skills, knowledge, and clinical choices of the individual clinician. Different parents or carers will be able to tolerate varying degrees of insight-giving interventions (p. 213). Fundamentally, the parent worker is offering the "capacity to empathise with both parental and child perspectives" and using the relationship built through parent work to inform "other kinds of conversation which have therapeutic potential" (p. 218).

In adolescence, developmental imperatives mean that the young person has to gain increased separation from his or her parents, mourn the loss of his or her parents as experienced and recalled in childhood, and develop a new relationship to the parents of his or her adolescence. In the context of depression, some adolescents may be melancholic in response to this developmental task, particularly the task of being able to bear knowing of his or her ambivalent feelings towards his or her parents, and struggle to turn more towards his or her peer groups and develop peer relationships, including of a sexual nature. This is a challenge not only for the adolescent but also for the parents, who, in a parallel process, need to make a developmental shift in their roles and in the nature of their intimacy with their child, now an adolescent. If there is a parental couple, this process usually brings movement and new considerations within the couple relationship. The parents may become immobilized, resistant, or conflicted in response to the pain aroused and the losses involved. In STPP, the work with parents may help in such a situation, enabling them to mourn the loss of their younger child and become interested in, and appreciative of, their adolescent child. They are then better placed to help their son or daughter to recognize the new emotional realities and gain confidence in the processes of development, including fresh, uncharted ways of relating to his or her parents.

Frame, setting, and contract
for the work with parents or carers

Although parents are generally offered far fewer sessions than the young person, parent work nevertheless offers them the opportunity to meet the parent worker regularly and reliably for the duration of their child's therapy. The usual expectation is for 7 sessions for parents, that is, one for every 4 sessions for the young person, at roughly monthly intervals. These are not fixed parameters in relation to the parent work, however, and the rhythm of parent sessions may be determined on a case-by-case basis. Some parents, particularly those of younger adolescents, or where the child is behaving in ways that pose a significant risk, may need more frequent parent sessions. It is also possible to vary the frequency of sessions during the course of the work, as more may be needed during one period and fewer at another point. It is usual for the parent work to begin concurrently with the young person's treatment, and it is particularly important to have a parent-work session near the end of the young person's treatment in order both to review the young person's progress and to address any anxieties that may arise in the parent about the work coming to an end. In some clinical situations, it may be that parents are more consistent in attending their sessions than their child is in attending their psychotherapy. Useful parent work can nevertheless be undertaken, and in some instances this may be the most vital aspect of the intervention.

Parent-work sessions, like therapy sessions, should ideally take place in the same room each time, and last 50 minutes. The room should be quiet, private, and free from interruptions. Best practice is to offer the same time and day for each appointment. It is often, but not always, best for parent sessions to take place at the same time as the young person's psychotherapy sessions, particularly if the parent is transporting the young person to his or her session.

Who should attend for parent work?

For the young person involved in treatment, there will be a wide range of parental and care contexts. Identifying who needs to attend for parent work is a primary issue, especially with families in conflict and young people who are looked after by the state (see "Working with looked-after children and their carers" in chapter 7).

Young people will also have various attitudes towards the involvement of parents or carers in their treatment and in parallel parent work. Some young people may be against parental involvement, and this may conflict with the professional view that contact with their parents is needed. In the UK, young people who are 16 years of age or over (and are assessed as having "capacity" based on their emotional maturity) are entitled to undergo treatment without parental involvement, and this right must be respected. For young people under the age of 16, negotiations may be needed to arrive at an arrangement that is more or less acceptable to all parties.

The range of a young person's family situations may include the following:

» an intact parental couple;
» separated parents (with or without current partners);
» one single parent;
» adoptive parents;
» friends or family carers;
» being in the care of the Local Authority that holds parental responsibility.

If there is an intact parental couple (who, of course, may be a heterosexual or a homosexual couple), it is best if both parents can attend sessions, although this may not always be possible. In addition to the potential helpfulness of gaining views from two perspectives, the young person's separate and different relationship with each parent can be brought alive in the work. The active participation of two parents also allows for the possibility of observation of how the young person's depression and adolescent development is impacting on the parental couple relationship, and for the therapeutic work to engage with this. It provides an opportunity to think about how any difficulties in the couple relationship may be affecting their child, including the anxieties and emotional states associated with depression. In some families, the source of the depressive difficulties may be in the parent/couple relationship as much as, or rather than, in the young person. Working with the parental couple may lead to an increased capacity in the couple to tolerate knowing more (in an emotional sense) about their child's depression. It can promote development of their containing capacities in relation to their child's distress and their own and lead to a more of a "couple state of mind" (Morgan, 2001; see also Morgan, 2005).

Where the parents are not an intact couple but each parent is still actively involved with their child (and still retains parental responsibility), it may make sense for each parent to be offered an initial consultation, either together or separately, depending on the degree of cooperation (or hostility) between them. Having a discussion about this can help to assess and establish who might attend parent-work sessions and whether this should be one parent on a regular basis, or each parent on a separate and less frequent basis. For single parents, sessions with a parent worker may help not only to relieve some of the emotional burden of the psychological complexities of parenting an adolescent, but also to mediate any dynamics of entanglement or a stark division between the parent and his or her adolescent child. Where a separated parent has a current partner (perhaps in a step-parent relationship to their adolescent child), it may be helpful that the mother–stepfather couple or father–stepmother couple attend the parent work.

Communication with therapist, supervisor, and other agencies

Given the potential for risk, the seriousness of the young person's psychological predicament, and the consequent anxieties likely to be generated, the young person's therapist and the parent worker need to have regular communication outside of the therapeutic sessions, in addition to review meetings with the family. Such communication needs to be sufficiently regular to lessen significantly the likelihood of acting out by the family, their workers, or the network. A pattern of meetings should ideally be agreed between the clinicians at the outset. These could take place face-to-face or by telephone. Additional communications (such as by telephone and email) will also be necessary in some cases. This has implications for the way confidentiality is discussed with the young person at the start of therapy.

The young person's therapist and the parent worker will probably need to share a developing formulation of the young person's internal world, paying attention to the nature of internal objects, anxieties, and defences. They will also discuss the impact of the treatment on the parents and family and the young person's functioning in the external world – such as at school, at college, or in a residential unit – and on his or her peer relationships. It will be necessary for the young person's therapist to know something of the psychological resources and limitations of the parents in order to understand the young person's home situation. Any issues concerning the young person's siblings and extended family members will also need to be shared between the two clinicians.

The therapist and the parent worker need to strike a balance in achieving good communication in this way without blurring the distinction between the two pieces of work. If there is a high level of discussion between them, this can, to some degree, serve a peer-supervisory function, including containment. The transference and countertransference experiences in which each clinician is participating (with the young person or parents) will, however, influence how each clinician hears the other's clinical material and also affect each clinician's identifications within the family dynamic. This holds the potential for distortion to understanding, and it may unhelpfully shape what each clinician offers to the other from a supervisory perspective. Too much discussion between the young person's psychotherapist and the parent worker runs the risk of an unhelpful amount of information and views from each of the family members being exchanged between the two. This can become lodged in the clinicians' minds and get in the way of their unprejudiced emotional availability in subsequent sessions.

Having the opportunity to discuss parent work with a supervisor, or with colleagues in a work discussion group, is therefore extremely helpful, and this is discussed in chapter 6. To this end, and for processing hitherto unknown aspects of the experience of the session, it is helpful to write up process-recording notes of each session, as often as is possible. This can help to generate new thinking regarding the parents and their relationships with their adolescent child.

The parent worker may also be the case manager for the clinic involved, and he or she will need to balance the different (though linked) responsibilities of each role. In order that the integrity of the young person's treatment framework with his or her therapist can be maintained, and particularly when the parent worker is the case manager, it is most likely that the parent worker will be the primary point of contact with external agencies regarding the young person. This may involve joint work with those agencies, particularly education and social services. (See "Case management, collaborative working, and psychiatric issues" in chapter 3.)

Setting-up, reviews, communication,
and routine outcome monitoring

Assessment and setting-up

It is most likely that the process of referring the young person will begin with an initial joint meeting between the therapist offering STPP, the young person, and the parent or parents (as was described in relation to Anna in chapter 4); this should also be attended by the parent worker. It is helpful for the parent worker to start the parent sessions while the young person is in the assessment phase of the treatment. This may help the parents with their anxieties about the process, and it is also useful in gathering additional information to support the assessment, in giving the parents an initial experience of parent work, and in helping the parent worker to assess the likelihood that the parents will support their child's therapy (whether by attending for parent work or in other ways). There is likely to be another meeting of all parties once this assessment phase is completed, to agree the way forward.

These initial meetings as part of the setting-up process provide the opportunity to make a good therapeutic engagement with the family, to share important information, to make observations, and to develop a preliminary formulation regarding the parents/carers and young person.

The initial joint meeting usually needs to include:

» preliminary exploration of family situations and relationships, and how the young person's depression is impacting on the family;

» explanation of the treatment framework of STPP for the young person and the parents/carers;

» initial assessment of parental functioning and the couple relationship, where appropriate;

» assessment and discussion of who should attend and participate in the parent work – this is particularly pertinent with separated and reconstituted families and looked-after children;

» discussion of the practicalities around attendance;

» agreement about the need for and the nature and frequency of review meetings.

The optimal frequency of parent-work meetings and what is feasible will also sometimes be discussed at this point, although more often this will be considered during the first parent-work session rather than in the young person's presence.

In some cases, this initial meeting may be an opportunity for the parent worker to confirm the extent to which information about depression, and basic psycho-education about the relationship between depression, exercise, diet, and sleep, has already been provided to the parents in the initial contact with the clinic. Psycho-education is not part of the model of parent work in STPP, but where it has not been given to parents already, this meeting may be an opportunity to point them briefly in the direction of relevant information.

In this initial parent session, preliminary agreement will also be reached on the dates for future meetings. If the psychotherapist knows in advance of anything that will disrupt the agreed dates, then as much notice as possible needs to be given. Particular attention must be paid to the impact on the relationship between the parents and parent worker generated by breaks, such as for holidays or related to sickness.

In setting up parent work, it is important for the parent worker to attend closely to his or her countertransference for indications about the parents' or carers' possible emerging transference (which may be to the clinic, the child's therapist, or the parent worker). This is the best clue to the degree of unconscious consent in the parents. The consent of the parents or carers to the level of work in which they want to engage, however, will continue to develop during the course of the work. Sutton and Hughes (2005) recommend that the parent worker attend to three questions: "what is useful for the child, what is useful and possible for the parents and what is possible for the therapist?" (p. 175).

Anna's parents: assessment and setting-up process

Anna came to the initial meeting with the psychotherapist and parent worker (another child psychotherapist working in the clinic) along with her mother, Ms A. Like her daughter, Ms A presented as somewhat pleased that the offer of STPP was being made, and she was helpful and practical in relation to making arrangements for Anna to attend (with the agreement that the first three sessions would constitute an assessment, after which all parties would decide whether or not to proceed). The parent worker described the role of parent work and suggested, supported by the therapist, that Ms A might like to bring her partner, Anna's stepfather, to the parent sessions. Ms A agreed to this in a somewhat breezy way, leaving the parent worker wondering whether she would really attend and would indeed bring her partner. The parent worker decided to try to arrange at least one parent session to take place during the assessment phase of Anna's treatment, in order to gain a clearer picture of the parents' concerns and any difficulties, and to get a sense of the degree of support they might be prepared to give the therapeutic work in this way.

Once Anna's first individual session had been arranged, the parent worker contacted Ms A to arrange a meeting. Practical commitments, including the couple's younger children, made it difficult to arrange a session promptly, but Ms A did attend one session during the assessment phase of Anna's therapy, accompanied by her partner. During this session, Ms A continued to present in a rather light-hearted way, while it seemed to fall to her partner to express concerns about tension and rows within the family. Supported by the parent worker, Anna's stepfather eventually expressed his considerable concern not just about Anna but about her mother, and he spoke rather diffidently about his partner's recurrent bouts of depression. Ms A was clearly moved by this, while also rather embarrassed and ambivalent about it being discussed. The parent worker talked carefully about the remit of the parent work, that it was not to be "therapy" for the parents but to support them in parenting Anna, given Anna's current difficulties and their own; she acknowledged Ms A and her partner's worries about Ms A's depression being "passed on" to Anna as well as its importance in its own right. (She also ascertained that Ms A had some rather piecemeal contact with her own GP about her depression.) Ms A seemed to find this reassuring.

Reviews and routine outcome monitoring

Once it has been agreed that STPP will proceed, whether or not this will include parent work, an agreement needs to be reached as to the necessary frequency and timing of review meetings, along with provisional agreement about who is to be invited to them.

Good communication between the two workers as part of their clinical practice is a primary factor in holding the concerns and anxieties of the family and network. The purpose of a review meeting, however, is different (as discussed above), in that it provides an opportunity for contact between the young person's own therapist and the parents. The support of the parent worker for this process is crucial: he or she is in a position both to support the parents in speaking about their own perspectives and to hold on to the information relayed in the reviews, and its emotional significance, to work on in subsequent parent sessions. Review meetings may also be useful opportunities to reset, or reaffirm, the framework and boundaries of the therapeutic work with all parties. There will be some cases when few or no review meetings of this sort are indicated, particularly with older adolescents.

Review meetings also provide a good opportunity to conduct or review routine outcome-monitoring measures that will first have been introduced at the end of the assessment process. Outcome measures or simple measures of therapy process are a useful means of identifying and quantifying the young person's difficulties and progress. Not only may they be useful to demonstrate progress to colleagues or commissioners (and may indeed be required by the clinical service), but they may also be helpful to the young person or the parents in enabling them to consider any progress they are making.

Session-by-session outcome monitoring is not helpful in STPP, as it interferes unduly with the therapeutic process – in particular, the unfolding and resolution of negative transference. Regular use of measures at greater intervals, however, such as once a term, can facilitate the monitoring of the young person's progress in a way that may be clinically useful. Children and young people have been found to appreciate this, provided that it is conducted within an established therapeutic relationship (Stasiak et al., 2013). Measures that identify treatment goals or aims may be particularly useful in yielding clinical insights (Emanuel et al., 2014; Troupp, 2013).

Anna: first review meeting

For 15-year-old Anna, the first review meeting also functioned to mark the end of the assessment phase of STPP. (By this time, her mother and stepfather had attended a session with the parent worker: see above, "Anna's parents: assessment and setting-up process".) Her stepfather did not attend this meeting, but Anna came with her mother. Anna's therapist spoke briefly about Anna's attendance of the assessment sessions and how, in her view, continuing with the treatment would be helpful for Anna. Anna spoke up to say that she would like to continue. Ms A surprised both the therapist and the parent worker by asking rather anxiously and insistently about what Anna's sessions had covered; Anna visibly cringed and looked frightened at this point, as though unbearably intruded upon. Therapist and parent worker tried hard to navigate this awkward moment by explaining the boundary around the therapeutic work, which Ms A accepted to Anna's relief. The parent worker silently wondered whether Ms A's anxiety had been related to concerns about her own depression which had emerged in the first parent session: perhaps she was wondering whether this had been mentioned by her daughter in her therapy and was worrying about the extent to which it might have had an adverse effect on Anna.

The process of parent work in STPP

Therapeutic technique in STPP parent work

Unlike many other therapeutic approaches, many of which are skills-orientated, STPP parent work is not structured in terms of content. At times, and when necessary, the worker may ask facilitating questions in order to promote dialogue and communication. The parent worker may ask a parent, for example, "How are things going?", "What is on your mind today?", or "How are things with your son/daughter?". The parent worker may also ask a parental couple, "What is the impact on each of you/you as a couple, in response to what your son/daughter has said/done?" This may enable the parents to consider their individual relationships to the young person and how they are functioning as a couple. The aim is to open up a conversation and the possibility of thinking together about the emotional state of the parents and their adolescent child, and the relationships between them all (Rustin, 1998a). The parent worker will allow the clinical material to unfold with an even attention paid to all aspects of the parents' communication, including non-verbal, unspoken communication, and the experience in the countertransference.

The parent worker should not make the assumption that he or she knows the particular experience of each parent with their child; rather, there is a unique parent–child relationship to try to get to know in its particular detail. In this way of working with parents, direct advice, specific management strategies, targets, and homework are not employed. On occasion, however, parent workers may find themselves offering suggestions and ideas about parenting. When this occurs, it is important that the parent worker tries to understand why he or she is doing it. Sometimes the parent worker may feel driven to providing a concrete solution in response to parental distress or anxiety. In such instances, this is often likely to be a defensive enactment ("acting in") by the worker and (ultimately) unlikely to be helpful. On other occasions, however, it can be helpful in stimulating the parents to find their own new approaches to managing the parent–child dynamic.

Careful thought is needed by the parent worker to discriminate between the two situations outlined above. It is quite common in this work for parents to be interested in what is happening in their adolescent child's therapy. They may ask questions about this. In these circumstances, the parent worker needs to acknowledge their interest and explore what may be underlying their question. For instance, it may be that a parent is struggling to manage recognizing that his or her child has a separate mind and independent experience, or to allow this. Alternatively, it may be that the young person has told his or her parent that the therapist is unhelpful and the treatment unnecessary. Additionally, the parent may have anxieties about whether the young person's therapist is sufficiently alert to risk and safeguarding issues. The parent worker might expect to feel undermined or anxious in the face of such questioning. In response, the primary stance of the worker needs to be one of sensitivity, curiosity, reflection, and exploration, rather than attempting to provide reassurance or answers.

The parent worker will need to be alert and thoughtful regarding that which has been projected by the young person into the parents, the parents' possible identification with this, and parental projections into the young person. Where possible, the parent work can help the parents to distinguish their own emotions and anxieties from those of their child and thus re-establish the possibility of more adequate emotional containment (Bion, 1962a). If there is not an intact parental couple attending, then the therapist needs to be alert to the potential for projection or attribution of anxieties and feelings into the absent parent and be aware of what they may represent to the parent who is being worked with.

Early stages of parent work

For all parents or carers, the young person embarking on treatment is likely to generate anxieties, fears, and hopes. This may not be the first treatment the parents or young person have sought out or engaged in. The core questions (not necessarily spoken about or even conscious) in parents' minds may be, "Is this going to work?", "Is it going to make things worse?" or "Will nothing change despite the effort by all involved?". These anxieties, fears, and hopes will inform the parents' transference to the clinic and hence to the parent worker, as well as to the young person's therapist. They are also likely to affect the current relationship with their child, and the parents' attitude towards the young person's own treatment. The parent worker will need to help contain these anxieties and uncertainties in order to begin to build an alliance with the parent(s) and to prevent acting out and disruption of the therapy.

The young person's depression may well be long-standing, and the referral may come at a point of crisis. Seriously depressed young people raise extremely difficult management problems for parents: faced with suicide threats it is not easy to be firm regarding behavioural issues, such as those relating to school attendance or the use of drugs and alcohol, or the maintenance of ordinary family boundaries. The situation is further complicated by the conscious or unconscious guilt and anxiety of the parents, who may question why their child is ill and whether or not this has links to events early in the child's life, to current situations of stress (such as family illness or parent conflict), or to their own relationship with their child (as may have been the case with Anna's mother in the vignette above).

It is inevitable that for parents whose son or daughter has reached adolescence, there will be emotional resonances and dissonances at times. Parental identifications may be helpful or unhelpful, depending on their nature and to what degree the parent is taken over by them (Whitefield & Midgley, 2015). Parental anxieties, if too intense or extensive, can lead to a restriction in their capacity to think about their young person. This can impair judgement as to what are reasonable expectations and can bring distortions in the parents' capacity to see things from their adolescent child's point of view and negotiate matters such as boundaries and acceptable standards of behaviour. Parent work provides a relationship within a clear therapeutic frame in which the therapist can work to help the parents experience some emotional containment of anxieties, address areas of identification with adolescent states of mind, and provide an understanding of the feelings of strain, bewilderment, and helplessness. This helps create mental space in their minds, allowing them to see their child more clearly, or anew, and to reflect upon their own past adolescent experiences and any current adolescent states of mind within themselves. As Green (2000) argues, "the initial phase of working with parents entails working towards the point where they can awaken their emotional awareness of their child and begin to reflect on their relationship" (p. 29).

Parents who are too caught up in their identifications with, and anxieties about, their adolescent child may relate to the young person in ways that impede his or her development of a newly growing sense of identity and self. This includes renewed exposure to, and adolescent renegotiation of, oedipal conflicts and anxieties, now in the context of a sexually developing body and identity. This requires space for relationships with peers and peer groups, as well as emotional space and flexibility in the relationship with his or her parents. As part of this, adolescent behaviour can veer suddenly between excitability and despair, between impulsivity and feeling anxiously immobilized. There is a complex, changeable interplay between infantile dependency needs and the drive towards increased autonomy or, if in an omnipotent state of mind, complete emotional self-sufficiency. These dynamics are difficult for parents to keep up with and remain (more or less) emotionally responsive to. Inevitably, a parental couple can find themselves suddenly shifting from a shared understanding and agreed position regarding their son or daughter to one of polarized positions and associated parental conflict. Parent-work sessions can help considerably in containing the parents and making some sense of the fluctuating nature of their adolescent child's experience and their own as parents.

Given all this, it is likely that parental anxiety will be raised and intensified, particularly in the context of current high levels of concern about adolescent depression in the wider society. There may have been unease over a protracted period of time. Parents may have managed this anxiety in different ways. These might, for example, include feeling crushed and overwhelmed by despair; uninterested or apparently unconcerned; depressed and guilty; driven to seek manic solutions (which may include the attitude towards getting help); or experiencing a loss of confidence in their own parental capacity, leading to over-identification with their adolescent child's point of view or state of mind.

Any or all of these concerns and dynamics may become apparent in the early stages of the parent work in STPP. In these early stages, the parent worker needs to be emotionally receptive and containing, especially of acute parental anxieties, fears, guilt, and phantasies regarding their child's depression. The young person in therapy may be struggling to engage, and this is likely to have the effect of increasing parental anxiety. Alternatively, the young person may be engaging with enthusiasm, perhaps idealizing the therapist, and experiencing a sense of relief or even excitement at his or her internal feelings being attended to so carefully and seriously. This, too, may be difficult for parents, who may feel rejected. The gathering and sorting out of projections within the family, couple, and towards the clinic and the STPP treatment will most likely be central, along with the process of clarifying the boundaries of the work and relationship and the therapeutic task. The nature of the parental concerns for their son or daughter, including any sense of helplessness or denial, will start to take shape.

Anna's parents: early parent work sessions

Ms A attended the next parent session without her partner, explaining that he was too busy at work to come. She talked anxiously about Anna's low mood and irritability and seemed very worried about Anna having forgotten two of her STPP sessions at the start: perhaps Anna was simply not going to "get into" the therapy and was not going to take it seriously. The parent worker reminded Ms A that Anna had agreed to proceed with the therapy, but took up Ms A's anxiety about whether STPP would really be able to help Anna and also (she added) whether the parent work would be able to help Ms A and her partner in their current situation. Ms A, perhaps relieved by this, went on to disclose that her partner had been reluctant to attend another parent session. She thought that perhaps he had felt overwhelmed by his anxiety about her (Ms A) and not sure whether he should have spoken so freely about it. Ms A spoke more about her recurrent depression and difficulties surrounding Anna's birth, when she had felt very stressed and low about having the baby on her own.

Middle stages of parent work

The middle stages of parent work offer an opportunity, as they do in the STPP therapy, for the parents to settle in to the work, ideally on the basis of having established a reasonably solid relationship with the parent worker in the first few sessions. Because there are fewer parent sessions (a total of 7) than sessions for the young person, there will be a limit to how much can be covered, and a clear focus for the work is helpful here. Whether the sessions are evenly spaced or not will be a matter of individual choice. Some parents or parental couples may find it helpful to attend weekly or fortnightly for a time, which builds a fuller picture for the parent worker more quickly and enables the parents to establish a sense of trust in the worker and clinic, before reducing to much less frequent contact. However the sessions are spaced, there is likely to be a sense of a beginning, middle, and ending, with the middle stages ideally bringing a sense of going more deeply into the most relevant areas and feelings.

Being alert to oedipal dynamics and how these are manifesting themselves within the triad (or wider family, where there are siblings), and the ways in which their child is positioned within the minds of the parental couple, can be a useful and often essential area of parent work which may become particularly manifest during the middle stages. Adolescent relational and sexual explorations, and development of a sexual identity, can generate questions and anxieties in the parental couple regarding intimacy and sexuality within their own relationship. This may precipitate a re-working or renegotiation of the couple relationship. In some instances, it may bring about a crisis for the parental couple. The parents' capacity to tolerate feeling excluded (either singly or as a couple) from their adolescent child's life is seriously tested. The young person's developing ambitions, newly discovered sexual feelings and impulses, and preoccupation with peer relationships may lead the parents to reflect on and reassess their own achievements and choices and past, lost possibilities and desires. This can lead to emotional work involving mourning, or it may lead to some acting out in an effort to evade pain and seek a return to an earlier stage of life. Such processes can lead to a keener consciousness of mortality. They can also bring a reinvigorated attitude, focusing on what is good and possible, and energy to make the most of mature adult life.

In all of these situations, the parent worker can hold in mind that the young person carries within him or her a relationship to an internal parental couple. The form and nature of this internal couple will be shaped by an ongoing, dynamic interaction in the young person's mind involving his or her lived experience with his or her parent(s) and their own ways of understanding, managing, and relating to the psychic reality of a parental couple, whatever the current external circumstances. Some thinking about oedipal matters may help the parents to recognize the significant emotional work required by the young person to manage feelings and anxieties regarding his or her own growing potential, within new social structures of peer groupings, for sexual coupling, and perhaps eventual parenthood for his/herself.

In the middle stages of parent work, the therapist thus needs to have increased awareness of and pay close attention to the parents' experience of themselves as the parents to their child, and to themselves as a parental couple. Their sense of separateness from their adolescent child is also key, as are the changes and limits to their role as parents to an adolescent, and their own experiences as adolescents. Oedipal dynamics in the family and in their couple relationship may come more into view.

Anna's parents: middle stages of parent work

Anna's mother, Ms A, attended regularly for four sessions during the middle stages of Anna's treatment, but she was unable to persuade her partner to make the necessary arrangements with his work to return. While she tended to avoid talking in too much detail or depth about her own depression, she did expand a great deal on her own childhood. She revealed that her elder sister, who had been more than 10 years her senior, had largely brought her up, along with their father, when their mother died at a young age. This was Anna's aunt who had, in turn, had a significant responsibility for sharing the upbringing of Anna. Feeding this information back to the therapist was helpful in informing the professionals' understanding of the intergenerational dynamics involved, the impact that the death of this aunt had had on mother and daughter, Anna's occasional seemingly unconscious acceptance of a mothering role in relation to her younger siblings, and difficulties in allowing Anna's stepfather to assume a full parental function in relation to Anna.

The parent worker also reflected on the differences in cultural background between her and Ms A. When Ms A made an apparently passing reference to how it was more common in her own mother's culture to share childcare among the extended family or across the generations, the parent worker was able to take this up with interest. Ms A seemed relieved by this implicit permission to acknowledge cultural difference. She admitted that she had worried that the white parent worker might think that these practices had in themselves been problematic for Anna. In the discussion that followed, they were able to distinguish between the helpful experiences of care that Anna (and indeed her mother) had had and their very painful experiences of loss.

In the next session, the parent worker was able to think with Ms A about the tendency for Anna to sleep in her bed, leaving her stepfather needing to sleep elsewhere, that had been taking place while Anna was at her lowest and most anxious. They were able to relate these to the multiple experiences of loss that Anna had suffered.

The ending stages of parent work

In all psychoanalytically informed clinical work, great attention is paid to the emotional experience and meaning to the patient of the end of the therapy, and this is an essential focus of parent work too. In time-limited work such as STPP, the ending will need particularly close attention, care, and thoughtfulness. The parent worker will be expected to keep the ending in mind throughout the work and make specific references to it from the mid-point of the work onwards. This may be especially significant in the light of unresolved experiences of loss in the parents (as was key, for instance, for Anna's mother). As the parents feel safer within the relationship with the parent worker, they may feel more able to raise painful issues such as guilt and the sense of feeling blamed. The parent worker will need to be alert to how unresolved matters regarding separation and loss may threaten to disrupt the ending of the young person's treatment and the parent work. The monitoring of responses to holidays or other gaps in the treatment will be helpful in tackling these issues.

In addition to the overall frame, each session includes the emotional experience of arriving and leaving, of beginning and ending. It is important for the parent worker to observe closely the emotional attitude of the parents towards arriving, leaving, and gaps between sessions, which may have associations with abandonment and loss, or with experiences of belonging, inclusion, and being held in mind. Understanding how the parents manage gaps may illuminate how difficulties in separating from their adolescent child, or difficult feelings about separation, may interfere with or seriously undermine the work.

In the ending stages, it needs to be borne in mind that what is approaching is an ending not only for the parents but also for the young person in the treatment. This may be experienced by the parents as a satisfactory completion of a treatment process or as a relief. The parent worker's attention will be on how the ending resonates with previous parental separations and losses, how these were managed and are thought about now, and parental anxieties about the loss of the clinicians and clinic. Questions may arise for the parents about their own emotional resources and their confidence or concerns as to whether these are sufficient for the continuing parental tasks. Depressive anxieties may arise. Together with the parent worker, the parents need to review their situation and gain a realistic view of their capacities and what is needed. In a few instances, this may lead to additional parent-work sessions being required, but usually this is not the case. More usual is that, despite the anxieties generated by the ending process, the parents will feel better placed within themselves in their emotional parenting capacities and more confident in how to relate to their adolescent son or daughter.

Anna's parents: the ending stages of parent work

As described above, Anna became rather distressed as she entered the ending stages of her STPP therapy, and she experienced a panic attack at school which made her fear that she was "going back to the beginning again" with her difficulties. Anna's mother picked up on this anxiety and asked the parent worker whether she could arrange a consultation with the clinic psychiatrist. By the time of this session, the parent worker knew from the therapist that the panic attack had not been repeated, and also that the therapist had understood it as a communication of Anna's panic about being "abandoned" at the end of her therapy, as she had been when her aunt and the family friend had died. Without disclosing the content of Anna's sessions, she was able to help Ms A to reflect on these events and their significance, and on the timing of the panic attack in relation to the approaching end of therapy. She made it clear that a psychiatric consultation could be arranged if desired, but Ms A decided to wait and see how things developed for Anna.

With the end of the parent work as well as of the therapy in sight, the parent worker took up again the question of whether Anna's stepfather might be able to arrange to attend. Perhaps this was more palatable to him because it seemed to offer a chance to review progress before ending, or perhaps Ms A's stronger relationship with the parent worker also enabled her to represent the idea to her partner in a way that inspired his confidence in the process. He attended two parent sessions before the end of the treatment, along with a final review with the therapist. During the parent sessions, Ms A and her partner voiced their relief that Anna seemed so much better and happier than she had before, both at home and, as far as they could tell, in her peer relationships. They also seemed to communicate more freely with each other and articulated that they had each individually worried about the impact of Anna's difficulties on them and their relationship. (This seemed to match the concerns about their relationship which Anna had picked up and articulated previously.)

Common themes, difficulties, and variations

Intergenerational difficulties

Given the severity of the young person's difficulties, loss can frequently be a significant issue within parental histories or the present family, as in the case of Anna. There may have been multiple bereavements and losses, even traumatic losses, as was seen in the IMPACT trial. For some families, there will have been parental separation and divorce, as well as other situations of parental conflict, including domestic violence. Many may be single parents, which may or may not put additional pressure on any difficulties they and their adolescent child are experiencing. In some cases, the parent may have a significant mental health problem with which he or she may or may not be receiving help from other services.

It could be said that intergenerational anxieties, conflicts, and experiences of loss, dislocation, and trauma are inevitably carried forward to some degree in every family. There is no such thing as a family where past sorrows and troubles are not passed on to some extent. The intergenerational impact of the Holocaust, for instance, is well known (Karpf, 1996), as are the psychological sequelae of migration (Varchevker & McGinley, 2013). In work with parents and carers, it is necessary to bear this in mind and be alert to the potential influence such matters may be having upon the current family constellation, parental struggles, and the young person's depression. In some cases, raw or unresolved intergenerational family experiences will be writ large in the work with the young person and the parents. In many clinical situations, however, such associations and dynamics are not so obvious or distinct. Often, parents have not made emotional links or seen the connections, and when these do become clear during a parent session, the new awareness and knowledge may be painful as well as helpful.

The parent worker will need to be alert to the potential for the young person's treatment to arouse adolescent feelings in the parents themselves. It is possible that as the young person begins to show signs of improvement, the family dynamics may be altered and the parents may be faced with their own problems more starkly, such as their own depression or conflicts around their own adolescent development. Sibling dynamics may also play a part: as one child develops, another may become more evidently vulnerable. The parent worker may be able to help the parents to find suitable help, support, or therapy in their own right or for other members of the family, and, if clinically indicated, refer on.

Maintaining therapeutic boundaries

Given the inevitable anxieties for parents regarding their child's physical and psychological vulnerability and the risk of dangerous acting out, there may be great pressure from parents to intrude upon the confidentiality of their child's psychotherapy. This is likely to place strain on the parent worker. It is, however, the parent worker's job to protect the confidentiality of the young person's therapy and the space they need for it, and to contain parental anxieties and frustrations about this.

In rare cases, parents may "act out" their conflicted feelings about their child's difficulties or therapy by taking action that directly or indirectly impacts on the therapy. They may end the therapy, for instance, and this may be based on a stated reason that the therapy is not helping or, on the contrary, that it is no longer necessary. Alternatively, a parent may outwardly support the therapy but "sabotage" it by talking to his or her adolescent child in a way that undermines the young person's attempts to help him/herself through therapy or that undermines the therapist. Such processes may be subtle and require careful attention from therapist or parent worker. Good communication between the parent worker and the therapist and team are needed. In many cases, the parent's actions may be driven by his or her own depression, or by unresolved envy of his or her child as a therapy patient; where possible, this will need to be carefully understood within the parent work.

Difficulties in the external world of school or college

Engaging in treatment may impact on the young person in a way that leads to difficulties in the external world of school or college. The parent worker, in collaboration with the young person's therapist and parents, needs to be alert to such difficulties. As is usual in good clinical practice, liaison and communication with schools and colleges can be very helpful. One function of this contact is to protect the young person's therapy. There may be instances where the parents ask for the parent worker's help in negotiations or contact with school or college. The parent worker may also attend network meetings as appropriate, particularly when there are concerns that the young person may be at risk.

Dropping out of therapy: implications for parents

In some cases, the young person may drop out of treatment prematurely (as discussed in "Containment failure and drop-out" in chapter 7). When this happens, the parents and parent worker will need to review their work together. They may decide to continue to pursue the work for some further sessions or to bring this to an end. This decision will be made on a case-by-case basis, and will usually require communication within the clinical team. It may be that the work with the parents is seen as having a helpful impact on their understanding of their child's depression, their family dynamics, and their own capacity to tolerate the anxieties associated with their current parenting task. Such continuing work may provide essential emotional containment of parental needs and anxieties and may help them be more receptive, alert, and thoughtful in relation to their child's depression and any risks associated with this. How long this work continues for will also be a case-by-case decision. Remaining within the originally agreed STPP time frame is most helpful, however, with a review at the end of this period to decide if there are sufficient clinical reasons for additional parent-work sessions.

Parents' need for help in their own right

In some instances, the parent worker may assess that the parent is in need of psychological, medical, or social care in his or her own right (an example of this is given in chapter 7). It is the parent worker's responsibility to discuss this with the parent and either suggest how her or she can access such help or make the referral directly on his or her behalf – for instance, to a GP, to psychology services, or to social services. Sometimes, a degree of help may already have been obtained, as with Anna's mother, but the question of additional treatment (such as psychotherapy where none has been offered previously) may become key. This may also become more palatable to the parent as he or she gains some insight into the nature of psychological work through the experience of the parent work.

Working with adopted and looked-after children and their carers

Working with young people who are adopted or looked after by the state, and who are depressed and needing treatment, raises particular issues, even where the adoption is long-standing. Although in some respects the situations of adopted and looked-after young people are significantly different – with those who have been adopted likely to be in a much more stable environment in which the possibility of multiple transitions may not be a key issue – for both groups the renegotiation of oedipal conflicts and anxieties, and the associated questions and uncertainties regarding their developing identity, takes place in the context of belonging to more than one set of parents, more than one family (Fagan, 2011; Hindle & Shulman, 2008; Rustin, 1999). For the adoptive parents or carers, understanding the young person's depression and developmental struggles will inevitably raise anxieties about the young person's familial origins and early experiences. This may lead to questions about what role "genetically inherited traits", early environmental deficits, or trauma may be playing in the current depression – questions that may also feature in the young person's mind or in his or her unconscious anxieties. In such circumstances, thinking about the multiple parental and familial figures in the young person's mind and how this may complicate and influence his or her identity development is an important task for the therapist, while helping the adoptive parents or carers to think about this will also be part of the parent worker's role.

For adoptive parents, parent work may be a valuable opportunity to help them consider the ways in which, through their parenting, they have helped repair or mediate any damage or deficit from the young person's early years, and also perhaps recognize what has not (as yet) been possible. If the adoption has arisen through parental infertility, and if the depression in the young person is thought to be associated with early experiences, losses, and displacements (such as within the care system), this may generate painful emotional resonances within the parents (Ludlam, 2008). They may find themselves experiencing a resurgence of feelings of loss and disappointment in relation to their infertility, and in relation to the experiences their adopted child had in the earliest period of life, from which they were not able to protect him or her.

With looked-after young people in either foster or residential care, thought must be given to the question of who can be engaged with in a meaningful way to support the young person in his or her therapy. This may be a foster carer, residential key worker, social worker, independent visitor, residential unit manager, or a combination of some of the above. For looked-after young people, the decision about who is most appropriate to engage in this work needs to be made with the involvement of the young person. It is important to engage the support of the social worker with statutory parental responsibility for the young person.

In determining who should attend for parent work, parallel to the looked-after young person's therapy, and with whom the parent worker should liaise, the guiding principles are:

» who is legally responsible for the young person;
» who is responsible for the young person's "parental" emotional care and development;
» the young person's preference as to who should be involved in parent work;
» what is indicated clinically in order to support the young person's treatment;
» what is indicated clinically to ensure that any concerns about risk are shared, understood, managed, and monitored.

In working with foster carers, thinking and discussion regarding the emotional aspects of their "parental position" in relation to the young person in their care will need particular sensitivity and an understanding of the boundary between social workers' and foster carers' responsibilities. The looked-after young person may be in a foster care placement, in a residential unit, or in supported accommodation. Some may be unaccompanied asylum seekers. In principle, all looked-after children in the UK should have an allocated social worker or leaving care worker. In reality, however, this is not always the case. Given these variations, decisions will need to be made on a case-by-case basis as to who, if anyone, could attend meetings with a parent/carer worker in parallel with the young person's STPP treatment. The discussion that leads to this decision should always include the young person's view. Whom he or she identifies within the networks as serving a parental function is key.

The aim is for the parent worker to be meeting with someone who has concern for the emotional life of the young person, some parent-like interest in the young person's development, and some authority within the network structure. In some instances, it may be decided that it is appropriate and helpful to meet jointly with the concerned adults, such as a social worker and foster carer, or a residential key worker and manager.

In working with foster carers, particularly if the young person is in a well-established placement, careful thought will need to be given to the degree of emotional consent communicated by the foster carers regarding the level of interest in their own emotional lives and family history that they may welcome or be able to tolerate. Experience suggests that this is an area of great variability in work with foster carers. Exploration of this area of emotional consent will require much sensitivity. There is also plenty of casework evidence, in the work of child psychotherapists and others, showing how the internal worlds and object relations of looked-after young people can shape relationships within the network (Emanuel, Miller, & Rustin, 2002; Sprince, 2008). This serves a communicative function but can also significantly distort relationships and functioning. The so-called corporate-parent (Briggs, 2012, p. 5) functioning held within the Local Authority network may sometimes need attention from the parent/carer worker, in addition to any individual carer work.

Arrangements for work with carers or the network may take a range of forms, within the designated 7 sessions: one-to-one "parental carer" sessions with the foster carer(s), plus telephone or email communication (as needed) with the young person's social worker and the foster carer's supervising social worker or support worker; consultation meetings with the foster carer and social worker and/or family placement worker; consultation meetings with the social worker and residential unit manager and/or the key worker; consultation meetings with the social worker, foster carer, unit manager, or key worker, and the school special educational needs coordinator, or a member of the college pastoral care staff; no formal consultations or sessions but occasional review meetings, which may include the young person and/or any of the above adults, dependent on clinical need and the young person's preference; or no involvement of the network, in cases where this is the preference of the young person if they are old enough to make this decision.

STPP with a looked-after adolescent boy

The following vignette shows some of this thinking at play in the STPP treatment of "Danny", a 16-year-old looked-after boy, and the parallel work with his carers and the network.

> Danny was taken into the care of the Local Authority when he was 6 years old, due to protracted experiences of neglect and emotional unavailability in his early years with his birth parents. Both parents were depressed and addicted to alcohol, and there were reported incidents of domestic violence. There was evidence of Danny being left on his own, unsupervised, for many hours at a time. When he came into care, Danny presented as highly anxious, easily agitated, and emotionally uncontained. After a number of short-term foster care placements, Danny moved into a foster family, which became a long-term placement for him. Although there were many difficulties over the years, at home and at school, the placement was sustained.

> Danny was referred for STPP when he was 16. He was still living in his established foster placement, although this was under considerable strain. He was in his last year of secondary school, which, throughout his time there, had been challenging for him in terms of managing the academic demands and the ordinary requirements around communication with teachers, peer relationships, and behaviour. Danny's aggressive relating and occasional violent incidents with peers had increased over the previous 12 months. When Danny's girlfriend ended their relationship, his

mood deteriorated and he started to talk about wanting to hurt himself. Danny's social worker referred him to a service where he was assessed for STPP and then seen for treatment. His foster parents were offered supportive parent sessions alongside.

During the period of his 28 sessions, there were a number of highly significant life events for Danny. In addition to the end of his time at school, the transition to college, and the unforeseen loss of his girlfriend, Danny's long-term foster placement broke down. This was due to his aggression and lying and the despair engendered in his foster parents by the chronic nature of Danny's difficulties. The loss of his foster placement, with carers whom he considered as family, was a painful blow to Danny. This led to his moving into a shared, supported semi-independent living unit.

Throughout these difficult events, Danny's attendance at his STPP sessions was generally good, albeit with some sudden gaps. What became clear through the work was how Danny's early experiences of neglect, uncertainty, fright, and unavailable parental objects had had a profound impact on his development. This had left him deprived of a solid sense of who he was and of robust internal objects that could help him manage losses, change, and developmental transitions. This in turn contributed to his failure sometimes to identify and make good use of what was being offered by interested adults around him. Over the years, Danny had managed his anxieties, confusion, and fears through developing an aggressive carapace that readily presented itself whenever he felt his identity and psychic survival to be threatened. This inevitably led to many conflicts with others and to associated persecuted states of mind in Danny. A further complicating deficit was that Danny struggled to symbolize his emotional experiences and to put things into words.

In his STPP treatment, Danny's tendency to become suspicious of others and to manage painful emotions through denial, avoidance, and hostile relating all became active in the transference. The therapy situation managed to hold sufficiently for work to be done on some of the ways in which his melancholia of despair and grievance was linked to, and arose from, early experiences with his birth parents. Danny's defensive use of aggression to protect him from what he anticipated to be unbearable emotional pain and anxiety was able to be observed, identified, talked about, and at times interpreted in the transference. Given Danny's high level of anxiety and the aggressive heat often present in the room, more usually it was necessary for the therapist to hold the projected states and comment from this position. The other area in which work was possible was the making of some tentative links between the raw feelings generated by Danny's current losses and those of early life.

The sustaining of Danny's treatment was significantly helped by the separate, parallel work being undertaken by a clinic colleague with people from Danny's network. This included his foster carers, social worker, and in due course the manager from the semi-independent living unit to which Danny moved. The nature of these sessions was consultative and collaborative. This work supported Danny's attendance at therapy and helped him "see the point" in continuing with his STPP treatment, despite all that was going on in his life. The consultation sessions enabled the small network of adults around him to develop a shared, coherent understanding of Danny and supported the principle of collective thinking prior to the taking of actions. For the foster parents, however, the parent sessions had a particular function in helping them to try to bear the pressure of Danny's behaviour on them and, subsequently, to manage their distress at his move to the unit.

Given the reality of Danny's life experiences, both past and present, it is important to note that his STPP treatment could not be expected, and did not aim, to work through all the losses and consequences of the deficits in Danny's experience, nor did it lead to an integration of all the various aspects of his rather troubled personality. What was possible, however, in the context of his adolescent developmental crisis, made tensely acute by his position as a young person in care, was some containment of his immediate anxieties related to his current situation; some attention to his deep fears about what sort of a man he might become (he was very anxious not to repeat familial history); and some new awareness of the reality of his depression and how it was related to his aggressive relating style and outbursts. As the timing of Danny's treatment coincided with both planned transitions and unplanned severances, it provided an opportunity (albeit with limitations) to help through a developmental crisis and begin to make sense of how badly he felt about himself.

Where the young person is looked after, like Danny, there will be a range of issues to resolve regarding who should attend parent work sessions, and with whom the parent worker should liaise, as well as regarding the nature of the work that can be undertaken with a carer who is neither the biological nor the adopted parent of the patient. In the case of Danny's carers, who had taken him into their family over a long period, there was clearly important work to be done in helping them attempt to manage, first, their dismay and anxiety over his behaviour and, later, their distress at the breakdown of the placement. Throughout this process, the need to maintain contact with the responsible social worker was also paramount.

CHAPTER SIX

Supervision of Short-Term Psychoanalytic Psychotherapy

S upervision is an essential component of psychoanalytic psychotherapy and of STPP. It supports the psychotherapist's developing understanding of the patient, addresses technical issues, and provides a space for processing countertransference difficulties. Supervisors are experienced senior colleagues whose work aims to facilitate the thinking of their supervisees. Their respect for the therapist and his or her patient is an essential component of the supervisory relationship and the background to the development and maintenance of trust between supervisor and supervisee.

The aim of psychoanalytic supervision in STPP as in longer term psychoanalytic psychotherapy is to facilitate the maintenance of a non-directive, observing, and enquiring stance in the therapist, by providing an opportunity for the therapist to discuss and understand the clinical material brought by the patient, on a regular basis and in a safe and reliable setting. Supervision is an agreed commitment for supervisor and therapist alike and depends on the proper preparation of therapeutic session notes ("process notes" or "process recordings") by therapists. Supervision meetings involve a close examination of such notes, including attention to the therapist's countertransference responses to the patient.

Principles and aims of psychoanalytic supervision

In psychoanalytic psychotherapy, supervision has a particular role and relevance because of the importance accorded to the understanding of unconscious processes and dynamics. The aim is to understand the patient's manifest and unconscious communications and the psychological processes underlying the material that emerges. The work thus aims to contain, identify, and analyse internal affective experience and to relate it to the current clinical situation. This involves both cognitive and emotional work, integrating feeling and thinking on the part of both therapist and supervisor. It is a fundamentally collaborative endeavour undertaken by two professionals, with the twin aims of understanding the complexity of the patient's communications and internal world and supporting the development of the supervisee.

The supervisor provides a reliable frame in which the case material can be explored. The starting point is the observation and close attention devoted to elucidating the anxieties and defences seen in the patient's material and the therapist's response. The therapist's confusion, worry, or, for example, sense of incompetence need to find a home in the supervisor's mind. Also crucial is the provision of a space in which to approach the clinical material in a spirit of curiosity. Being alive to what is occurring in the patient–therapist relationship and in the therapist–supervisor relationship allows for a focus on the possible interplay between the two.

The supervisor's stance therefore aims to bring together the following features:

» a serious professional atmosphere;
» a facilitating listening attitude, non-judgemental, thoughtful, and accepting: this can enable the therapist to contain, identify, and analyse his or her own experience in relation to the clinical situation and to develop autonomy and an "internal supervisor";
» a collaborative approach – the supervisor is not the therapist's therapist, but a senior colleague;
» the value of experience – although preferably not didactic in tone, reference may be made to similar cases the supervisor has treated in order to elucidate a point of technique, which can be particularly useful if the therapist feels in difficulty with the case or persecuted

by the scrutiny that supervision involves (it can be embarrassing to see in supervision what has been "missed" in the session);

» a non-directive technique – this allows the account of the therapeutic hour to unfold, with an even attention paid to all aspects of the therapist's communication, not just to the written process material but to all that emerges;

» respect for both the therapist's and the patient's material – this includes the therapist's emotional response to the patient, which needs to be taken seriously;

» reflectiveness – the emphasis is on understanding rather than doing, and on expanding the therapist's frame of reference which can be utilized in subsequent work with the patient;

» confidentiality – clinical material and the supervisee's interpretations and further comments during the supervision are treated as private to the supervisory relationship.

The supervisor avoids making comments about the therapist's own emotional difficulties which may sometimes obtrude, and he or she does not encourage regression. If the therapist's own difficulties seem to be interfering in the work, a comment that recognizes this may help the therapist to undertake the necessary work in personal analysis or private self-analysis. The supervisor's focus remains that of helping to make sense of the patient's material in the light of his or her history, current presentation, and the therapist's response to the patient. Discussion of whether or how much the therapist's emotional response "belongs" to the patient (i.e., is a countertransference response) and how much "belongs" to the therapist is an ongoing feature of supervision.

There is a considerable literature on supervision in psychoanalytic psychotherapy with adults, but comparable attention has not been paid to supervision in child psychotherapy. One useful introduction is the volume edited by Martindale, Cid Rodriguez, Morner, and Vidit (1997) in which the chapter by Sedlak (1997) is particularly helpful in exploring emotional dynamics linking case, supervisee, and supervisor. Some of the concepts in the broader supervisory literature are made use of in current practice (Napier, 2015) – for example, the idea that the relationship between supervisee and supervisor can at times mirror that between patient and therapist – but these have not by and large been elaborated in the child psychotherapy literature.

Since most child psychotherapists in reflecting on their training give pride of place to their experiences of supervision, this is somewhat surprising. There is a limited number of papers, however, looking at aspects of supervision, including some of particular relevance to the demands of time-limited work.

Harris (1977) summarizes the approach to supervision thus:

> [It] aims to direct the attention of the student towards increasingly close observation of the details of interaction between himself and the individuals he is studying. . . . [It] intends to increase the student's capacity to tolerate uncertainty, to contain, to think about and to use his countertransference, hereby becoming more sensitive to emotional as well as cognitive communication. [p. 21]

In *Enabling and Inspiring* (Harris Williams, Rhode, Rustin, & Williams, 2012), there is a wide range of papers from across the world discussing Harris's teaching methods and her personal supervision in particular. Recurrent linked themes are a background in infant observation, the importance of the concept of maternal containment, and the way that Harris's profound interest in the potential for human development infused her supervision. The dual focus on the development of patient and supervisee, noted above, stands out as a central feature in the recollections of the many contributors. The differentiation between the tasks of personal analysis and supervision, which are characteristic of psychoanalytic training and supervision, emerge time and again.

In the *Handbook of Child & Adolescent Psychotherapy* (Lanyado & Horne, 2009), there is no chapter on supervision as such, but there are important references to its function in the chapters on inpatient work (Flynn, 2009), sexual abuse cases (Horne, 2009), and trauma (Lanyado, 2009). These contexts are, of course, ones of exceptional clinical stress and also ones where acting out by professionals is most likely to occur because of the intensity and disturbing quality of the projections that require containment. Trowell's work (1977) drew attention to the systemic implications of this with respect to child sexual abuse, and this theme was later taken up by Rustin (2005) in her paper on the Victoria Climbié case. There has, in fact, been perhaps more writing drawing on the psychoanalytic model of supervision, both to analyse particular limitations in practice with children and families and to delineate possibilities for development than about clinical supervision as such (Rustin & Bradley, 2008).

One collaborative supervisory research project among senior clinicians was reported in the *Journal of Child Psychotherapy* (Rustin, 2010). The original plan to investigate the experience of service supervision among a group of colleagues entailed work on differentiating forms of supervision with inevitably overlapping features. The concepts that were particularly fruitful included the potential conflicts of interest between the supervisor's responsibility to the supervisee and the responsibility to the patient and the clinical service, the risks of infantilization of supervisees, the issues of confidentiality, and the importance of kindness. While the patient's right to confidentiality is clear, the supervisor may well have a managerial as well as a professional development role with the supervisee, and these two responsibilities may sit uneasily with each other. The overriding importance of trust in a supervisory relationship is self-evident, since in order to learn we must bear with our ignorance and failings, but this precious quality is not always easy to foster or protect. The paper also looked at what can go wrong in a supervision arrangement. Bad matches between supervisor and supervisee, or between one of them and the patient under discussion do occur. An interesting contrast to the problem of the bad match is provided by a paper that describes a benign and ultimately creative link between supervisor, supervisee, and patient in the intensive treatment of a small boy (Rustin, 1998b), in which the supervisor's emotional response to the clinical situation (countertransference at one remove) is described. In his play, Bernard, the young patient, had made the Lego Mother shout repeatedly from the rooftop of the damaged Lego House, "Don't worry!"

> The Lego Daddy appears but seems to be paralysed by the atmosphere of denial: Bernard makes him sleep through it. In the supervision I felt I had to function as somewhat like a father who can see that some active worrying is an urgent necessity. Bernard's relief when [his therapist] disputed his claim that the Daddy was injured and had to go to hospital was palpable: at that moment [his therapist's] refusal to be conned by the shifting story line revived Bernard's contact with her independent functioning. [Rustin, 1998b, p 443]

This was what the supervisory dialogue had brought into being, helped along by a much-needed meeting with the parents, which calmed their anxieties.

The self-definition arrived at by the service supervisors' group aptly summarizes what this chapter aims to describe in its emphasis on collaboration in clinical supervision:

> We were not here to propose better comments on the clinical material [than the supervisor had in fact offered] but to study the process of supervision and to identify the leading anxieties and defences which characterised the supervisory relationship. [Rustin, 2010, p. 6]

There is a small number of publications of special relevance to supervision of time-limited psychotherapy and to working with depressed young people. The earliest of these (Emanuel, Miller, & Rustin, 2002) described supervision of work with sexually abused girls aged between 6 and 14 years. These cases were seen in the context of a research study, and they uniformly involved high levels of disturbance in the children and their families. The paper discusses the particular technical issues in work with this client group (the "annihilation of the symbolic", p. 592) and the implications of time-limited work for both therapists and patients. The pressures of the time limit were painful for the therapists working with such troubled children, and the supervisor needed to combine some hopefulness about the value of the therapy with realism about what could be achieved.

In *Childhood Depression* (Trowell & Miles, 2011), which describes the European research study of depression in young adolescents (Trowell et al., 2007), three chapters particularly relevant to STPP stand out. Miles (2011) describes the intensity of the anxieties and the powerful projections encountered in work with such severely depressed young people and their parents. This makes access to supervision vital for clinicians to sustain thinking under great pressure. Rhode (2011) notes the particular impact of transgenerational loss and trauma in many of the family and suggests that a particular transference may arise in relation to such cases – namely, the role of supportive grandparent:

> Supervision is often thought of as providing the triangulation of an additional point of view, with the supervisor in the role of a supportive partner to the therapist in her task of addressing the child's problems. . . . In addition, however, the supervisor could be seen to be fulfilling the role of a supportive grandparent, and

. . . this may have played a significant role for families in which transgenerational issues were so prominent. [Rhode, 2011, p. 135]

Hall (2011) presents a case study in which her clinical material and the elaboration in supervision are shown to create a new level of understanding. This is a very fine record of what psychoanalytic supervision hopes to achieve. She describes how in her supervision with Anne Alvarez, "the emphasis of holding negative projections and paying attention to a sense of agency when it appeared in my patient's communications and behaviour stand out as particularly important" (p. 75).

STPP supervision: the framework and process

The room in which the supervision takes place needs to be quiet, private, and as free from interruptions as is possible. Best practice is to meet in the same room each time, in order to keep the setting the same, not a source of distraction. The supervision "hour", like the therapy hour, has a pre-defined length and starts and ends on time. The supervisor and supervisee should prepare for breaks, giving notice on both sides. The collegial atmosphere of the supervision often involves some brief, more personal exchange at the start, which allows for the shift of focus from all the other everyday pressures of the clinical and professional context.

In learning to provide STPP, fortnightly direct case supervision is optimal. More experienced clinicians may find that monthly supervision meets their needs in a realistic framework. If a small-group supervision is the most practical way to work, a 90-minute period is ideally needed to discuss two cases adequately. Each therapist reads process recordings of one or more sessions in the group for group discussion. Therapists are asked to write a detailed process record for sessions brought to supervision, with briefer notes of intervening sessions if possible. The process recordings are as full as possible a reconstruction of the therapy hour. As well as bringing the case to life, they also serve a key function in the therapist's processing of the transference and countertransference in the clinical work with the patient, which can then be continued in supervision (Creaser, 2015).

The supervisor takes responsibility for initiating attention to a psychoanalytic formulation of the case and thinking about this over time, as well as attending regularly to discussion of issues of risk. The first supervision meeting is an introductory meeting and is likely to cover the following topics:

» supervision arrangements: dates, timing, and so on;
» establishing a format for the supervision group: depending on the time frame, one or two supervisees may be expected to present each time, but time will be allowed for other therapists to bring up any matters of urgency or concern;
» outlining requirements for process recordings;
» the parameters of responsibility for risk.

In subsequent supervision sessions, the therapist reads a process recording or recordings for the supervisor and supervision group to consider; the supervisor decides whether the entire process recording should be read first in its entirety or whether it may be interrupted for clarification or for detailed discussion of points as they arise. There is no overriding right way to tackle the material, as this is likely to depend both on the case and on the individual supervisor and supervisee. The comments of the supervisor and the supervision group are based on this process material, the responses to it evoked in the supervisor and the other supervisee(s), and additional information provided by the therapist in retrospect.

One of the tasks of the supervision group is to develop over time a psychoanalytic understanding of the nature of the young person's depression and other difficulties. The initial attempt at formulation will usually be made by the third or fourth supervision meeting, and revisions to this are then made across the life cycle of each individual therapy case.

It is the supervisor's responsibility to ensure an atmosphere of serious reflection. If the supervision is within a group, it is vital that it feels safe for therapists to explore their work and anxieties. Respect for the work and any therapist vulnerabilities expressed is fostered as a group ethos. Group reflection and consideration of the material is encouraged, with other group members being invited to contribute their views.

Supervising Anna's therapist

Anna's case study presented in chapter 4 drew attention to some of the issues discussed in the supervision group, but it is perhaps useful to link together aspects of the role of supervision in the evolution of this case.

At the start, the therapist expressed doubts about whether Anna would in fact take up the sessions, because of her disquiet about the too-compliant atmosphere of the initial meeting with Anna and her mother. Gone was the raw sense of Anna's difficulties. In fact, the first session was cancelled by text at the last minute, and in supervision the group could note that this aptly represented Anna's ambivalent feelings, a session both "forgotten" and remembered. Thinking about the mass of words Anna poured out when she did arrive, and its impact on the therapist, who felt too full and unable to think, with the pressure of this reminding her of Anna's symptom of severe headaches, gave rise to thoughts about Anna's somatization of anxiety and her experience of feeling too full of the projections of family members to which she was painfully open. What was the basis for her feeling that she had to contain so much for others? An answer to this question emerged very quickly when she described her intention to become a mentor at school and requested a change of session time to allow her to do this. She had very quickly become the one to provide help to vulnerable others, and this seemed to be linked to a competitive response to having a therapist for herself. She preferred to be the giver of help, not the receiver.

The supervision group was often to note that something was interfering in the therapist's access to her own mind, such as when she felt unable to describe Anna's appearance. The group became alert to attacks on linking in the early sessions, and by the time the middle phase of therapy was reached there had been a significant growth in Anna's trust and in her therapist's confidence. Anna's internal parental figures became more clearly etched: a mother demoted to being like a sister, a beloved aunt, the "second mother", lost just before Anna's puberty, a father never known, and a stepfather kept at a distance so that Anna could sustain the image of the cosiness of the mother–daughter couple in which generational differences were obscured. The therapist discussed in supervision her fear and consequent tentativeness in interpreting Anna's unconscious attacks on a creative couple.

The group's sharp awareness of Anna's deep-seated rivalry with the maternal figure provided support and bolstered the therapist's courage in confronting this issue, and the therapist was able to use the shared work of the supervision group directly as she spoke to Anna about the problem of being able to recognize that their work could only be done if the two of them worked together.

The final phase brought a dramatic collapse, reminiscent of Anna's earlier "melt-downs", faced with school-leaving exams. The therapist felt anxious and guiltily asked herself whether this collapse signalled the inadequacy of the time-limited treatment. The supervision group helped to steady her and allow for the idea that the ending was not premature and could be an experience different from the sudden losses of Anna's life. It was also interesting to consider that the patient's fear of exam failure was echoed in the therapist's fear of the therapy being a failure. The vulnerability of the therapist to identification with Anna's anxiety about what she could cope with was relieved when this insight was discovered, and it was very striking to hear in the final sessions of a first possible boyfriend, suggesting the opening up of more ordinary adolescent concerns and of a new kind of couple in Anna's mind.

Dealing with risk

The supervisor will often, though not always, be a member of the wider clinic multidisciplinary team, but is also helpfully thought of as an auxiliary member of the team working on the case. The supervisor's role in relation to risk management needs to be defined in the light of the overarching risk-management protocol for the service as a whole. In the initial supervision, there can be discussion of what is to be considered as deliberate self-harm or taken as evidence of suicidality, and how this fits into the policy and management of risk in the therapist's multidisciplinary team. Arrangements for informing colleagues of significant risk will be reviewed, and the responsibilities of therapist, supervisor, and the senior clinician responsible for the case will be clarified.

The therapist has primary responsibility for informing the clinic psychiatrist and any other multidisciplinary colleague responsible for coordinating issues of clinical risk. With younger adolescents, consultation with the parent worker is paramount. The supervisor can be consulted in between supervisory sessions if the therapist feels in need of urgent support in understanding the clinical situation with the patient, in managing the relationship to the team, or in dealing with differences of opinion about the action required if these arise.

In supervision, the focus will be on the psychodynamic significance of the risk-taking behaviour, or potential behaviour, and how it might be related to the transference situation.

Problems of management in STPP supervision

In managing the supervisory relationship within a group, equity of attention to the members of the group and their cases needs to be maintained. This may entail a rota of presentation or equal time to be allocated to each presentation at each supervision session, although from time to time urgent or pressing matters may take up more time. There will be some cases of greater difficulty, or that involve more crises, which inevitably take more than a strictly equitable share of the time available. These factors can be discussed openly.

Problems can arise in supervision when there is persistent non-attendance or significant lateness by the supervisee, or other difficulties with sticking to the framework, such as recurrently presenting process notes that lack adequate detail. The supervisor should tackle such issues in a tactful but firm way and explore whether there is an element of parallel process giving rise to such phenomena (as discussed below). Lapses of this sort are likely to be pointers to something that needs to be understood.

Supporting therapists' management of countertransference

The necessity to support the therapist's exploration of his or her countertransference response to the patient is a feature of all psychoanalytic supervision, as described above. This may feel particularly urgent when difficulties in understanding and bearing the countertransference arise, as in the following vignette.

> "Steve" was a boy whose cool demeanour and extensive prior experience of professional help – a drugs counsellor to help him give up heavy drug use, and counselling in his secondary school – evoked particular uncertainty in his therapist. She found it hard to believe she had anything to offer this apparently sophisticated boy, and she found herself asking a string of questions and making "sensible" suggestions rather than exploring the transference implications of what he said. Inexperience in work with disturbed adolescents played a part in this. She felt more at home with younger children.
>
> She was aware of being intimidated by his references to always having been an angry person. He "knew" he was the source of his parents' frequent arguments, and he "could not help" creating trouble and getting into fights. His conviction about the power of his aggression was matched by stories of extensive sexual activity, which disturbed her. He was now 15, but he reported that he had got his girlfriend pregnant last year and had then slept with her best friend "to make himself feel bad".
>
> At the end of an early session, Steve said, "One of the things that worries me most is being ignored, because I am used to getting attention." His therapist felt unable to address the significance of this communication coming at the end of the session. In supervision, the group talked about the extent of the fear he stirred up in her: could she withstand the pressure of his aggressive sexuality and possessiveness? What would happen if she tried to gather these passions into the transference relationship? Did she feel strong enough to cope?
>
> Steve continued to patronize her, "You all right?" being his opening greeting and "After you" as he held the door of the consulting room open for her. It was hard for her to grasp the anxiety underlying his need to look after her. This interfered with her being able to respond to alarming material about a friend Steve told her had just committed suicide by stepping in front of a train. Steve could not believe the friend was dead: he was always the one who cheered everyone up. Steve continued to chat in a lively way, explaining that he knew his friends would not like his depressed side and wondering whether he would be as missed as his dead friend was.

It was all too evident that the supervisor's increasing worry, faced with the therapist's problem in tackling things, must be an indication of how the seriousness of the situation had to be pushed as far away as possible. It was not being contained in the consulting room. What seemed particularly problematic was the absence of space for the therapist to become aware of her own feelings of worry, anger, and at times horror in response to Steve's account of his manic state of mind.

Gradually, the experience of feeling taken for a ride by this boy began to take shape in the therapist's mind. As he talked grandiloquently about the various diagnoses he had acquired and announced how "intrigued" he was by the suggestion she had made that he pushed uncomfortable things out of his mind, she felt on firmer ground. Noting his trembling knee, she spoke of his discomfort and anxiety when there was a moment of silence in the room. Steve replied, "I'm not good at silences. That's why I always have to listen to music or watch TV. Silence makes me feel alone, empty." The starkness of this now seemed tolerable, however painful it was for both of them to see just how much trouble he was in.

Parallel process in supervision

An interesting further point about countertransference is the significance of the supervisor's response to the supervisee's use of the supervisory relationship. Supervisors can, for example, sometimes feel bored, irritated, or anxious, or, by contrast, they can get carried away by how exciting their insights seem to be. Brenman Pick (unpublished paper, 2012) reported observations of her reactions in supervision, concluding that the working-through of her countertransference unlocked hitherto hidden aspects of the clinical material and the patient's difficulties. This theorizes in a particular way the phenomenon often referred to as "mirroring" between the therapist and supervisor or supervision group, a parallel process reflecting the dynamics between the therapist and patient. This can alert the supervisory pair or group to the unconscious dynamics in play in the case. When this is addressed constructively, it can contribute to the therapist's understanding of the clinical material and capacity to engage with it. In any group (rather than one-to-one) supervision, the supervisor will also need to be aware of group processes, and these too may pick up some of the parallel process, with different members in touch with diverse elements of the patient's inner world.

Rhode (2011), reflecting on the experience of supervising for the study of STPP for childhood depression (Trowell et al., 2007), comments that such parallel processes may be particularly powerful in working with severely depressed children or adolescents, where there are intergenerational experiences of loss, and where using a time-limited model brings feeling of loss to the fore. She gives an example of the feeling of inadequacy in the depressed patient being experienced in both the therapist's and the supervisor's countertransference:

> one therapist repeatedly said how inadequate she felt and how convinced she was that she was not doing her job properly. . . . [B]efore long I began to feel acutely that my best efforts to help her were not succeeding, that my suggestions were incomprehensible – in fact, that I was not doing *my* job properly. These feelings were so immediate and distressing that it took some weeks before I could see them as a reflection of the patient's own overwhelming feeling of inadequacy, communicated to her therapist and, by her therapist, to me. [Rhode, 2011, p. 135]

Such mirroring is illustrated in the following vignette:

A fifth session of STPP was brought to a small STPP supervision group. The patient, "Millie", presented with symptoms of depression overlaid with significant and ongoing visible self-harm through cutting her skin. Unsurprisingly, this generated considerable concern among the professional network, which included the multidisciplinary team and the local emergency department. Her parents were also terribly anxious for their daughter. Millie was able to let her therapist know some of the emotional conflicts that she experienced powerfully in relation to her body, and about her profound confusion. Fleeting moments of sharing and acknowledging thoughts in the initial sessions had opened up a germ of possible containment and a recognition that the therapist could stand alongside her through her desperate states of mind.

In the fifth session, Millie talked boldly about how she had cut her body since the last session and how she had gone on a drinking binge, making herself vulnerable to exploitation and assault. In supervision, the supervisor was struck by how Millie's therapist seemed to talk a lot more in this session than she had in earlier ones. Millie's therapist, unusually, had made quite directive statements, telling her patient that what she was doing was dangerous and thoughtless and pointing out the worry she was generating in her parents. This was strikingly out of character for the therapist as well as outside the psychoanalytic frame. As the supervisor listened to the clinical process notes being read out by the therapist, she noticed an increasing feeling of anger towards her, thinking, "Why is she not the thoughtful clinician she usually is?" The supervisor wanted to interrupt Millie's therapist reading out the detail of the session to ask her why she was talking to her patient like this and why she was not noting and making use of her countertransference in the session. She did not interrupt the therapist, as it was not her usual practice to do so, but found herself wondering how she, as supervisor, was going to be able to create a thoughtful space to make sense of the therapist's uncharacteristically judgemental and prescriptive approach.

Once the session notes had been read out, the group discussion helpfully began with a member kindly commenting on how Millie's therapist had been very active in the session. The therapist acknowledged this and described how baffled she was herself by it. The supervisory discussion developed into thinking about how the therapist might have found herself pushing anxiety back into her patient. Then a group member made a comment that was rather less tactful and likely to arouse guilt in the therapist. The supervisor noticed that a parallel process had developed in the group that was worthy of consideration, and which reflected her own emotional response to hearing the session material. The group dynamics of anger and guilt seemed to mirror Millie's unconscious experience and how she was pushing fear and anger into all the adults around her. Exploring this dynamic was helpful in thinking about the possible meaning and underlying dynamics of Millie's provocative and desperate communications.

Supervision of parent work

Clinical discussion of STPP parent work is recommended as part of good clinical governance around the patient and family. As with the supervision of psychotherapy, supervision or a work discussion group for parent-work cases provides a space for the clinician to engage in a third arena of thinking.

Within the clinic, the young person's therapist and the parent worker may choose to have a detailed discussion about their respective areas of work with the family, or they may decide that clinically it is best not to exchange too much information or clinical thinking beyond what is required for good case management. Whatever their practice, separate parent-work supervision is likely to be invaluable. One of the obvious advantages – and, some would say, essential features – of parent-work supervision is that it introduces a colleague who is not directly involved with the patient or family who can bring a fresh mind to the clinical situation and the session material. This triangulation (another core concept in thinking about supervision overall) allows for some freedom in exploration of the parent-work sessions in their own right, rather than as a secondary adjunct to the young person's treatment. More specifically, in relation to issues of risk, it can be a forum in which the dynamics of risky behaviour (which may be particularly pressing for the parents) can be thought about and the need for any action be considered carefully. This helps guard against preemptive decisions and actions.

Supervision for STPP parent work needs to reflect the fact that this is a psychoanalytic model of treatment. The supervisor should have a high level of training in psychoanalytic principles and conceptual frameworks and significant relevant clinical experience. The structure of this supervision will inevitably be shaped by local clinic and service possibilities and limitations, and it may take a variety of forms:

» regular individual supervision of the parent work either in its own right or as part of the established supervision of a clinician's overall caseload;

» peer supervision (one-to-one or as a group) with colleagues who are also engaged in psychoanalytically informed parent work, either specifically within the STPP model or as part of a generic caseload;

» one-off consultations with a psychoanalytically trained psychotherapist, on an as-and-when-needed basis;

» the work discussion group model, where a group of clinicians (often multidisciplinary) meet on a regular and committed basis, with a group facilitator who has psychoanalytic experience of this area of work.

In the work discussion model, group members take it in turns to present detailed case material for collective thinking and discussion. In addition to the consideration of clinical material, the discussion usually gives attention to the therapeutic frame, the role of the clinician, and the overall context for the work (Rustin & Bradley, 2008).

In conclusion, it is interesting to note that in the IMPACT trial, many of the clinicians, despite their considerable prior clinical experience, spoke of the importance of the supervision provided. While this was likely to arise in part from natural anxieties about being part of a research study, and uncertainties about unfamiliar aspects of the STPP model, it also seemed to have a lot to do with the exceptional pressure of the serious levels of depression encountered, together with the consequent strain in sticking to a thinking clinical stance and resisting the temptation to discharge anxiety through action of one sort or another.

CHAPTER SEVEN

Short-Term Psychoanalytic
Psychotherapy in clinical practice

Managing psychiatric difficulties and risk

Self-harm and suicidal ideation

Issues of risk in STPP, as with other approaches to therapy with severely depressed young people, usually focus on deliberate self-harm, such as cutting, and on expressions of suicidal ideation and actual suicide attempts. As discussed in chapter 3, the therapist will have a clear line of communication with multidisciplinary colleagues, including the child psychiatrist, about issues to do with risk in the treatment of depressed young people, and she or he will also be clear with the patient about the limits of confidentiality around risk, including involving their parents where necessary. Supervision is crucial in helping the therapist think through all the implications of such actions. If parents are to be alerted to the risk level, for instance, the therapist will need to think in supervision about how this can be done in a way that does not undermine the young person's relationship with his or her therapist.

Discussions of risk in supervision will focus not only on management but also on the unconscious communication involved in the young person's risk-taking behaviour. The theoretical assumption behind this approach is that all risk-taking behaviour has a psychic or emotional meaning which can be explored in psychotherapy. It may, for example, be an enactment of the young person's difficulty in being able to reflect on destructive impulses and on the over-whelming nature of the anxieties that the behaviour is intended to modify – cutting, for instance, may be felt to reduce extreme levels of tension or anxieties about feeling real. The role of the supervision is to support and expand the therapist's capacity to perceive the under-lying belief system (e.g., that the patient's hatred is too powerful to be safely acknowledged). This enables the therapist either to name it for the young person where this seems likely to be meaningful, or to contain the understanding within the therapeutic relationship – for instance, by describing to the patient his or her projections of danger-ous destructiveness into the therapist or others.

Psychotic symptoms

Younger adolescents are much more likely than older ones to report psychotic symptoms, such as hearing voices. A recent study found that between 21% and 23% of younger adolescents (aged 11 to 13 years) reported such symptoms, compared to only 7% of mid-adoles-cents (aged 14 to 16 years) (Kelleher et al., 2012). Psychotic symptoms need to be assessed carefully in order to determine whether they are of a clearly transitory nature, such as can sometimes arise in the course of treatment, or whether they indicate a psychotic disturbance that requires medication or other psychiatric input. Such symptoms may be "markers" for severe psychopathology and co-morbidity, rather than specifically for a psychotic disorder, particularly for older adolescents (Kelleher et al., 2012).

It is not unusual for adolescence to throw up intense, passionate, and polarized states of mind (Waddell, 2006). These seem to be a more common feature as mental illness has come into mainstream media, culture, and education. The idea of a named condition can seem to offer the comfort of a diagnosis that will explain all difficul-ties. Young people can become acutely anxious about their intense emotional experiences of anxiety, self-consciousness, and confusions about identity as being evidence of a psychiatric disorder such as bipolar or psychotic illnesses. Alternatively, feelings of detachment or struggles with forming relationships can be pigeon-holed as evidence of autistic spectrum disorder. The very situation of embarking on STPP because of a depressive "illness" stirs up concerns that this may mean that they have an underlying psychotic disorder.

Such concerns were illustrated in the case of Anna, but they were also a feature in the work with 12-year-old "Leah":

> In her therapy, Leah described vivid nightmares that at times were like waking dreams. She would see scenes of violence before her eyes or have an intense feeling of being watched. This was coupled with either feeling intensely hopeless and distressed or extremely happy, as if she didn't have a care in the world. This all added to Leah's view that she was suffering from a psychotic illness. Experiencing Leah's powerful and emotionally vivid accounts left her therapist too concerned that she might have an undiagnosed underlying illness. Yet when the material was thought about in more detail, the picture became less polarized and it became possible to gain insights into the contexts and quality of Leah's anxiety. Supervision was important in thinking about this, particularly as Leah's worry was threatening to get lodged in her therapist's mind in an unhelpful way. Once this was contained, therapist and supervisor could think together about how Leah was presenting, about liaising with the parent worker, and about seeking additional consultations with a child psychiatrist. These consultations also helped to contain the therapist's anxiety and provide a useful, non-intrusive monitoring of Leah's mental state alongside her therapist's direct clinical experience and judgement. As Leah progressed through STPP, she gained greater emotional insight which enabled these extreme states of mind to be borne and thought about.

Inpatient admission and day hospital treatment

Most cases of child or adolescent depression can be safely and effectively treated on an outpatient basis. This will be contingent, however, on having access to intensive and frequent review, as necessary, in periods of crisis.

While admitting a young person to an inpatient unit can seem like a safe alternative, and is sometimes clearly necessary, there are also risks associated with admission. Admission may lead to the young person having a reduced sense of responsibility for him/herself, and young people may also learn or amplify maladaptive coping strategies, such as self-harm, from each other. Admission will also disrupt the young person's ongoing education. Nevertheless, there are times when admission is necessary, including when the depression is very severe and not responding to outpatient treatment; when it is not possible to manage the level of risk safely, despite best efforts, in outpatient services; when there is diagnostic doubt and there is a need for more intensive observation and examination than is possible in outpatient settings; and when aspects of the home environment seem to play a major role but cannot be clarified in the outpatient setting. STPP can in principle be combined with such an inpatient admission, but this will require careful professional liaison and planning. Close attention will need to be paid to this in supervision, even at times when the patient is unable to attend sessions, in order to help the therapist hold the young person in mind.

Day patient care, when available, offers a halfway house between residential inpatient care and outpatient care and can be useful where it seems particularly important for the young person to remain in his or her home and community; where admission on a residential basis is not acceptable to the young person or his or her family; where a brief admission on a day-patient basis can be used for more intensive assessment; or as a prelude to admission.

An example of the use of inpatient admission is provided by 15-year-old "Jack".

Jack was hospitalized after five sessions of STPP. He had deliberately stepped out into moving traffic while waiting at a bus stop with his mother. The high level of impulsivity of this act, and concerns about risk and the severity of his depression, resulted in a four-month admission to a local inpatient unit.

In the five STPP sessions prior to Jack's admission, he had attended regularly and had been able to let his therapist know about his self-destructive behaviours and quite extreme states of mind. For example, Jack had described how sexually promiscuous he had become over recent months, thoughtlessly sleeping around and then feeling quite hysterical, wanting to pull his hair out. He had become unrecognizable to his friends, who were concerned about him. Jack had described how, growing up, he had felt closest to his father, and as the eldest child had been no trouble and easy-going. His father became depressed and attempted suicide by a massive overdose when Jack was 9 years old. Over the last couple of years, his parents had been going through the process of splitting up, and Jack had been increasingly worried about his mother and how upset and fragile she had become. Jack's therapist was able to maintain contact with Jack initially by telephone two weeks into his admission and then through several letters. This was thought about carefully in supervision to make sure that a reasonable level of contact was maintained – enough to sustain the relationship with Jack without undermining the work he was doing in the unit.

It was possible to resume STPP once Jack was discharged from hospital and he was able to make good use of the remainder of his sessions. His therapist had initially thought he would require an extension to STPP or an adjustment into open-ended, long-term psychotherapy. Approximately 10 sessions into STPP, however, it became clear how important and helpful it was to Jack to sustain the time boundary of the intervention. The prospect of returning to his studies, friends, and family as a young person and not as a patient was an important aim for Jack, but with an idea that further psychotherapeutic support in the future might well be helpful.

Some common problems

Silent patients

Some patients find it very difficult to speak freely in their sessions, perhaps particularly in the initial sessions. Silence needs to be carefully understood and indeed may be communicative (Segal, 1997b). Silent patients need help from the therapist – in the form of interpretation based on the therapist's observation of the patient's bodily presence, any brief verbal or non-verbal cues, and the "total situation" (Joseph, 1985) of the transference and countertransference – in order to find ways to express themselves. While for some young people only a little help may be needed, others may use "no-entry" defences (Williams, 1997b) to indicate a shutting down of vitality and desire.

Such patients may experience words coming from the therapist very concretely, "like being force-fed" (Magagna, 2000, p. 230). It will be essential to "understand the prevailing mood derived from . . . the therapist's conscious and unconscious responses to the child" (p. 249) and to "[receive] verbalised and non-verbalised experiences – present in tone, rhythm, volume, and velocity of speech, the bodily states, pictorial images, gestures, actions, and play" (Magagna, 2012, p. 103).

> "Becky" was 16. She often found it hard to speak in her therapy sessions, and her therapist had to work hard to help her communicate.
>
> A session shortly before a Christmas holiday began with a period of silence, while Becky picked at her nails. Her therapist broke the silence to ask what she was thinking, to which she replied "Nothing". Further enquiries elicited "No thoughts" and then "Nothing". Becky sounded irritated. The therapist suggested that in recent weeks Becky had felt bothered by not being able to think and had wanted help to understand this, but today she seemed to feel distant and feel that her therapist would not or could not help. Becky did not respond, and her face looked shut down.
>
> After a further long pause, the therapist said she thought Becky was irritated by what she was saying – "No." The therapist then added, "Perhaps you really do not want to be here today." This seemed to stir Becky's interest, and she responded to encouragement by saying, "That would be rude." The therapist suggested that Becky feared that she (the therapist) would not be able to cope with that. Becky then said: "I have nothing to say because nothing has happened and so [*said rather tartly*] there is no reason to be here." The therapist acknowledged that Becky felt that she had failed to help her with this state of being unable to think. Becky glanced first at her and then at her own shoes, thoughtfully, retying the laces. After another silence, feeling Becky to be less cut-off at this point, the therapist asked, what she was thinking about. "Yoga, which I am going to later this evening. I like yoga." The therapist suggested that she felt yoga was a good way of looking after herself, whereas therapy seemed not to help, perhaps particularly as the Christmas holiday and the half-way point in the therapy approached. She linked this to Becky's earlier description

of how she had withdrawn from her parents and shut herself away in her room. "This is what seems to be happening here today." Becky replied, "Mm, maybe." The therapist continued: "This seems to be at the heart of your problems, but it is difficult to bring it here because you shut down and become impervious to things." Betty looked puzzled and asked what "impervious" meant. "It means impenetrable . . . Something that can't be got through, like the shut door of your bedroom." "Mm, perhaps?" "Then you feel your parents can't help and just now you feel I can't either." Becky looked up, and as the session ended the mood felt somewhat lighter.

In discussing this session in supervision, the therapist and supervisor explored the projection of irritation and disappointment into the therapist. They came to see how it was only when the extent of Becky's angry rejection of the therapist's painstaking efforts, even her capacity to be frankly rude, was really palpable, that her therapist became robust enough to tackle matters head-on. This allowed for Becky's curiosity to be sparked. The aggression behind the apparently despairing silence and withdrawal could be out in the open and, with it, some energy and engagement. Becky had then cancelled the next session by text message – a huge contrast to her faithful attendance hitherto. The supervisor and therapist debated whether this was a further dose of hostility or an important step towards Becky being able to own her negative feelings. The text message said that she was having dinner with her family, so a warmer atmosphere seemed likely to have developed in Becky's relationship with her parents, of whom she had lately been so dismissive. One might suggest that the negative transference was now being held in the patient–therapist relationship, leaving more space for something better in the external world.

Parent work following trauma

Where there has been a trauma or multiple traumas in the immediate or wider family, these will have a bearing not only on the young person's therapy but also, inevitably, on the parent work and will need to be sensitively handled. Relational trauma within the parental relationship may, as in the following case of "Thomas", mean that there is only one parent available or appropriate to be worked with, although the trauma may continue to feel "alive" in the internalized sense of a parental couple in the adolescent child's mind or the parent's conception of parenting.

> The parents of 14-year-old "Thomas" were separated and his mother, Ms T, was his sole carer. Thomas was of dual heritage: Ms T was Eritrean and had a history of traumatic loss, fleeing violent conflict in her country of origin; Thomas's father was white British. There had been domestic violence in the parental relationship, leading to its eventual breakdown, and Thomas had only sporadic contact with his father. Ms T had had to work hard in her dual role as sole parental provider to Thomas. This had included dealing with episodes of discrimination within her local community. Following a period in which Thomas's mother became concerned that he was increasingly withdrawn and uncommunicative, Thomas was referred to the clinic after cutting himself rather seriously and describing to the psychiatrist in the hospital emergency department some feelings of wishing to end his life.
>
> In the initial meeting, Ms T clearly communicated her distress and her need for some parent-work sessions. She was frightened by Thomas's mood and his frequent angry outbursts, and she was unsure how best to help him develop as an adolescent. Once it had been agreed that Thomas would attend an assessment for STPP, the parent worker suggested an individual appointment for Ms T a week later to think about parent work, described as "support".
>
> Ms T did not attend the agreed session and did not make contact. The parent worker wrote a short letter to her, offering another appointment. Later that week, Thomas attended his first session. Ms T attended her next session. In contrast to the initial meeting, in which she had been clearly distressed, she was anxious and hesitant. The parent worker spoke about this, and about Ms T's concern for Thomas and her uncertainty in approaching this potential new relationship (with the parent worker). This helped Ms T to become less tense and speak about the strain of being a single mother raising Thomas as he grew into becoming a young man. There was also some discussion about Ms T's rather isolated social position and how little contact she had with the communities of people from her country of origin who were living in the

same city. This allowed the parent worker and Ms T to acknowledge some differences between them, culturally and ethnically.

The next session was two weeks later, and Ms T attended. She
spoke at length about her relationship with Thomas's father,
which included aggressive interactions and violent behaviour.
Ms T said she was no longer frightened of him and he did not
"bother" her. She was concerned, however, that their difficulties
now in communicating about Thomas put Thomas in a vulnerable
position. Ms T was also concerned that Thomas might be hurting
himself rather than becoming aggressive to women, as his father
was. They considered at length the possible difficulty for Thomas
of working out how to develop ordinary potency as a young man
rather than turning to aggression towards himself (or others). The
parent worker and Ms T also wondered whether or not Thomas's
father should be invited to the clinic for a session on his own with
the parent worker. (They later agreed this, but Thomas's father
declined to attend.)

Once Thomas's assessment for STPP had been completed and an
agreement had been made for him to proceed to work with the
same psychotherapist for STPP, the parent worker confirmed with
Ms T that they would continue to meet separately, at more or less
monthly intervals. In the next few sessions, more work was done
on Ms T's worries about her position as a single mother and how
to help Thomas develop confidence in his capacities to make good
relationships with girls. This became linked with Ms T's questions
about the impact of the parental conflict and violence on Thomas
as a young boy. Ms T was angry and upset in remembering this
time, and she felt guilty that she had not been able to provide a
better male role model for her son.

With parent-work sessions now once a month, Ms T spoke of her
own upbringing, the loss of her settled birth-family life due to a
civil war, the traumatic disappearances of family members and
friends, and her flight from her community and country. Thinking about these many losses and experiences of conflict enabled
Ms T to consider how Thomas might be very frightened of his
move into adolescence, particularly in the light of his experiences
growing up with warring parents and the absence of an effective father. This work helped Ms T separate out her own tragic

experiences from Thomas's struggles, and this enabled her to be more available emotionally to him. It was recognized that previously Thomas's despair and his suicidal act had joined up in Ms T's mind with her own emotional experiences. This had been overwhelming for her and rendered her emotionally unavailable to Thomas. In addition to thinking about her place as his parent and her own history, there was discussion as to how Ms T might make more social contacts for herself, including increasing her connection to her own community locally. Later on in the work, some thought was given to the possibility of Ms T being referred to an adult psychological therapy service following the end of Thomas's STPP treatment.

"Acting out" and "acting in"

Within the session, interpretation is sometimes not enough to address actions that could be dangerous to the young person and/or to the therapist. This is likely to arise mostly in those young people whose depression manifests as anger or externalizing problems. The therapist's response to this will be governed partly by the young person's age, but it will always be important to emphasize the distinction between a feeling or impulse that is being communicated by the behaviour, which it is essential for the therapist to know about, and the behaviour itself. One of the therapist's essential tasks is to ensure his or her own safety as well as that of the young person. For this reason, it needs to be stated clearly what kind of behaviour is unacceptable and why, as well as to interpret the unconscious communication. The vital distinction to be made is between the verbal expression of violent feelings and desires and any actual physical enactment ("acting out").

In the case of very young adolescents who are prone to act violently or who threaten or attempt to run out of the therapy room, it may be helpful to enlist the cooperation of parents, who may, for instance, be asked to sit discreetly nearby. The patient's knowledge that this additional help has been enlisted may be very helpful for him or her. With older adolescents, it is important to make clear that there are colleagues to whom the therapist can turn for support if this is necessary, which includes support with ending the session, either for a five-minute "breather" or until the next appointment. It is helpful to model this kind of cooperation between adults in the young person's interest, and to demonstrate that aggressive impulses can be managed as well as understood.

"Acting in" takes place when the therapist, under the pressure of countertransference feelings, speaks or behaves in way that goes beyond the usual framework for psychoanalytic psychotherapy. This may be a particular risk when such countertransference pressures have not been fully recognized. This might take the form of offering advice, not because it is the therapist's considered judgement that this would be helpful (although giving advice is usually contraindicated in psychoanalytic psychotherapy), but under pressure to be seen as "helpful" or because of finding the patient's distress unbearably painful, or of taking an unhelpful action outside the parameters of the therapy (such as communicating unnecessarily with parents or school) driven by countertransference pressure. The danger of acting in is one of the reasons for the paramount importance of ongoing clinical supervision.

"Acting out" by the young person *outside* the session, such as getting involved in problematic or delinquent behaviour, may require liaison with the wider team alongside attempting to elucidate the meaning of the behaviour with the young person during sessions. Where this involves risk of significant harm to the young person or others, this will necessitate close attention to risk management, as discussed below.

The following vignette illustrates, first, the acting in during the session engaged in by the therapist working with "Michael" under the pressure of her countertransference frustration; and then Michael's "acting out" that followed.

13-year-old Michael was referred with a request for psychotherapy by his social worker and his father, who were both concerned about his profound depression. He had been abandoned by his mother on the steps of the local social services organization when he was 8 years old. He had lived in foster care since then, with a single foster carer who was of the generation to be his grandmother. He attended a school for children with moderate learning difficulties. His father, who had had several other children with different partners, remained in regular contact with him, and Michael also saw these half-siblings from time to time. His extreme quietness had led to the provision of speech therapy at his school, with no observable increase in verbal communicativeness.

In his weekly therapy sessions, Michael's passivity, near-silence, and immobility were the main features. He always sat in the same chair and could remain exceptionally still, with a blank expression on his face and his eyes seeming open to absorb whatever the therapist might do. She experienced a range of feelings and thoughts, which she was able to draw on in order to understand her countertransference. Her initial technique was to combine comments based on observation (e.g., comments on his keeping an eye on her and waiting to see what to expect, what sort of thing therapy might be, and what sort of person she was) with some interpretations of the transference situation based on the emotional atmosphere of the sessions as she perceived it (e.g., comments on his doubt about whether she remembered him from week to week or was interested in what was in his mind).

The slow pace of the sessions contrasted painfully with Michael's physical growth: he was a big-boned, tall boy, making her think of him as a gentle giant at times when the sadness of his state was more evident. At other times, however, a terrible sense of urgency and irritation would take hold of the therapist, a worry that his life would simply slip by: she came to understand this as a fear of psychic death. She found herself unable to wait the necessary time for any response he might make to a comment, as he sometimes did after minutes had elapsed, and would hear herself repeating or rephrasing what she had said as if he had not heard it or were stupid and needed things to be said twice. It was then possible, through supervision, to observe that this pressure was counterproductive: Michael would seem to shrink back and become more silent rather than be energized by this too-eager or too-anxious therapist. This observation enabled her to resist becoming active on Michael's behalf and to wait more calmly to see what would emerge.

At a later point in Michael's therapy, he started to develop more of a sense of agency and also became able to "act out". He was now making the journey from school to the clinic under his own steam instead of being escorted. He was usually somewhat late. The therapist interpreted his wish to make her wait for him and his investigation of how she felt to be kept waiting: perhaps he wondered whether she would be worried that she had been forgotten? Would she be angry with him for not being the good boy who always did what grown-ups wanted? Once, when he unusually arrived on time, she noticed his glancing pointedly at the corridor clock after she had kept him waiting for two minutes in the waiting room. He began to be able to tell her what happened on his journey to make him late: he would be distracted by looking in a shop window on the way to the station, or interested in the trains going in the opposite direction from the one he needed to take. He became able to act out both in the everyday sense of being a mildly delinquent adolescent and the psychoanalytic sense of expressing feelings through action outside the session rather than communication within it. But almost simultaneously he became able to take note of what passed through his mind and to become interested in discussing it.

Michael's deep depression was giving way to a sense of some inner aliveness, which included access to his capacity for self-assertion or aggression, in the context of the developing therapeutic relationship, which he no longer believed to be available only if he presented himself as passive, undemanding, and compliant.

In this example, Michael's development of a capacity to act out moderately during and around the session (coming late) was evidence of his reduced anxiety about his aggression and was accompanied, in the therapy, by his increasing ability to be aware of his own thoughts and feelings, with his therapist's support. For Michael, to be able to enact something aggressive represented progress beyond his earlier passive state, which had involved the loss of parts of himself through projective identification, whereby any feelings of agency and energy, for example, had been lodged in his therapist with the result of her feeling irritated and impatient. Had the acting out outside the therapy – his more delinquent behaviour – been more extreme, this might have become seriously counterproductive, as may happen of course in some cases (as discussed above in relation to self-harm and risk and below in relation to non-attendance).

Negative transference, therapeutic impasse,
and negative therapeutic reaction

Negative transference is expected to be a feature of STPP work requiring careful handling on the part of therapist and supervisor alike. For the supervisor, a central supervision dilemma may concern how to be sensitive and open to the negative transference, particularly in the early stages of the STPP treatment when the therapist is concerned with building a therapeutic relationship with the patient that will carry them through the work. There may be tension around the important question of how best to recognize and perhaps respond to the part of the young person that comes to sessions with anticipation and hope for help and recovery (Cregeen, 2012). Therapists may worry that to identify and name expressions of uncertainty and ambivalence in the patient, early in treatment, may create or increase the patient's anxiety in such a way as to jeopardize his or her engagement. Therapists may need help from the supervisor and supervision group to acknowledge the patient's doubts or scepticism sensitively, by framing it as an understandable expression of mixed feelings that the therapist can accept. This may highlight for the therapist how uncomfortable, aggressive, and attacking experiences in the work with the young person can be usefully explored, as the following vignette illustrates.

> 15-year-old "Jake" came to his first session full of enthusiasm to receive help to recover from his depression, which was making him feel that there was no point in investing in his friendships, family, or education. He talked about how open he was to the idea of talking about his experiences, as he had a male learning mentor at school who had been really helpful. Jake described how this mentor had been readily accessible throughout the school day and had actively sought Jake out to check that he was OK. The mentor had also lent Jake some novels to read which the mentor thought would help Jake to understand his feelings better. In supervision, Jake's therapist explained how she had responded to this by picking up his hope for this new therapy, and she described how impressed she felt about Jake's openness and motivation to think together. When this was thought about in more detail in the supervision group, a contrast emerged between a readily accessible male mentor who gave Jake books and checked up on him

and STPP with a middle-aged woman who had just explained the frame of weekly sessions at a set time in a rhythm of breaks and gaps. Jake's therapist readily understood the more anxious communication once given the chance to think about it in more depth, but she was worried about the likely impact of commenting on it in such early sessions, and the supervision group tried to explore with her the possible benefits of doing so.

In the following session, Jake talked about how he had been able to contact a friend in the middle of the night when he was feeling really angry about an incident at school that day. His therapist picked up on his feeling aware of the limitations of this new therapy that was not available in the middle of the night or at school: a therapy that did not provide actual things, like recommended books. She commented that he might quite understandably be questioning how an hour of therapy once a week would help him and whether it would be enough. Although a little self-conscious, Jake gave a steady nod and the space opened up for him to talk about how he felt unsupported, inadequately prioritized, and poorly understood. Expressions of complaint and some grievance came to the fore which felt emotionally more substantial and helpfully contrasted with his earlier pleasing expressions of hope.

The example of Jake illustrates the ordinary difficulty of using negative transference in work with severely depressed young people, particularly in the early stages of the therapy. By contrast, the concept of therapeutic "impasse" describes those situations within an ongoing therapeutic relationship in which the possibilities for communication between patient and therapist have broken down. This can occur for a variety of reasons. These include both factors in the patient's personality – and additionally, in the case of young people, aspects of the patient's external circumstances, particularly his or her family situation – which intrude into the therapeutic relationship, and factors in the therapist which interfere with good functioning in his or her professional work.

In the following vignette, the STPP treatment of "Peter" came close to breaking down.

Peter, 17 years old, was referred for STPP because of long-standing depression and an escalation in self-harming behaviour during the previous six months. He had been supported in the multidiscipli-nary clinic for some time by a nurse, who thought that STPP might help to address his self-harm, which was primarily expressed through cutting and occasionally through drinking binges. Peter seemed relieved at the offer of an assessment and was then keen to continue with STPP, using the sessions to explore his at times extremely overwhelming feelings. While his single mother seemed very supportive of his attending, he and she were both in agree-ment that parent work was not needed: that Peter, at the age of 17, would prefer the privacy of attending the clinic without his moth-er's involvement, and that she respected this. It was agreed that she would attend only for regular reviews, which would also be attended by the nurse, who continued to be Peter's case manager.

After an initial "honeymoon" period in which Peter seemed to make good use of his therapy and his self-harm reduced con-siderably, he started to miss sessions on a regular basis, citing college commitments, difficulties in his peer group that required his immediate attention, and, on other occasions, simply feeling too wretched to attend. His therapist felt increasingly troubled by these missed sessions and by the suspicion he had when Peter did attend that he might be self-harming again. A review of the therapy was suggested, and this was attended by Peter and his mother, as well as the case manager. This meeting was diffi-cult: Peter's mother talked at length about Peter's unmanageable behaviour, which clearly distressed and angered Peter to hear, and he eventually responded in an explosive way. The therapist and his colleague found themselves somewhat powerless to intervene in the escalating row between mother and son. They agreed later that they had both felt angry with Peter's mother for not encour-aging him to attend his sessions (despite, in reality, appreciating how difficult it would be for her to do so). The situation was barely resolved within the review meeting.

In supervision, the therapist spoke about this difficult clinical encounter. Supported by the supervision group, he gradually real-ized that his overwhelming response was of guilt: somehow, he should be able to help Peter to attend; somehow, he should have improved Peter's mental state by now. In fact, he confessed, he had been wondering whether he had been mistaken in offering time-limited work to this boy in the first place; perhaps he needed more, and the therapist was therefore also guilty of depriving his patient. The group then became able to explore the central role of guilt in the family dynamics between Peter and his mother, and they wondered whether Peter's determination not to involve his mother in his treatment, other than minimally through review meetings, had been designed to protect her. The case manager subsequently made contact with Peter's mother and established a strong line of regular communication about Peter's progress, while the therapist was able to talk with Peter in their next session about Peter's guilty feelings in relation to his mother. A break-down in the work was thus narrowly avoided.

There is a considerable psychoanalytic literature on the "negative therapeutic reaction", following the important formulation by Riviere (1936). This work explores factors in the patient which threaten progress in ongoing analytic work and may also undermine progress that has previously occurred. A persisting negative therapeutic reaction is one way of describing an impasse arising from destructive forces within the patient. This clinical situation is characterized by an absence of insight or thoughtfulness in the patient and by the therapist's inability to reestablish contact with a part of the patient able and willing to reflect on the difficulties between himself and his therapist. Active hostile rejection of the therapist can arise, for example, from the analysis of a delusion (such as disappointment when an eroticized transference is not reciprocated); from intolerance of painful envy of the therapist, making the therapist's good work a source not of relief but of severe mental pain for the patient; and from severely split-off areas of disturbance that are too frightening to acknowledge. More temporary negative therapeutic reactions are common following separations that have been painful for the patient, and this is particularly frequent in work with adolescents who do not return to their sessions following a break. These more temporary hostile enactments only develop into a state of impasse when it proves impossible to recover from them.

It is interesting to note that in work with adolescents, a break-down or premature ending in therapy is much more common than a therapeutic impasse. This may be linked to the natural pressure in adolescence towards asserting independence through the rejection of adults' expectations, and towards finding out about themselves and the world through exploration rather than introspection.

The young person's continued dependence on family support means that difficulties rooted in the personalities or relationships of parents and occasionally also siblings may have the power to disrupt ongoing therapeutic work. This is particularly so when the individual has been unable to protect him/herself from ongoing projections from family members which undermine a sense of personal mental space (of having a mind of one's own). Examples would include an ongoing sadomasochistic relationship with someone in the family from which the patient is unable to detach him/herself, or a highly vulnerable parent for whose safety and well-being the young person feels responsible and whose needs can be overwhelming when mental or physical breakdown is feared or actually takes place. This is why STPP includes parent work, which includes attention to the family as a whole. Access to a wider professional network is a bulwark against a breakdown in treatment as a consequence of the young person's exposure to family difficulties. The young person's inner state may nonetheless threaten an impasse when his or her sense of vulnerability becomes too exposed to such long-standing recurrent stressors.

Factors in the therapist contributing to impasse were extensively explored by Rosenfeld (1987) following on from Bion's (1963) insight into the distinction between communicative and evacuative forms of projection. This work has had particular resonance in child and adolescent psychotherapy because of the severe levels of neglect and abuse that characterize the backgrounds of many children referred for treatment in recent decades. Following Rosenfeld's work, a body of work has built up focusing on clinical techniques that take account of traumatic factors and deprivation in the patient's history and the risks of reenactment in the analytic work. This includes:

» the importance of paying serious attention to the patient's early history;
» a tolerance of idealization in the transference (Alvarez, 1992b);
» care in the interpretation of envy and in modulating the pain that patients can tolerate, particularly feelings of guilt and humiliation (Pick, 1985);

» distinguishing between "thick" and "thin skinned" forms of narcissism (Britton, 1998; Rosenfeld, 1987);

» scrutiny of countertransference responses (with the vital support of supervision).

An apparent regression and loss of the progress made are particularly common in the final stages of STPP. This might be considered as a pseudo-therapeutic impasse, as it is likely to shift in the direction of "working through" insights gained in earlier sessions. This phenomenon can be difficult for therapists to bear when the time limit has to be respected and when the whole sequence is taking place at quite a fast pace, rather than across a number of months.

Negative transference and medical consultation

Young people in STPP treatment may request or seek the advice of the child psychiatrist about a range of concerns relating to medication and/or physical symptoms: panic attacks, shakes or tremors, or the severity of the depression itself. Such requests may be helpful and within the collaborative framework of the multidisciplinary team and the specific team around the individual patient. They may also, on the other hand, be an expression of the negative transference or of anxiety in the young person or family about the potential helpfulness of the therapy. As already noted, the emergence of the negative transference is usually seen within psychoanalytic psychotherapy as a sign that the treatment is progressing, but it may be accompanied by a worsening of mood or by complaints against the therapist. For this reason, it is important to evaluate carefully on a case-by-case basis what the factors in such a situation appear to be, rather than always to assume that a temporary worsening or a slow initial response indicates treatment failure. Such an approach supports the young person and family's development of thoughtfulness about the young person's symptoms, and it also minimizes the risk of inviting a passive acceptance of prescribed medication and of fostering a dependence on such medication. The following vignette illustrates a thoughtful psychiatric assessment that facilitate a useful trial of medication during the course of STPP.

16-year-old "Mark" communicated long-standing experiences of alienation that predated his entry into adolescence. Although emotionally articulate, he was also intense and he brooded over his thoughts and feelings. He could easily become frustrated and angry by the ordinary short-comings and fallibilities of relationships and the world around him. Mark talked only fleetingly about his childhood, his descriptions having a traumatic quality. When he became distressed or frustrated, he conceptualized this as a chemical imbalance in his brain that required antidepressants. He could recognize how his therapy helped, but he also explained how challenging he found it and described his feeling that medication would more simply and directly attend to his emotional pain. Several sessions would go by when the issue of medication would fade into the background, but inevitably his plea would become the central feature of the work.

At about the tenth session, his therapist began liaising with a child psychiatrist colleague, and they found a way of setting up a psychiatric assessment that enabled both Mark's therapist and the psychiatrist to think about the function of splitting and Mark's underlying anxieties. The psychiatrist suggested a trial period of antidepressant use, while giving Mark the clear message that this needed to be done alongside his continued engagement in the psychotherapy. Mark was relieved that he had been taken seriously, and his therapist felt that Mark had experienced the collaboration between psychotherapist and psychiatrist, on a deeper level, as a robust and collaborative coupling that attended to all aspects of him.

Non-attendance and the STPP time frame

It needs to be made clear to both the young person and his or her parents that missed sessions count towards the total 28 sessions that are available. That is, missed sessions are not made up at another time unless the session has been missed or cancelled by the therapist, except in certain circumstances which it is helpful to define from the start if possible. Family holidays fixed prior to the start of treatment or school exams might well be accepted as unavoidable cancellations and a replacement session offered, in line with standard clinical practice. The role of the parent worker in clarifying these parameters is central in the case of younger adolescents. With older adolescents, it can also be helpful to engage with the wider network, for example GP, school, or college, who may be able to support attendance. In all cases, the therapist focuses on attempting to understand the reason for any non-attendance and on working on this with the young person. It should not immediately be assumed that patchy attendance is a sign of treatment impasse, although this may be the case. It may also be the vehicle for important communications about different attitudes that coexist within the young person or signal an absence of parental support.

A recurring theme in STPP is how challenging it can be to pick up the patient's aggression in the session and how this may be side-stepped or redirected into confusions and subverting of the boundaries related to the time limit. This is particularly acute with young people who present with a great deal of risky behaviour, who often become the focal point for concern and anxiety in the clinical team. In such circumstances, therapists who would ordinarily be very mindful and protective of the psychoanalytic frame may struggle to stay within the usual parameters of the treatment. This may manifest itself in confusion and inconsistency in how missed sessions are defined, and this is an issue that can be usefully picked up in supervision. It may seem relatively straightforward that a patient cancelling a session to do a mandatory school exam would not be counted as one of the 28 STPP sessions. Vaguer and less legitimate reasons for missed sessions, however, may lead the therapist to confuse the session count by "stopping the clock". Supervision will be crucial here in helping to understand the struggle about whether the time boundary can be experienced as containing or an unreasonable imposition on a vulnerable patient. Is the therapist who maintains the frame in such a situation exercising a clear paternal function based on reality, or is he or she cruelly "acting out" a more troubling transference dynamic?

It is useful to think about these technical issues in supervision as enactments related to the therapists' profound anxieties generated by working with these severely depressed patients. Supervision supports the therapist to engage with the anxiety and to be thoughtful and containing about it within the structure of the STPP treatment already agreed with the patient and family. Discussion in supervision will need to focus on the risks inherent in undermining the frame for the work, particularly the risk that it will push the patient into further action of the same kind and away from therapeutic thinking and processing. Where the therapist is able to stick to the framework and trust it, thus advocating it to the patient, the patient is likely to respond by attending more straightforwardly and relying on the therapy and the therapist.

Oedipal dynamics

Many of the difficulties described above may usefully be thought about in relation to oedipal dynamics and how these resurface in adolescence. Concrete themes brought to therapy may illustrate such concerns, such as absent fathers, parents having babies when the young person reaches puberty or early adolescence (as was the case with Anna), or rather enmeshed and intensely dependent relationships with one parent. Oedipal dynamics may manifest themselves in more symbolic ways, however, such as a young person's struggles to observe in a triangular space (not feeling obliterated by not being the centre of attention), or to bear the reality of time, boundaries, and loss.

Such dynamics are likely to present a challenge for therapists and require careful attention in supervision. They may be linked with an intensity of sexuality in the transference relationship or, by contrast, its apparent complete absence. Supervision is helpful in teasing out the specifics and detail of possible unconscious dynamics, so that the therapist is able to speak more clearly and confidently about the young person's oedipal experiences.

Difficulties in engaging parents

The illustrative case study of Anna we have used demonstrates the fluctuations in engaging both parents (or, in her case, a parent and step-parent) in parent work. In Anna's case, her stepfather attended one initial session and then re-engaged, helpfully, with the parent work once the end was in sight. The following case of "Lucinda" illustrates a more conventional process by which one parent, initially more reluctant to attend, engaged in the parent work.

The parents of 17-year-old Lucinda were middle-class professionals who were interested in their children and concerned about
Lucinda's difficulties. Lucinda's severe depression had led to her
taking an overdose and being briefly admitted to hospital. The
level of risk had reduced as she had subsequently engaged with
the outpatient clinic, but she remained seriously depressed.

In the initial meeting with the therapist and the parent worker,
Lucinda's mother, Ms L, expressed confusion about the severity
of Lucinda's difficulties. The parent worker was receptive to her
distress and bewilderment. He was also alert to a sense of underlying panic and her effort to try to control emotions and events.
Ms L agreed to attend some parent-work sessions, and Lucinda –
perhaps unusually for an older teenager – agreed to this too,
expressing some relief that her mother would have some space to
air her concerns about what had been happening.

Ms L attended the first parent-work session on her own. She was
very positive about what she saw as improvements in her daughter's mood and activity. The parent worker was unconvinced by
the evidence for such a view and thought that Ms L was communicating a desperate need to think that all was well, perhaps as a
defence against seeing despair or depressive feelings in Lucinda.
The parent worker gently explored this possibility. Ms L was able
to respond to this approach. This allowed some acknowledgement
and brief conversation about her recent loss of her own mother
and the collapse of the family business. The parent worker also
focused on enabling Ms L to open up some mental space for considering depressive feelings in herself as well as in her daughter.
The possibility was raised of Lucinda's father attending with Ms
L next time.

For the following meeting, two weeks later, Ms L attended on her
own again. There was some discussion of how Lucinda was, especially in the light of the distressing events at the end of Lucinda's
session two weeks previously, when she had become very angry
and threatened to take another overdose. The fact was discussed
that Lucinda's father, Mr L, had never attended a parent-work session; in fact, he had not been to the outpatient clinic at all, although
he had spent all of Lucinda's brief hospital admission at her side.
Ms L seemed keen to continue asking him to come. Following

the thinking in the previous parent meeting, Ms L and the parent worker had a more involved and searching conversation about Ms L's loss of her mother, how Lucinda might have experienced this loss, and the effect this might have had on Ms L's capacity as a mother to Lucinda. This was linked to Ms L's experience of post-natal depression following the birth of Lucinda's brother, when she was 2 years old. Again, Lucinda's possible experience of her mother during this period was thought about and discussed.

The next session, three weeks later, was attended by Mr and Ms L together. The parent worker acknowledged that this was Mr L's first experience of coming to a session, and then they discussed the recent strains upon them as a couple and as a family. Ms L spoke of some of the things discussed in the previous sessions. The focus in this first joint session was on the impact of recent losses and of Lucinda's depression on them as a couple and on their parenting capacity from an emotional point of view. Mr L was vocal about his shock and distress when Lucinda took the overdose and about his reluctance to think about her continuing to experience depression after this initial devastating shock. This enabled some movement towards the restoration of mental space between them as a parental couple.

The following session, four weeks later, was again attended by Mr and Ms L. Mr L now seemed relieved to have the opportunity to reflect on the family relationships and the effects of losses upon them. In this meeting, the discussion quickly turned to Lucinda's depression in the context of her development into adolescence. A link was made with her experience as a 2-year-old when Ms L was postnatally depressed and Mr L was preoccupied with the baby's care and his wife's depression. Much of the discussion was about the new developmental challenges not only for Lucinda but also for the family as a whole, in encountering their eldest child moving towards a more independent way of life and searching for an adolescent identity. The oedipal issues for Mr and Ms L as a couple were touched upon. This allowed Mr L to begin to reflect on his own adolescent experience of trying to disentangle himself from his relationship with his mother in the context of an absent father.

Mr and Ms L continued to attend sessions as a couple. These became monthly in frequency. The themes arising in the first few meetings were elaborated and explored in greater depth. Separate independent couple work was not necessary, though they were both interested in exploring ways to keep their conversation going and in thinking more about how best to help Lucinda in her adolescent development.

It is inevitable that some parents will apparently agree to attend parent-work sessions but not in fact turn up. Sometimes this will be a repeated pattern. In these circumstances, it is essential that the parent worker make a determined effort to contact the reluctant parent. The decision as to whether to do this by telephone or by letter will be determined by the individual situation, the nature of the relationship with the parent, and the stage of the work.

Containment failure and drop-out

Young people who are severely depressed, particularly where there are high levels of emotional deprivation and intergenerational difficulties, may find it extremely difficult to take in their therapist's commitment and concern. They may have painfully little faith in the adult world, or in the relationships offered by their peers, and lack any conception of containment (Bion, 1962a), even for the purposes of evacuation and relief rather than understanding. For these young people, developing such a conception in STPP may feel like a revelation. For some, however, there may be such a sense of pain in engaging in any human relationship that the therapy feels or becomes unbearable. These patients may miss a high number of sessions or, despite their therapists' best efforts, drop out. In so doing, these patients may be enacting a feeling of being dropped out of adults' minds (or out of their lives, where there has been a great deal of actual rejection or abandonment of the young person as may have been the case for some who are looked after by the state). Such young people may be unlikely to have the kind of parental or carer support that would solidly support the STPP work (e.g., by encouraging attendance).

"Tony" was 17 years old. His parents had been long-term heroin addicts, and his father had recently died. Tony began to have bad arguments with his mother and left home. He took an overdose and ended up in the local emergency department, and social services became involved. He was referred by his social worker, who described him as "a survivor" but was concerned about his depression. He was temporarily living with an aunt in a different part of the city, far from his friends, while waiting for a hostel placement.

The original clinician was male, and Tony was put out to find that his STPP therapist was a woman. Despite a thorough discussion of the referral with that clinician, Tony said in the initial meeting with the STPP therapist that he had not been told what kind of therapy he would have and added that he had no choice. He found it difficult to talk but did say he had found it hard to concentrate since his father died. He said he did not like questions. He looked very neglected and unwell.

When it was time to stop at the end of his first session, he did not get up to leave but silently stared at his therapist for a long time. She felt disturbed and concerned about him and contacted the psychiatrist on the case. Meanwhile, Tony went to the local hospital and, despite his suicidal threats, was discharged to his aunt's care, with no link made to the CAMHS clinic by the hospital. His aunt could not cope, and Tony quickly became homeless. His therapist no longer had any way to contact him and his social worker also seemed at a loss.

Some weeks later, Tony made contact with the team psychiatrist, asking for medication. He then reappeared for two more STPP sessions in a row, complaining about the "useless" (male) psychiatrist and torturing his therapist with threats to swallow the sleeping pills he had brought with him. The therapist was extremely alarmed and went to her supervision in a very troubled state, having been unable to think during Tony's sessions or write them up, and feeling almost psychotic herself, at a distance from everything. The supervision group thought this spaced-out state might well echo Tony's experience of being with his drug-addicted parents. We could see that the main communication was Tony's terror that no one could help him, which indeed the therapist felt herself. The multiple losses, of his father, his home, and his place at college combined to break up any sense of containment. The therapist's main task seemed to be to mobilize the professional team whose own communication system had broken down, possibly as a consequence of Tony's violent splitting and projection which they had not been able to think about. Ultimately, a hostel place was found, and Tony was able to attend psychiatric appointments as he wanted medication to make him "feel more in control". Possibly if the psychiatrist and therapist had been more closely linked (they did not work in the same place, and Tony therefore had to go to two different places for his appointments), Tony might have been able to attend sessions. As it was, the therapy framework seemed only to remind him of how senseless his life now seemed and to terrify him.

Working with such high levels of emotional deprivation in young patients is draining for therapists and a challenge for supervisors, who need to support the therapist while also keeping in mind the darkest aspects of the work, in the hope that by helping the therapist to confront these, the young person may come to feel better contained and the therapy be salvaged. It should not be forgotten, however, that where such young people are helped to begin to conceive of a helpful adult, or a thinking capacity in themselves, the effect may be both powerful and profound.

"Priscilla", aged 16, was the eldest of three siblings of a single mother. Both her siblings were boys, and one of them, aged 15, was non-speaking and autistic and the other, much younger, developmentally delayed. At referral, she was very depressed, almost unable to speak. She felt that there was "no point" in life and that coming for therapy would be a waste of the therapist's time. The only thing that helped, she said, was talking online to a friend who also had to look after her younger siblings because her mother was ill.

Her therapist talked about her loneliness and her wish to be understood, having noted how Priscilla evoked considerable warmth and sadness in her. Priscilla then said that she did want to come but had not known how to say it. It soon became clear that she was bitterly angry with her mother, who had tried to conceal a recent pregnancy which had ended in a miscarriage. This situation in the family had left Priscilla having to look after everyone.

Priscilla frequently cancelled her sessions due to her needing to look after her brothers. Her therapist arranged for her to have weekly text reminders from the clinic administrator to help to sustain the reality of her therapist's availability. Despite the frequent gaps between sessions, Priscilla's hope that talking could help never entirely disappeared.

Gradually her anger with her father, who had left because of mother's having a lesbian affair, and her autistic brother, whose "specialness" had deprived her of much of her childhood, gave way to small steps towards adolescent exploration. Priscilla felt sure she was a completely boring person, always excluded from the excitements of teenage life, but one day, after missing three sessions in a row, she arrived with blue hair and a request for a change of session time. This could accommodate the fact that the school term had now ended: she wanted to come *earlier* in the day so that she would have time to do other things!

Holding on to the potential value of the therapy seemed to have had a particularly meaningful impact on this girl's sense of being of interest to someone and hence to herself.

Afterword

It was early in 2009 that the authors of this book first sat down together, to begin work on writing a treatment manual of Short-Term Psychoanalytic Psychotherapy for adolescents suffering from depression. Funding had been secured for the IMPACT trial (Goodyer et al., 2011), and although an earlier clinical trial (Trowell et al., 2007) had offered evidence for the effectiveness of the approach – albeit with a relatively small sample – and a treatment manual had been used in that study (Trowell, Rhode, & Hall, 2010), there was still much work to be done. Between them, the members of the STPP manual writing group had many years of clinical experience working with depressed young people, in a variety of clinical settings, but for most of us it was the first time to be involved in a research study of this scale and, in particular, to be involved in writing a treatment manual. What kind of document were we hoping to create?

It is fair to say that, traditionally, there has not been a very favourable view among the psychoanalytic community towards treatment manuals (Taylor, 2015). The increasing demand for treatment manuals has occurred in the context of the rise of the evidence-based practice movement and, in particular, as part of the emphasis on RCTs as a means of evaluating the effectiveness of therapy. Treatment manuals are valued in research because they offer a replicable and systematized approach to therapeutic interventions, which supports one of the key features of clinical trials: the measurement of fidelity to the treatment being studied (Perepletchikova & Kazdin, 2005). After all, what is the value of saying whether a therapy is effective if you cannot say what the therapy entails?

But for a variety of reasons many clinicians have long been suspicious of manuals, often viewing them as inflexible, rigid, and restricting therapists from tailoring their intervention according to the needs of the individual client (Barron, 1995; Strupp & Anderson, 1997). Treatment manuals have also been criticized as potentially undermining the therapeutic relationship (Arnow, 1999), and they have been seen as especially unsuitable for less structured approaches to treatment, such as psychoanalytic psychotherapy, where the therapist's clinical intuition and creativity is seen as a core component. For example, Goldfried and Wolfe (1998) argued that the key skills of a psychoanalytic psychotherapist run counter to the idea of manualized therapy, while others have suggested that to manualize a psychoanalytic treatment would be an over-simplification of the rich dynamics between client and therapist (Addis & Krasnow, 2000).

It was therefore with some trepidation that our group began this work. In a study that tried to capture some of the experience of this process (Henton & Midgley, 2012), an independent researcher undertook interviews with those involved in the STPP manual writing group. In those interviews, members spoke about feeling daunted, hesitant, and un-skilled. As one of the writing team put it: "I think how one properly represents what is a very private activity in a public area, well that's problematic. And it does raise all kinds of anxieties about wanting to be sure that one does justice to practice . . ." (p. 207). Likewise, when we later interviewed some of the STPP IMPACT therapists themselves, many spoke about how nervous they had been about what "working with a manual" would be like. When one was asked what came to mind when she thought of treatment manuals, she replied: "a bit rigid, and you know, having to stick to the book . . . rather than be . . . free". Another said that before starting work on the IMPACT trial, she simply "couldn't understand how you could create a manual [for psychoanalytic psychotherapy]" (Vadera, 2014).

So how did we as a group overcome these doubts? As one of us put it, "we educated ourselves – we had to read, and understand, and come to grips with the issues" (Henton & Midgley, 2012, p. 208).

Part of that was reaching an understanding of what kind of treatment manual it should be. In the middle of the process, one of the writing team explained:

> [In] a prescriptive manual . . . you *will* do so and so, and so and so, and you *won't* do so and so . . . and you are to educate yourself in the treatment. And then the other way of thinking . . . is a way of describing and capturing normal practice . . . providing the framework, around which to say . . . this is what psychotherapy would look like if you did *this*; and if you did *that*, it wouldn't be STPP. [Henton & Midgley, 2012, p. 209, emphasis in original]

Having reached some kind of understanding of what kind of treatment manual we hoped to write, and also a shared view of *why* we were writing it, the process itself proved to be remarkably stimulating, offering us the opportunity to reflect on our practice and try to reach a shared understanding of the core elements of STPP with young people. The therapists who used the manual also reported positively on the experience (Vadera, 2014). Their experience was in line with research that has suggested that many therapists tend to have negative views of treatment manuals *before* they have had personal experience of using them, but they then develop more positive attitudes *after* they have had the opportunity to do so (Forbat, Black, & Dulgar, 2015). This has turned out to be true for psychoanalytic therapists as well. For example, Busch, Milrod, and Sandberg (2009) found that being directly involved with the manual developed a richer understanding of the practical use of implementing treatment manuals and seemed to challenge some of their own preconceptions, while Taylor (2015) argues, based on the experience of developing a manual for the Tavistock depression study (TADS; Fonagy et al., 2015), that such manuals can contribute significantly to the advancement of psychoanalytic knowledge. A similar trajectory was found in the present findings, with the manual described by some of the child psychotherapists involved in the IMPACT trial as "workable" and "a useful resource" (Vadera, 2014), which they drew on to inform their work, without feeling as if they were being told "how to be a child psychotherapist".

The work presented in this book is the result of this process, and it was further enriched and informed by the experience of those clinicians who worked on the IMPACT trial, as well as colleagues from Norway who are using the STPP manual as the basis for their own research study, known as FEST-IT (Ulberg, Hersoug, & Høglend, 2012). Through supervision meetings, and through regular gatherings of the therapists working with the manual, we obtained feedback on which areas were insufficiently developed; what key aspects were missing; and where we had simply got it wrong. With the valuable editorial support of Jocelyn Catty, the group was able to refine and revise the manual, enriching it with vignettes based on composite cases drawn from the IMPACT trial.

This book is our attempt to share what we have learned about working psychoanalytically in a time-limited way with depressed adolescents. It joins a growing number of treatment manuals attempting to describe psychoanalytic therapy with children and young people, including important work by Milrod, Busch, and Shapiro (2004) on psychodynamic approaches to the adolescent with panic disorder; Gottken and von Klitzing's (2014) manual for short-term Psychoanalytic Child Therapy (PaCT); and Hoffman, Rice, and Prout's (2016) manual of regulation-focused psychotherapy for children with externalizing behaviours. Although very different from each other, each of these books attempts to offer a clear and clinically meaningful account of psychoanalytic therapy with children and young people.

There are a number of reasons why we want to make this manual available more widely. First, we hope to share some of the experience of psychoanalytic therapy with children and young people with a wider audience, in a form that can help to demystify some elements of our work. We also know that treatment manuals such as this provide a basis for empirical research – something that is urgently needed in the field of psychoanalytic child psychotherapy. When the findings of the IMPACT trial are published, we hope they will provide a better understanding of which young people benefit from STPP – and which do not. In due course, the data from this clinical trial will be combined with data from the various "sibling" studies to the IMPACT trial, which have explored the experience of the young people and families taking part (IMPACT-ME; Midgley, Ansaldo, & Target, 2014), as well as studies looking at the genetics and the neuroscience of adolescent depression (Hagan et al., 2013) and how these may both mediate the response to therapy and also change as a result of a successful therapeutic intervention. We hope that bringing together these different types of data will enable us to understand more about the nature of adolescent depression itself; the key moderators and mediators that impact on treatment outcome; and the change mechanisms that explain the process by which psychotherapy facilitates growth and development. More specific questions about STPP that we hope researchers will come back to include the role of transference interpretation (a question that is being specifically focused on by the FEST-IT study in Norway); the reasons why some young people drop out of therapy (currently being explored by a doctoral student working with data from the IMPACT and IMPACT-ME studies); and the role of parent work in short-term psychoanalytic therapy with adolescents.

And it is not only researchers who we hope can take this work forward. Over the coming years, it will be important for child psychotherapists to find out whether STPP can be successfully offered in a range of clinical settings and with a range of young people with depression. The Association of Child Psychotherapists (ACP) has shown great support for the approach, including the setting up of an Implementation Group and assistance with the creation of a network of STPP supervision groups around the UK to support clinicians' STPP work and to promote the development of the model. Some of these groups may want to explore whether the model of STPP set out in this book can be adapted to other clinical populations, such as adolescents who self-harm or those who have eating disorders or emerging personality disorders. If so, what adaptations to the model would be needed, and how effective would such work be? Others may want to find out whether it will be possible to train less highly qualified professionals in STPP. Preliminary analysis of the treatment tapes from the IMPACT trial has already indicated that qualified child and adolescent psychotherapists in the UK, who until now have had relatively little experience of working with treatment manuals, were able to offer the therapy with a relatively high level of treatment fidelity. But given the limited number of child psychotherapists in the UK – and elsewhere – there is also scope to consider training other professionals with appropriate clinical experience and personal therapy in the STPP model and to evaluate whether these less-qualified professionals would be able to offer the therapy in an equally effective way. This issue would be important if STPP were ever to be offered as part of nation-wide programmes such as the UK's CYP-IAPT programme, given the relatively limited number of specialists in CAMHS clinics around the UK. If this approach were shown to be effective, then child psychotherapists might thus enable more services to offer STPP through providing training and ongoing supervision to a broader CAMHS workforce. But would such a development work, or would it lead to the quality of therapy being lost, at the cost of poorer outcomes for young people?

As these questions make clear, we hope that the publication of this STPP manual is not only the end of a long, but rewarding, piece of work, but also the start of a whole range of new activities – all of which can ultimately contribute to improving the mental health and well-being of children and young people.

Nick Midgley

The Association of Child Psychotherapists (ACP) is the main professional body for psychoanalytic child and adolescent psychotherapists in the UK and is registered with the Professional Standards Authority (PSA). It was established in 1949 and has over 900 members working in the UK and abroad. Psychoanalytic psychotherapy is internationally recognized. ACP-registered child psychotherapists have completed an NHS child mental health–based training which lasts for at least four years and are therefore experienced and able to work with some of the most complex difficulties and disorders. ACP members work with children, adolescents, parents, and families, individually or in groups, with a range of complex psychological difficulties and disorders.

ACP members have considerable experience of treating:

- Anxiety
- Attachment problems
- Abuse
- Self-harm
- Eating disorders
- Depression
- Trauma
- Looked-after and adopted children and young people

They also provide consultation to professionals in education, social care, and the voluntary sector.

The ACP is committed to promoting and upholding high standards of child and adolescent psychoanalytic psychotherapy in the NHS and in community and private settings. It aims to do this through:

- Maintaining and monitoring ACP-accredited trainings and the overarching continued professional development of our members.
- Working in partnership with the public and a range of other groups including relevant professional bodies, to increase awareness and understanding of, and the need for, psychoanalytic psychotherapy with children and young people.
- Protecting the public from misconduct and unethical behaviour by its members in clinical practice. It implements this by providing an Ethics committee, comprised of a majority of Lay members, that oversees a Code of Professional Conduct and Ethics.

REFERENCES

AACAP (2012). Practice parameter for psychodynamic work with children. *Journal of the American Academy of Child & Adolescent Psychiatry, 51* (5): 541–557.

Abbass, A. A., Hancock, J., Henderson, J., & Kisely, S. (2006). Short-term psychodynamic psychotherapies for common mental disorders. *Cochrane Library* [www.cochranelibrary.com].

Abbass, A. A., Rabung, S., Leichsenring, F., Refseth, J. S., & Midgley, N. (2013). Psychodynamic psychotherapy for children and adolescents: A meta-analysis of short-term psychodynamic models. *Journal of the American Academy of Child & Adolescent Psychiatry, 52* (8): 863–875.

Abbass, A. A., Town, J., & Driessen, E. (2011). The efficacy of Short-Term Psychodynamic Psychotherapy for depressive disorders with comorbid personality disorder. *Psychiatry: Interpersonal and Biological Processes, 74* (1): 58–71.

Abraham, K. (1924). A short study of the development of the libido, viewed in the light of the mental disorders. In: *Selected Papers on Psychoanalysis* (pp. 418–501). London: Hogarth Press, 1927.

Addis, M. E., & Krasnow, A. D. (2000). A national survey of practicing psychologists' attitudes toward psychotherapy treatment manuals. *Journal of Consulting and Clinical Psychology, 68*: 331–339.

Alvarez, A. (1992a). *Live Company: Psychoanalytic Psychotherapy with Autistic, Borderline, Deprived and Abused Children*. London: Routledge.

Alvarez, A. (1992b). The necessary angel: Idealization as a development. In: *Live Company: Psychoanalytic Psychotherapy with Autistic, Borderline, Deprived and Abused Children* (pp. 118–126). London: Routledge.

Alvarez, A. (2012). *The Thinking Heart: Three Levels of Psychoanalytic Therapy with Disturbed Children*. London: Routledge.

Anastasopoulos, D. (2007). The narcissism of depression or the depression of narcissism and adolescence. *Journal of Child Psychotherapy, 33* (3): 345–362.

Anderson, R. (2008). A psychoanalytical approach to suicide in adolescents. In: S. Briggs, A. Lemma, & W. Crouch (Eds.), *Relating to Self-Harm and Suicide: Psychoanalytic Perspectives on Practice, Theory and Prevention* (pp. 61–71). London: Routledge.

APA (1980). *Diagnostic and Statistical Manual of Mental Disorders, Third Edition (DSM-III)*. Washington, DC: American Psychiatric Association.

APA (2013). *Diagnostic and Statistical Manual of Mental Disorders, Fifth Edition (DSM-5)*. Washington, DC: American Psychiatric Association.

Arnow, B. A. (1999). Why are empirically supported treatments for bulimia nervosa underutilized and what can we do about it? *Journal of Clinical Psychology, 55*: 769–779.

Bailey, T. (2006). There is no such thing as an adolescent. In: M. Lanyado & A. Horne (Eds.), *A Question of Technique: Independent Psychoanalytic Approaches with Children and Adolescents* (pp. 180–199). London: Routledge.

Barron, J. (1995). Treatment research: Science, economics and politics. *Independent Practitioner, 15*: 94–96.

Bell, D. (2008). Who is killing what or whom? Some notes on the internal phenomenology of suicide. In: S. Briggs, A. Lemma, & W. Crouch (Eds.), *Relating to Self-Harm and Suicide: Psychoanalytic Perspectives on Practice, Theory and Prevention* (pp. 45–61). London: Routledge.

Bemporad, J., Ratey, J., & Hallowell, E. (1986). Loss and depression in young adults. *Journal of the American Academy of Psychoanalysis and Dynamic Psychiatry, 14*: 167–179.

Bibring, E. (1953). The mechanism of depression. In: P. Greenacre (Ed.), *Affective Disorders: Psychoanalytic Contributions to Their Study* (pp. 13–48). New York: International Universities Press; reprinted 1961.

Bibring, E. (1954). Psychoanalysis and the dynamic psychotherapies. *Journal of the American Psychoanalytic Association, 2*: 745–770.

Bick, E. (1968). The experience of the skin in early object relations. *International Journal of Psychoanalysis, 494*: 484–486. Reprinted in: A. Briggs (Ed.), *Surviving Space: Papers on Infant Observation* (pp. 55–59). London: Karnac, 2002.

Bick, E. (1986). Further considerations on the function of the skin in early object relations: Findings from infant observation integrated into child and adult analysis. *British Journal of Psychotherapy, 2* (4): 292–299. Reprinted in: A. Briggs (Ed.), *Surviving Space: Papers on Infant Observation* (pp. 60–71). London: Karnac, 2002.

Bifulco, A., Brown, G., & Harris, T. (1987). Childhood loss of parent, lack of adequate parental care and adult depression: A replication. *Journal of Affective Disorders, 12* (2): 115–128.

Bion, W. R. (1957). Differentiation of the psychotic from the non-psychotic personalities. *International Journal of Psychoanalysis, 38* (3–4): 266–275. Reprinted in: *Second Thoughts: Selected Papers on Psycho-Analysis* (pp. 43–64). London: Heinemann, 1967; reprinted London: Karnac, 1984.

Bion, W. R. (1959). Attacks on linking. *International Journal of Psychoanalysis, 40* (5–6): 308–315. Reprinted in: *Second Thoughts: Selected Papers on Psycho-Analysis* (pp. 93–109). London: Heinemann, 1967; reprinted London: Karnac, 1984.

Bion, W. R. (1961). *Experiences in Groups and Other Papers*. London: Tavistock Publications.

Bion, W. R. (1962a). *Learning from Experience*. London: Heinemann; reprinted London: Karnac, 1984.

Bion, W. R. (1962b). A theory of thinking. *International Journal of Psycho-analysis, 43*: 328–332. Reprinted in: *Second Thoughts: Selected Papers on Psycho-Analysis* (pp. 110–119). London: Heinemann, 1967; reprinted London: Karnac, 1984.

Bion, W. R. (1963). *Elements of Psycho-Analysis*. London: Heinemann.

Bion, W. R. (1967). Notes on memory and desire. *The Psychoanalytic Forum, 2*: 272–273, 279–290. Reprinted in: *Cogitations* (New extended edition, pp. 380–385). London: Karnac, 1994.

Birmaher, B., Brent, D., & the AACAP Work Group on Quality Issues (2007). Practice parameter for the assessment and treatment of children and adolescents with depressive disorders. *Journal of the American Academy of Child and Adolescent Psychiatry, 46* (11): 1503–1526.

Blatt, S. (1995). The destructiveness of perfectionism: Implications for the treatment of depression. *American Psychologist, 49*: 1003–1020.

Blatt, S. (1998). Contribution of psychoanalysis to the understanding and treatment of depression. *Journal of the American Psychoanalytic Association, 46*: 722–752.

Blatt, S. J., & Luyten, P. (2009). A structural–developmental psychodynamic approach to psychopathology: Two polarities of experience across the life span. *Development and Psychopathology, 21* (3): 793–814.

Bleichmar, H. (1996). Some sub-types of depression and their implications for psychoanalytic treatment. *International Journal of Psychoanalysis, 77*: 935–961.

Blos, P. (1967). The second individuation process of adolescence. *Psychoanalytic Study of the Child, 22*: 162–186.

Bordin, E. (1979). The generalizability of the psychoanalytic concept of the working alliance. *Psychotherapy: Theory, Research, and Practice, 16* (3): 252–260.

Boston, M., & Szur, R. (1983). *Psychotherapy with Severely Deprived Children*. London: Routledge.

Bott Spillius, E. (1988). *Melanie Klein Today: Developments in Theory and Practice: Volume 2*. London: Routledge.

Bott Spillius, E. (1994). Developments in Kleinian thought: Overview and personal view. *Psychoanalytic Inquiry, 14* (3): 324–365.

Bowlby, J. (1960). Grief and mourning in infancy and early childhood. *Psychoanalytic Study of the Child, 15*: 9–52.

Bretherton, I. (1992). The origins of attachment theory: John Bowlby and Mary Ainsworth. *Developmental Psychology, 28*: 759–775. Reprinted in: S. Goldberg, R. Muri, & J. Kerr (Eds.), *Attachment Theory: Social, Developmental, and Clinical Perspectives* (pp. 45–84). New York: Analytic Press, 2000.

Briggs, A. (2012). Introduction. In: A. Briggs (Ed.), *Waiting to Be Found: Papers on Children in Care* (pp. 1–22). London: Karnac.

Briggs, S., Maxwell, M., & Keenan, A. (2015). Working with the complexities of adolescent mental health problems: Applying time-limited adolescent psychodynamic psychotherapy (TAPP). *Psychoanalytic Psychotherapy, 29* (4): 314–329.

Britton, R. (1989). The missing link: Parental sexuality in the Oedipus complex. In: R. Britton, M. Feldman, & E. O'Shaughnessy (Eds.), *The Oedipus Complex Today: Clinical Implications* (pp. 83–101). London: Karnac.

Britton, R. (1995). The Oedipus complex and the depressive position. *Sigmund Freud House Bulletin, 9*: 7–12.

Britton, R. (1998). Subjectivity, objectivity and triangular space. *Belief and Imagination* (pp. 41–58). London: Routledge.

Brown, G., & Harris, T. (1978). *The Social Origins of Depression*. London: Tavistock.

Busch, F. N., Milrod, B. L., & Sandberg, L. S. (2009). A study demonstrating efficacy of a psychoanalytic psychotherapy for panic disorder: Implications for psychoanalytic research, theory, and practice. *Journal of the American Psychoanalytic Association, 57* (1): 131–148.

Busch, F. N., Milrod, B. L., & Slinger, M. B. (1999). Theory and technique in psychodynamic treatment of panic disorder. *Journal of Psychotherapy Practice and Research, 8*: 234–242.

Busch, F. N., Rudden, M., & Shapiro, T. (2004). *Psychodynamic Treatment of Depression*. Washington, DC: American Psychiatric Publishing.

Buxbaum, E. (1950). Technique and termination of an analysis. *International Journal of Psychoanalysis, 31*: 184–190.

Canham, H. (2004). Spitting, kicking and stripping: Technical difficulties encountered in the treatment of deprived children. *Journal of Child Psychotherapy, 30* (2): 143–154. Reprinted in: A. Briggs (Ed.), *Waiting to Be Found: Papers on Children in Care* (pp. 119–132). London: Karnac, 2012.

Carr, A. (2007). Depression in young people: Description, assessment and evidence-based treatment. *Developmental Neurorehabilitation, 11* (1): 3–15.

Casaula, E., Coloma, J., Colzani, F., & Jordan, J. F. (1997). Bi-logic of interpretation. *Journal of Melanie Klein and Object Relations, 15*: 563–574.

Cassidy, J. (2011). Lost boys: Aspects of projective identification, countertransference, and enactment with three boys. In: J. Trowell & G. Miles (Eds.), *Childhood Depression: A Place for Psychotherapy* (pp. 57–73). London: Karnac.

Catty, J. (2006). "The vehicle of success": Theoretical and empirical perspectives on the therapeutic alliance in psychotherapy. In: D. Loewenthal & D. Winter (Eds.), *What Is Psychotherapeutic Research?* (pp. 215–228). London: Karnac.

Chambless, D. L., & Hollon, S. D. (1998). Defining empirically-supported psychotherapies. *Journal of Consulting and Clinical Psychology, 66*: 7–18.

Connolly Gibbons, M. B., Crits-Christoph, P., & Hearon, B. (2008). The empirical status of psychodynamic therapies. *Annual Review of Clinical Psychology, 4*: 93–108.

Copley, B. (1993). *The World of Adolescence: Literature, Society and Psychoanalytic Psychotherapy*. London: Free Association Books.

Corveleyn, J., Luyten, P., & Blatt, S. (Eds.) (2005). *The Theory and Treatment of Depression*. Belgium: Leuven University Press.

Costello, J., Erkanli, A., & Angold, A. (2006). Is there an epidemic of child or adolescent depression? *Journal of Child Psychology and Psychiatry, 47* (12): 1263–1271.

Creaser, M. (2015). *A Comparison of Audio Recordings and Therapists' Process Notes in Child and Adolescent Psychoanalytic Psychotherapy.* PhD thesis, Psychoanalytic Child and Adolescent Psychotherapy, London, Tavistock Centre/University of East London.

Cregeen, S. (2009). Exposed: Phallic protections, shame, and damaged parental objects. *Journal of Child Psychotherapy, 35* (1): 32–48.

Cregeen, S. (2012). Innate possibilities: Experiences of hope in child psychotherapy. In: A. Briggs (Ed.), *Waiting to Be Found: Papers on Children in Care* (pp. 152 –171). London: Karnac.

Cuijpers, P., van Straten, A., Andersson, G., & van Oppen, P. (2008). Psychotherapy for depression in adults: A meta-analysis of comparative outcome studies. *Journal of Consulting and Clinical Psychology, 76* (6): 909–922.

Davanloo, H. (1978). *Basic Principles and Techniques in Short-Term Dynamic Psychotherapy.* New York: Plenum.

de Jonge, A. L. J., Van, H. L., & Peen, J. (2013). The role of patient characteristics in the selection of patients for psychodynamic psychotherapy. *Tijdschrift voor Psychiatrie, 55* (1): 35–44. [In Dutch]

de Maat, S., de Jonghe, F., Schoevers, R., & Dekker, J. (2009). The effectiveness of long-term psychoanalytic therapy: A systematic review of empirical studies. *Harvard Review of Psychiatry, 17* (1): 1–23.

de Maat, S., Dekker, J., Schoevers, R., van Aalst, G., Gijsbers-van Wijk, C., Hendriksen, M., et al. (2008). Short psychodynamic supportive psychotherapy, antidepressants, and their combination in the treatment of major depression: A mega-analysis based on three randomized clinical trials. *Depression and Anxiety, 25* (7): 565–574.

Driessen, E., Cuijpers, P., de Maat, S. C. M., Abbass, A. A., de Jonghe, F., & Dekker, J. J. M. (2010). The efficacy of short-term psychodynamic psychotherapy for depression: A meta-analysis. *Clinical Psychology Review, 30*: 25–36.

Dubicka, B., Goodyer, I., Wilkinson, P., Kelvin, R., Roberts, C., Byford, S., et al. (2008). The adolescent depression antidepressant and psychotherapy trial (ADAPT). *European Neuropsychopharmacology, 18*: S181.

Edwards, J., & Maltby, J. (1998). Holding the child in mind: Work with parents and families in a consultation service. *Journal of Child Psychotherapy, 24* (1): 109–133.

Emanuel, L., & Bradley, E. (Eds.) (2008). *What Can the Matter Be? Therapeutic Interventions with Parents, Infants and Young Children*. London: Karnac.

Emanuel, R. (2001). A-void – an exploration of defences against sensing nothingness. *International Journal of Psychoanalysis, 82* (6): 1069–1084.

Emanuel, R., Catty, J., Anscombe, E., Cantle, A., & Muller, H. (2014). Implementing an aim-based outcome measure in a psychoanalytic child psychotherapy service: Insights, experiences and evidence. *Clinical Child Psychology & Psychiatry, 19* (2): 169–183.

Emanuel, R., Miller, L., & Rustin, M. E. (2002). Supervision of therapy of sexually abused girls. *Clinical Child Psychology and Psychiatry, 7* (4): 581–594.

Erikson, E. (1950). *Childhood and Society*. New York: W. W. Norton.

Fagan, M. (2011). Relational trauma and its impact on late-adopted children. *Journal of Child Psychotherapy, 37* (2): 129–146.

Fava, M., Alpert, J. E., Borus, J. S., Nierenberg, A. A., Pava, J. A., & Rosenbaum, J. F. (1996). Patterns of personality disorder comorbidity in early-onset versus late-onset major depression. *American Journal of Psychiatry, 153* (10): 1308–1312.

Feldman, M. (2009). Manifestations of the death instinct in the consulting room. In: B. Joseph (Ed.), *Doubt, Conviction and the Analytic Process: Collected Papers of Michael Feldman* (pp. 96–117). London: Routledge.

Flynn, D. (2009). The challenges of in-patient work in a therapeutic community. In: M. Lanyado & A. Horne (Eds.), *The Handbook of Child & Adolescent Psychotherapy: Psychoanalytic Approaches. Second Edition* (pp. 261–276). London: Routledge.

Fonagy, P. (1999). Memory and therapeutic action. *International Journal of Psychoanalysis, 80*: 215–223.

Fonagy, P., Cottrell, D., Phillips, J., Bevington, D., Glaser, D., & Allison, E. (2014). *What Works for Whom? A Critical Review of Treatments for Children and Adolescents. Second Edition*. New York: Guilford Press.

Fonagy, P., Fearon, R. M. P., Steele, M., & Steele, H. (1998). Mentalization as a core component of parental sensitivity [Abstract]. *Infant Behaviour and Development, 21* (Suppl.): 66.

Fonagy, P., Rost, F., Carlyle, J., McPherson, S., Thomas, R., Fearon, R. M. P., et al. (2015). Pragmatic randomized controlled trial of long-term psychoanalytic psychotherapy for treatment-resistant depression: The Tavistock Adult Depression Study (TADS). *World Psychiatry, 14*: 312–321.

Forbat, L., Black, L., & Dulgar, K. (2015). What clinicians think of manualized psychotherapy interventions: Findings from a systematic review. *Journal of Family Therapy, 37* (4): 409–428.

Freud, A. (1953). Some remarks on infant observation. *Psychoanalytic Study of the Child, 8:* 9–19.

Freud, A. (1966). *Normality and Pathology in Childhood: Assessments of Development.* London: Karnac.

Freud, S. (1895d). *Studies on Hysteria. Standard Edition, 2.*

Freud, S. (1900a). *The Interpretation of Dreams. Standard Edition, 4–5.*

Freud, S. (1909b). Analysis of a phobia in a five-year-old boy. *Standard Edition, 10:* 3–149.

Freud, S. (1912b). The dynamics of transference. *Standard Edition, 12:* 97–108.

Freud, S. (1914g). Remembering, repeating and working-through. *Standard Edition, 12:* 145–156.

Freud, S. (1917e). Mourning and melancholia. *Standard Edition, 14:* 239–258.

Freud, S. (1920g). *Beyond the Pleasure Principle. Standard Edition, 18:* 7–64.

Freud, S. (1930a). *Civilization and Its Discontents. Standard Edition, 21:* 59–145.

Freud, S. (1937c). Analysis terminable and interminable. *Standard Edition, 23:* 211–253.

Freud, S. (1940a). *An Outline of Psycho-Analysis. Standard Edition, 23:* 141–207.

Frick, M. E. (2000). Parental therapy – in theory and practice. In: J. Tsiantis, S. B. Boethious, B. Hallerfors, A. Horne, & L. Tischler (Eds.), *Work with Parents: Psychoanalytic Psychotherapy with Children and Adolescents* (pp. 65–92). London: Karnac.

Garoff, F. F., Heinonen, K., Pesonen, A.-K., & Almqvist, F. (2011). Depressed children and young people: Treatment outcome and changes in family functioning in individual and family therapy. In: J. Trowell & G. Miles (Eds.), *Childhood Depression: A Place for Psychotherapy* (pp. 226–237). London: Karnac.

Goldfried, M. R., & Wolfe, B. E. (1998). Toward a more clinically valid approach to therapy research. *Journal of Consulting and Clinical Psychology, 66:* 143–150.

Goodyer, I., Tsancheva, S., Byford, S., Dubicka, B., Hill, J., Kelvin, R., et al. (2011). Improving mood with psychoanalytic and cognitive therapies (IMPACT): A pragmatic effectiveness superiority trial to investigate whether specialised psychological treatment reduces the risk for relapse in adolescents with moderate to severe unipolar depression: Study protocol for a randomised controlled trial. *Trials, 12:* 175. Available at: http://link.springer.com/article/10.1186/1745-6215-12-175

Gottken, T., & von Klitzing, K. (2014). *Manual for Short-Term Psychoanalytic Psychotherapy (PaCT)*. London: Karnac.

Green, A. (1980). La mere morte. In: *Narcissisme de vie, narcissisme de mort* (pp. 222–253). Paris: Editions de Minuit. [The dead mother. In: *On Private Madness* (pp. 142–173). London: Hogarth Press, 1986; reprinted London: Karnac, 1996.]

Green, V. (2000). Therapeutic space for recreating the child in the mind of the parents. In: J. Tsiantis, S. B. Boethious, B. Hallerfors, A. Horne, & L. Tischler (Eds.), *Work with Parents: Psychoanalytic Psychotherapy with Children and Adolescents* (pp. 25–45). London: Karnac.

Green, V. (2013). Grief in two guises: "Mourning and Melancholia" revisited. *Journal of Child Psychotherapy, 39*: 76–89.

Greenson, R. (1967). *The Technique and Practice of Psychoanalysis*. London: Hogarth Press.

Greenson, R., & Wexler, M. (1969). The non-transference relationship in the psychoanalytic situation. *International Journal of Psychoanalysis, 50*: 27–39.

Gretton A. (2011). The wake-up call of adolescence: Time-limited clinical work with three young people. In: J. Trowell & G. Miles (Eds.), *Childhood Depression: A Place for Psychotherapy* (pp. 33–56). London: Karnac.

Hagan, C. C., Graham, J. M., Widmer, B., Holt, R. J., Ooi, C., van Nieuwenhuizen, A. O., et al. (2013). Magnetic resonance imaging of a randomized controlled trial investigating predictors of recovery following psychological treatment in adolescents with moderate to severe unipolar depression: Study protocol for Magnetic Resonance-Improving Mood with Psychoanalytic and Cognitive Therapies (MR-IMPACT). *BMC Psychiatry, 13*: 247.

Hall, J. (2011). Affirming a sense of agency: The influence of supervision in once-weekly, time-limited work with a depressed child patient. In: J. Trowell & G. Miles (Eds.), *Childhood Depression: A Place for Psychotherapy* (pp. 74–88). London: Karnac.

Halligan, S., Herbert, J., Goodyer, I., & Murray, L. (2004). Exposure to postnatal depression predicts elevated cortisol in adolescent offspring. *Biological Psychiatry, 55* (4): 376–381.

Hanley, C. (1994). Reflections on the place of the therapeutic alliance in psychoanalysis. *International Journal of Psychoanalysis, 75*: 457–467.

Harold, G. T., & Conger, R. D. (1997). Marital conflict and adolescent distress: The role of adolescent awareness. *Child Development, 68*: 330–350.

Harris, M. (1965). Depression and the depressive position in an adolescent boy. *Journal of Child Psychotherapy, 1* (3): 33–40. Reprinted in: E. Bott Spillius (Ed.), *Melanie Klein Today: Developments in Theory and Practice. Volume 2: Mainly Practice* (pp. 132–139). London: Routledge, 1988.

Harris, M. (1968). The child psychotherapist and the patient's family. *Journal of Child Psychotherapy, 2* (2): 50–63.

Harris, M. (1975). Some notes on maternal containment in "good enough" mothering. *Journal of Child Psychotherapy, 4* (1): 35–51.

Harris, M. (1977). The Tavistock training and philosophy. In: D. Daws & M. Boston (Eds.), *The Child Psychotherapist and Problems of Young People.* London: Wildwood House. Reprinted in: M. Harris Williams (Ed.), *The Tavistock Model: Papers on Child Development and Psychoanalytic Training by Martha Harris and Esther Bick* (pp. 1–24). London: Karnac, 2011.

Harris Williams, M., Rhode, M., Rustin, M., & Williams, G. (Eds.) (2012). *Enabling and Inspiring: A Tribute to Martha Harris.* London: Karnac.

Hartnup, T. (1999). The therapeutic setting: The people and the place. In: M. Lanyado & A. Horne (Eds.), *Handbook of Child & Adolescent Psychotherapy: Psychoanalytic Approaches* (pp. 93–104). London: Routledge.

Haynal, A. (1977). Le sens du despoir. Rapport XXXVIe Congrès de Psychanalystes de Langues Romanes. *Revue Française de Psychanalyse, 41*: 5–186.

Henton, I., & Midgley, N. (2012). "A path in the woods": Child psychotherapists' participation in a large randomised controlled trial. *Counselling and Psychotherapy Research, 12* (3): 204–213.

Hindle, D., & Shulman, G. (Eds.) (2008). *The Emotional Experience of Adoption: A Psychoanalytic Perspective.* London: Routledge.

Hoffman, L., Rice, T., & Prout, T. (2016). *Manual of Regulation-Focused Psychotherapy for Children with Externalizing Behaviors.* New York: Routledge.

Høglend, P., Bøgwald, K.-P., Amlo, S., Marble, A., Ulberg, R., Sjaastad, M. C., et al. (2008). Transference interpretations in dynamic psychotherapy: Do they really yield sustained effects? *American Journal of Psychiatry, 165*: 763–771.

Hopkins, J. (1999). The child and adolescent psychotherapist and the family: (a) The family context. In: M. Lanyado & A. Horne (Eds.), *The Handbook of Child & Adolescent Psychotherapy* (pp. 81–86). London: Routledge.

Horn, H., Geiser-Elze, A., Reck, C., Hartmann, M., Stefini, A., Victor, D., et al. (2005). Efficacy of psychodynamic short-term psychotherapy for children and adolescents with depression. *Praxis der Kinderpsychologie und Kinderpsychiatrie, 54* (7): 578–597. [In German]

Horne, A. (2000). Keeping the child in mind: Thoughts on work with parents of children in therapy. In: J. Tsiantis, S. B. Boethious, B. Hallerfors, A. Horne, & L. Tischler (Eds.), *Work with Parents: Psychoanalytic Psychotherapy with Children and Adolescents* (pp. 47–63). London: Karnac.

Horne, A. (2009). Sexual abuse and sexual abusing in childhood and adolescence. In: M. Lanyado & A. Horne (Eds.), *The Handbook of Child & Adolescent Psychotherapy: Psychoanalytic Approaches. Second Edition* (pp. 339–360). London: Routledge.

Houzel, D. (2000). Working with parents of autistic children. In: J. Tsiantis, S. B. Boethious, B. Hallerfors, A. Horne, & L. Tischler (Eds.), *Work with Parents: Psychoanalytic Psychotherapy with Children and Adolescents* (pp. 115–134). London: Karnac.

Hurry, A. (1998). *Psychoanalysis and Developmental Therapy.* London: Karnac.

Jacobson, E. (1972). *Depression: Comparative Studies of Normal, Neurotic, and Psychotic Conditions.* Madison, CT: International Universities Press.

Jarvis, C. (2005). Parenting problems: Research and clinical perspectives on parenting adolescents. *Journal of Child Psychotherapy, 31* (2): 209–220.

Joffe, R. (1991). Work with suicidal adolescents at a walk-in centre in Brent. In: S. Miller & R. Szur (Eds.), *Extending Horizons: Psychoanalytic Psychotherapy with Children, Adolescents, and Families* (pp. 165–182). London: Karnac.

Joseph, B. (1985). Transference: The total situation. *International Journal of Psychoanalysis, 66*: 447–454.

Joseph, B. (1998). Thinking about a playroom. *Journal of Child Psychotherapy, 24* (3): 359–366.

Kam, S., & Midgley, N. (2006). Exploring "clinical judgement": How do child and adolescent mental health professionals decide whether a young person needs individual psychotherapy? *Clinical Child Psychology and Psychiatry, 11* (1): 27–44.

Karpf, A. (1996). *The War After: Living with the Holocaust.* London: Heinemann.

Keats, J. (1817). Letter to George and Tom Keats, 21, 27 (?) December. In: R. Gittings, (Ed.), *Letters of John Keats* (pp. 41–43). Oxford: Oxford University Press, 1970.

Kelleher, I., Keeley, H., Corcoran, P., Lynch, F., Fitzpatrick, C., Devlin, N., et al. (2012). Clinicopathological significance of psychotic experiences in non-psychotic young people: Evidence from four population-based studies. *British Journal of Psychiatry, 201* (1): 26–32.

Kernberg, O. (1986). Borderline personality organization. In: *Essential Papers in Borderline Disorders* (pp. 279–317). New York: New York University Press.

Klauber, T. (1998). The significance of trauma in the work with parents of severely disturbed children, and its implications for work with parents in general. *Journal of Child Psychotherapy, 24* (1): 85–107.

Klein, M. (1929). Personification in the play of children. *International Journal of Psychoanalysis, 10* (2/3): 193–204. Reprinted in: *Love, Guilt and Reparation and Other Works 1921–1945* (pp. 199–209). London: Hogarth Press, 1975; reprinted London: Karnac, 1992.

Klein, M. (1933). The early development of conscience in the child. In: S. Lorand (Ed.), *Psychoanalysis Today*. New York: Covici-Friede. Reprinted in: *Love, Guilt and Reparation and Other Works 1921–1945* (pp. 248–257). London: Hogarth Press, 1975; reprinted London: Karnac, 1992.

Klein, M. (1935). A contribution to the pathogenesis of manic depressive states. *International Journal of Psychoanalysis, 16*: 145–174. Reprinted in: *Love, Guilt and Reparation and Other Works 1921–1945* (pp. 262–289). London: Hogarth Press, 1975; reprinted London: Karnac, 1992.

Klein, M. (1937). Love, guilt and reparation. In: M. Klein & J. Riviere, *Love, Hate and Reparation*. London: Hogarth Press. Reprinted in: *Love, Guilt and Reparation and Other Works 1921–1945* (pp. 306–343). London: Hogarth Press, 1975; reprinted London: Karnac, 1992.

Klein, M. (1940). Mourning and its relation to manic-depressive states. *International Journal of Psychoanalysis, 21*: 125–153. Reprinted in: *Love, Guilt and Reparation and Other Works 1921–1945* (pp. 344–369). London: Hogarth Press, 1975; reprinted London: Karnac, 1992.

Klein, M. (1946). Notes on some schizoid mechanisms. *International Journal of Psychoanalysis, 27*: 99–110.

Klein, M. (1948). A contribution to the theory of anxiety and guilt. *International Journal of Psychoanalysis, 29*: 113–123. Reprinted as "On the theory of anxiety and guilt". In: *Envy and Gratitude and Other Works 1946–1963* (pp. 25–43). London: Hogarth Press, 1975; reprinted London: Karnac, 1993.

Klein, M. (1952). Notes on some schizoid mechanisms. In: M. Klein, P. Heimann, S. Isaacs, & J. Riviere, *Developments in Psycho-Analysis*. London: Hogarth Press and the Institute of Psychoanalysis. Reprinted in: *Envy and Gratitude and Other Works 1946–1963* (pp. 1–24). London: Hogarth Press, 1975; reprinted London: Karnac, 1993.

Klein, M. (1957). *Envy and Gratitude*. London: Tavistock. Reprinted in: *Envy and Gratitude and Other Works 1946–1963*. (pp. 176–235). London: Hogarth Press, 1975; reprinted London: Karnac, 1993.

Kohut, H. (1977). *The Restoration of the Self*. New York: International Universities Press.

Kolvin, I., Macmillan, A., Nicol, A. R., & Wrate, R. M. (1988). Psychotherapy is effective. *Journal of the Royal Society of Medicine, 81*: 261–266.

Kovaks, M., & Sherill, J. T. (2001). The psychotherapeutic management of major depressive and dysthymic disorders in childhood and adolescence: Issues and prospects. In: I. M. Goodyer (Ed.), *The Depressed Child and Adolescent. Second Edition*. Cambridge: Cambridge University Press.

Lanyado, M. (1999a). Brief psychotherapy and therapeutic consultations: How much therapy is "good enough"? In: M. Lanyado & A. Horne (Eds.), *Handbook of Child & Adolescent Psychotherapy: Psychoanalytic Approaches. Second Edition* (pp. 191–205). London: Routledge, 2009.

Lanyado, M. (1999b). Holding and letting go: Some thoughts about the process of ending therapy. *Journal of Child Psychotherapy, 25* (3): 357–378.

Lanyado, M. (2009). Psychotherapy with severely traumatised children and adolescents: "Far beyond words". In: M. Lanyado & A. Horne (Eds.), *Handbook of Child & Adolescent Psychotherapy: Psychoanalytic Approaches. Second Edition* (pp. 300–315). London: Routledge.

Lanyado, M., & Horne, A. (2009). *Handbook of Child & Adolescent Psychotherapy: Psychoanalytic Approaches. Second Edition*. London: Routledge.

Laufer, M., & Laufer, E. (1975). *Adolescent Disturbance and Breakdown*. Harmondsworth: Penguin.

Lazar, S. (1997). The effectiveness of dynamic psychotherapy for depression. *Psychoanalytic Inquiry, 17* (Supp.): 51–57.

Leichsenring, F. (2005). Are psychodynamic and psychoanalytic therapies effective? *International Journal of Psychoanalysis, 86*: 841–868.

Leichsenring, F., & Rabung, S. (2008). Effectiveness of long-term psychodynamic psychotherapy. *Journal of the American Medical Association, 300* (13): 1551–1565.

Leichsenring, F., Rabung, S., & Leibing, E. (2004). The efficacy of short-term psychodynamic psychotherapy in specific psychiatric disorders: A meta-analysis. *Archives of General Psychiatry, 61*: 1208–1216.

Long, J., & Trowell, J. (2001). Individual brief psychotherapy with sexually abused girls: What can we learn from the process notes? *Psychoanalytic Psychotherapy, 15*: 39–59.

Luborsky, L. (1976). Helping alliances in psychotherapy: The groundwork for a study of their relationship to its outcome. In J. L. Cleghorn (Ed.), *Successful Psychotherapy* (pp. 92–116). New York: Brunner/Mazel.

Ludlam, M. (2008). The longing to become a family: Support for the parental couple. In: D. Hindle & G. Shulman (Eds.), *The Emotional Experience of Adoption: A Psychoanalytic Perspective* (pp. 177–184). London: Routledge.

Luyten, P., Blatt, S., & Corveleyn, J. (2005). Epilogue. Towards integration in the theory and treatment of depression: The time is now. In: J. Corveleyn, P. Luyten, & S. Blatt (Eds.), *The Theory and Treatment of Depression* (pp. 253–284). Belgium: Leuven University Press.

Magagna, J. (2000). Individual psychotherapy. In: B. Lask & R. Bryant-Waugh (Eds.), *Anorexia Nervosa and Related Eating Disorders in Childhood and Adolescence* (pp. 227–263). London: Psychology Press.

Magagna, J. (2012). The child who has not yet found words. In: J. Magagna (Ed.), *The Silent Child: Communication without Words* (pp. 91–113). London: Karnac.

Malan, D. H. (1976). *The Frontier of Brief Psychotherapy*. New York: Plenum.

Malan, D. H., & Osimo, F. (1992). *Psychodynamics, Training and Outcome in Brief Psychotherapy*. London: Butterworth.

Malhi, G. S., Adams, D., Porter, R., Wignall, A., Lampe, L., O'Connor, N., et al. (2009). Clinical practice recommendations for depression. *Acta Psychiatrica Scandinavica, 119* (Suppl. 439): 8–26.

Martin, D. J., Garske, J. P., & Davis, M. K. (2000). Relation of the therapeutic alliance with outcome and other variables: A meta-analytic review. *Journal of Consulting and Clinical Psychology, 68* (3): 438–450.

Martindale, B., Cid Rodriguez, M. E., Morner, M., & Vidit, J.-P. (Eds.) (1997). *Supervision and Its Vicissitudes*. London: Karnac.

Mathes, L. (2013). *Mourning and Melancholia Revisited: Reflections on Depression in Young People Aged 11–17 Years Old Treated with Short-term Psychoanalytic Psychotherapy*. Unpublished paper given at the Annual Conference of the Association of Child Psychotherapists (June).

Meltzer, D. (1967). The gathering of the transference. In: *The Psycho-Analytical Process* (pp. 1–12). London: Heinemann.

Meltzer, D. (1968). Terror, persecution and dread. *International Journal of Psychoanalysis, 49*: 396–400.

Meltzer, D. (1969). The relation of aims to methodology in the treatment of children. *Journal of Child Psychotherapy, 2* (3): 57–61. Reprinted in: A. Hahn (Ed.), *Sincerity and Other Works: The Collected Papers of Donald Meltzer* (pp. 171–176). London: Karnac, 1994.

Meltzer, D. (1973). *Sexual States of Mind.* Strath Tay: Clunie Press.

Meltzer, D. (1976). Temperature and distance as technical dimensions of interpretation. In: A. Hahn (Ed.), *Sincerity and Other Works: The Collected Papers of Donald Meltzer* (pp. 374–386). London: Karnac, 1994.

Meltzer, D., & Harris, M. (2013). *The Educational Role of the Family: A Psycho-analytical Model,* ed. M. Harris Williams. London: Karnac.

Midgley, N., Anderson, J., Grainger, E., Nesic-Vuckovic, T., & Urwin, C. (Eds.) (2009). *Child Psychotherapy and Research: New Approaches, Emerging Findings.* London: Routledge.

Midgley, N., Ansaldo, F., & Target, M. (2014). The meaningful assessment of therapy outcomes: Incorporating a qualitative study into a randomized controlled trial evaluating the treatment of adolescent depression. *Psychotherapy, 51* (1): 128–137.

Midgley, N., Cregeen, S., Hughes, C., & Rustin, M. (2013). Psychodynamic psychotherapy as treatment for depression in adolescence. *Child and Adolescent Psychiatric Clinics of North America, 22* (1): 67–82.

Midgley, N., Holmes, J., Parkinson, S., Stapley, E., Eatough, V., & Target, M. (2014). "Just like talking to someone about like shit in your life and stuff, and they help you": Hopes and expectations for therapy among depressed adolescents. *Psychotherapy Research, 5*: 1–11.

Midgley, N., & Kennedy, E. (2011). Psychodynamic therapy for children and adolescents: A critical review of the evidence base. *Journal of Child Psychotherapy, 37* (3): 232–260.

Midgley, N., Parkinson, S., Holmes, J., Stapley, E., Eatough, V., & Target, M. (2015). Beyond a diagnosis: The experience of depression among clinically-referred adolescents. *Journal of Adolescence, 44*: 269–279.

Mikulincer, M., & Shaver, P. R. (2012). An attachment perspective on psychopathology. *World Psychiatry, 11* (1): 11–15.

Miles, G. (2011). The work with the parents alongside individual therapy with the children/young people: Present and absent parents. In: J. Trowell & G. Miles (Eds.), *Childhood Depression: A Place for Psychotherapy* (pp. 110–124). London: Karnac.

Miller, L. (2001). Brief encounters: Work with parents and infants in an under-fives' counselling service. In: F. Grier (Ed.), *Brief Encounters with Couples: Some Analytic Perspectives* (pp. 55–68). London: Karnac.

Milrod, B. L., Busch, F., & Shapiro, T. (2004). *Psychodynamic Approaches to the Adolescent with Panic Disorder*. Malabar: Krieger.

Milrod, D. (1988). A current view of the psychoanalytic view of depression – with notes on the role of identification, orality and anxiety. *Psychoanalytic Study of the Child, 43*: 83–99.

Mitrani, J. (2001). Taking the transference. *International Journal of Psychoanalysis, 82* (6): 1085–1104.

Molnos, A. (1995). *A Question of Time: Essentials of Brief Dynamic Psychotherapy*. London: Karnac.

Morgan, M. (2001). First contacts: The therapist's "couple state of mind" as a factor in the containment of couples seen for consultations. In: F. Grier (Ed.), *Brief Encounters with Couples: Some Analytical Perspectives* (pp. 17–32). London: Karnac.

Morgan, M. (2005). On being able to be a couple: The importance of a "creative couple" in psychic life. In: F. Grier (Ed.), *Oedipus and the Couple* (pp. 9–30). London: Karnac.

Mufson, L., Dorta, K. P., Moreau, D., & Weissman, M. M. (1993). *Interpersonal Therapy for Depressed Adolescents*. New York: Guilford Press.

Muratori, F., Picchi, L., Apicella, F., Salvadori, F., Espasa, F. P., Ferretti, D., et al. (2005). Psychodynamic psychotherapy for separation anxiety disorders in children. *Depression and Anxiety, 21* (1): 45–46.

Muratori, F., Picchi, L., Bruni, G., Patarnello, M., & Romagnoli, G. (2003). A two-year follow-up of psychodynamic psychotherapy for internalizing disorders in children. *Journal of the American Academy of Child and Adolescent Psychiatry, 42* (3): 331–339.

Murray, L., Sinclair, D., & Cooper, P. (2001). The socioemotional development of five year old children of postnatally depressed mothers. *Year Book of Psychiatry & Applied Mental Health, 1*: 39–41.

Napier, J. (2015). On training supervision: Unravelling a tangled web. *Psychoanalytic Psychotherapy, 29* (4): 416–427.

NICE (2005). *Depression in Children and Young People: Identification and Management in Primary, Community and Secondary Care*. London: National Institute for Health and Clinical Excellence.

NICE (2015). *Depression in Children and Young People: Identification and Management in Primary, Community and Secondary Care* (Revised edition). London: National Institute for Health and Care Excellence.

Norcross, J. C. (2011). *Psychotherapy Relationships That Work: Evidence-Based Responsiveness*. Oxford: Oxford University Press.

Novick, K. K., & Novick, J. (2005). *Working with Parents Makes Therapy Work.* Lanham, MD: Jason Aronson.

Nuttall, J. (2000). Modes of therapeutic relationship in Kleinian psychotherapy. *British Journal of Psychotherapy, 17* (1): 17–36.

O'Shaughnessy, E. (1986). A three-and-a-half-year-old boy's melancholic identification with an original object. *International Journal of Psychoanalysis, 67* (2): 173–179. Reprinted in: R. Rusbridger (Ed.), *Inquiries in Psychoanalysis: Collected Papers of Edna O'Shaughnessy* (pp. 84–94). London: Routledge, 2015.

O'Shaughnessy, E. (1994). What is a clinical fact? *International Journal of Psychoanalysis, 75* (5–6): 939–947.

O'Shaughnessy, E. (1999). Relating to the superego. *International Journal of Psychoanalysis, 80*: 861–870.

Perepletchikova, F., & Kazdin, A. E. (2005). Treatment integrity and therapeutic change: Issues and research recommendations. *Clinical Psychology: Science and Practice, 12*: 365–383.

Pick, I. B. (1985). Breakdown in communication: On finding the child in the analysis of an adult, *Psychoanalytic Psychotherapy, 1* (2): 57–62.

Quagliata, E. (1999). Emotional turbulence during the ending of psychotherapy with an anorexic adolescent. *Journal of Child Psychotherapy, 25* (3): 411–427.

Rado, S. (1928). The problem of melancholia. *International Journal of Psychoanalysis, 9*: 420–438.

Rance, S. (2003). Report on the survey of ACP members about the outcome study. Part II: Summary of therapist activity and child data. *Bulletin of the Association of Child Psychotherapists, 133*: 25–32.

Rhoades, K. A. (2008). Children's responses to interparental conflict: A meta-analysis of their associations with child adjustment. *Child Development, 62*: 311–327.

Rhode, M. (1997). Discussion. In: M. Rustin, M. Rhode, A. Dubinsky, & H. Dubinsky (Eds.), *Psychotic States in Children* (pp. 172–186). London: Duckworth.

Rhode, M. (2011). Some reflections on the individual therapy: Themes and interventions. In: J. Trowell & G. Miles (Eds.), *Childhood Depression: A Place for Psychotherapy* (pp. 125–136). London: Karnac.

Richmond, T., & Rosen S. (2005). The treatment of adolescent depression in the era of the black box warning. *Current Opinion in Pediatrics, 17* (4): 466–472.

Riviere, J. (1936). A contribution to the analysis of the negative therapeutic reaction. *International Journal of Psychoanalysis, 17*: 304–320.

Rosenfeld, H. (1960). Symposium on "depressive illness". VI. A note on the precipitating factor. *International Journal of Psychoanalysis, 41*: 512–513.

Rosenfeld, H. (1971). A clinical approach to the psychoanalytic theory of the life and death instincts: An investigation into the aggressive aspects of narcissism. *International Journal of Psychoanalysis, 52*: 169–178.

Rosenfeld, H. (1987). *Impasse and Interpretation: Therapeutic and Anti-Therapeutic Factors in the Psychoanalytic Treatment of Psychotic, Borderline, and Neurotic Patients.* London: Routledge.

Roth, P. (2001). Mapping the landscape: Levels of transference interpretation. *International Journal of Psychoanalysis, 82*: 533–543.

Rustin, M. (1971). Once-weekly work with a rebellious adolescent girl. *Journal of Child Psychotherapy, 3* (1): 40–48.

Rustin, M. (1998a). Dialogues with parents. *Journal of Child Psychotherapy, 24* (2): 233–252.

Rustin, M. (1998b). Observation, understanding and interpretation: The story of a supervision. *Journal of Child Psychotherapy, 24* (3): 433–448.

Rustin, M. (1999). Multiple families in mind. *Clinical Child Psychology and Psychiatry, 4* (1): 51–62.

Rustin, M. (2000). Dialogues with parents. In: J. Tsiantis, S. B. Boethious, B. A. Hallerfors, A. Horne, & L. Tischler (Eds.), *Work with Parents: Psychoanalytic Psychotherapy with Children and Adolescents* (pp. 1–23). London: Karnac.

Rustin, M. (2001). The therapist with her back against the wall. *Journal of Child Psychotherapy, 27* (3): 273–284.

Rustin, M. (2004). Psychotherapy and community care. In: M. Rhode & T. Klauber (Eds.), *The Many Faces of Asperger's Syndrome* (pp. 249–259). London: Karnac.

Rustin, M. (2005). Conceptual analysis of critical moments in Victoria Climbié's life. *Child & Family Social Work, 10* (1): 11–19.

Rustin, M. (2009a). The psychology of depression in young adolescents: A psychoanalytic view of origins, inner workings and implications. *Psychoanalytic Psychotherapy, 23* (3): 213–224.

Rustin, M. (2009b). Work with parents. In: M. Lanyado & A. Horne (Eds.), *The Handbook of Child & Adolescent Psychotherapy: Psychoanalytic Approaches. Second Edition* (pp. 206–219). London: Routledge.

Rustin, M. (2010). The complexities of service supervision: An experiential discovery. *Journal of Child Psychotherapy, 36* (1): 3–15.

Rustin, M. (2012). Dreams and play in child analysis today. In: P. Fonagy, H. Kachele, M. Leuzinger-Bohleber, & D. Taylor (Eds.), *The Significance of Dreams: Bridging Clinical and Extraclinical Research in Psychoanalysis* (pp. 17–30). London: Karnac.

Rustin, M., & Bradley, J. (Eds.) (2008). *Work Discussion: Learning from Reflective Practice in Work with Children and Families*. London: Karnac.

Ruszczynski, S. (1992). Notes towards a psychoanalytic understanding of the couple relationship. *Psychoanalytic Psychotherapy, 6* (1): 3–48.

Ryz, P., & Wilson, J. (1999). Endings as gain: The capacity to end and its role in creating space for growth. *Journal of Child Psychotherapy, 25* (3): 379–403.

Safran, J. D., Muran, J. C., & Eubanks-Carter, C. (2011). Repairing alliance ruptures. In: J. C. Norcross (Ed.), *Psychotherapy Relationships That Work: Evidence-Based Responsiveness* (pp. 224–238). Oxford: Oxford University Press.

Salminen, J. K., Karlsson, H., Hietala, J., Kajander, J., Aalto, S., Markkula, J., et al. (2008). Short-term psychodynamic psychotherapy and fluoxetine in major depressive disorder: A randomized comparative study. *Psychotherapy and Psychosomatics, 77* (6): 351–357.

Salzberger-Wittenberg, I. (1977). Counselling young people. In: D. Daws & M. Boston (Eds.), *The Child Psychotherapist and Problems of Young People* (pp. 136–159). London: Wildwood House. Reprinted London: Karnac, 2002.

Sandler, J. (1976). Countertransference and role-responsiveness. *International Review of Psycho-Analysis, 3*: 43–47.

Sandler, J., & Joffe, W. (1965). Notes on childhood depression. *International Journal of Psychoanalysis, 46*: 88–96.

Schachter, A., & Target, M. (2009). The adult outcome of child psychoanalysis: The Anna Freud Centre Long-term Follow-up Study. In: N. Midgley, J. Anderson, E. Grainger, T. Nesic-Vuckovic, & C. Urwin (Eds.), *Child Psychotherapy and Research: New Approaches, Emerging Findings* (pp. 144–156). London: Routledge.

Schmidt Neven, R. (2014). Short-term focussed and time-limited psychodynamic psychotherapy with children, parents and families: A model for current times. *Bulletin of the Association of Child Psychotherapists, 254* (May): 4–11.

Sedlak, V. (1997). Psychoanalytic supervision of untrained therapists. In: B. Martindale, M. E. Cid Rodriguez, M. Morner, & J.-P. Vidit (Eds.), *Supervision and Its Vicissitudes* (pp. 25–37). London: Karnac.

Segal, H. (1973). *Introduction to the Work of Melanie Klein.* London: Hogarth Press.

Segal, H. (1997a). On the clinical usefulness of the concept of the death instinct. In: J. Steiner (Ed.), *Psychoanalysis, Literature and War: Papers 1972–1995* (pp. 14–21). London: Routledge.

Segal, H. (1997b). The uses and abuses of counter-transference. In: J. Steiner (Ed.), *Psychoanalysis, Literature and War: Papers 1972–1995* (pp. 111–119). London: Routledge.

Shedler, J. (2010). The efficacy of psychodynamic psychotherapy. *American Psychologist, 65* (2): 98–109.

Shortt, A. L., & Spence, S. H. (2006). Risk and protective factors for depression in youth. *Behaviour Change, 23* (1): 1–30.

Sinason, V. (1986). Secondary mental handicap and its relationship to trauma. *Psychoanalytic Psychotherapy, 2* (2): 131–154.

Smadja, C. (2005). Study of essential depression. In: *The Psychosomatic Paradox: Psychoanalytical Studies* (pp. 38–88). London: Free Association Books.

Sodre, I. (2005). The wound, the bow and the shadow of the object: Notes on Freud's "Mourning and Melancholia". In: R. J. Perelberg (Ed.), *Freud: A Modern Reader* (pp. 124–141). London: Whurr.

Soenens, B. Luyckx, K., Vansteenkiste, M., Luyten, P., Duriez, B., & Goossens, L. (2008). Maladaptive perfectionism as an intervening variable between psychological control and adolescent depressive symptoms: A three-wave longitudinal study. *Journal of Family Psychology, 22* (3): 465–474.

Sorenson, P. B. (1997). Thoughts on the containing process from the perspective of infant/mother relations. In: S. Reid (Ed.), *Developments in Infant Observation: The Tavistock Model* (pp. 113–122). London: Routledge.

Spillius, E., & O'Shaughnessy, E. (Eds.) (2012). *Projective Identification: The Fate of a Concept.* Hove: Routledge.

Sprince, J. (2008). The network around adoption: The forever family and the ghosts of the dispossessed. In: D. Hindle & G. Shulman (Eds.), *The Emotional Experience of Adoption: A Psychoanalytic Perspective* (pp. 99–114). London: Routledge.

Stasiak, K., Parkin, A., Seymour, F., Lambie, I., Crengle, S., Pasene-Mizziebo, E., et al. (2013). Measuring outcome in child and adolescent mental health services: Consumers' views of measures. *Clinical Child Psychology and Psychiatry, 18*: 519–535.

Steiner, J. (1993). *Psychic Retreats: Pathological Organizations in Psychotic, Neurotic and Borderline Patients.* London: Routledge.

Stern, D. (1985). *The Interpersonal World of the Infant: A View from Psychoanalysis and Developmental Psychology.* London: Karnac.

Strachey, J. (1934). The nature of the therapeutic action of psycho-analysis. *International Journal of Psychoanalysis, 15*: 127–159.

Strupp, H. H., & Anderson, T. (1997). On the limitations of therapy manuals. *Clinical Psychology: Science and Practice, 4*: 76–82.

Sutton, A., & Hughes, L (2005). The psychotherapy of parenthood: Towards a formulation and valuation of concurrent work with parents. *Journal of Child Psychotherapy, 31* (2): 169–188.

Svanborg, P., Gustavsson, J. P., & Weinryb, R. M. (1999). What patient characteristics make therapists recommend psychodynamic psychotherapy or other treatment forms? *Acta Psychiatrica Scandinavica, 99* (2): 87–94.

Szapocznik, J., Rio, A., Murray, E., Cohen, R., Scopetta, M., Rivas-Vazquez, A., et al. (1989). Structural family versus psychodynamic child therapy for problematic Hispanic boys. *Journal of Consulting and Clinical Psychology, 57* (5): 571–578.

Target, M., & Fonagy, P. (1994a). The efficacy of psychoanalysis for children: Prediction of outcome in a developmental context. *Journal of the American Academy of Child & Adolescent Psychiatry, 33* (8): 1134–1144.

Target, M., & Fonagy, P. (1994b). The efficacy of psychoanalysis for children with emotional disorders. *Journal of the American Academy of Child & Adolescent Psychiatry, 33* (3): 361–371.

Taylor, D. (2015). Treatment manuals and the advancement of psychoanalytic knowledge: The treatment manual of the Tavistock Adult Depression Study. *International Journal of Psychoanalysis, 96*: 845–875.

Taylor, D., & Richardson, P. (2005). The psychoanalytic/psychodynamic approach to depressive disorders. In: G. O. Gabbard, J. S. Beck, & J. Holmes (Eds.). *Oxford Textbook of Psychotherapy* (pp. 127–136). Oxford: Oxford University Press.

Todd, R. D., Reich, W., Petti, T. A., Joshi, P., DePaulo, J. R., Nurnberger, J., et al. (1996). Psychiatric diagnosis in the child and adolescent members of extended families identified through adult bipolar affective disorder probands. *Journal of the American Academy of Child & Adolescent Psychiatry, 35*: 665–671.

Trevatt, D. (2005). Adolescents in mind. *Journal of Child Psychotherapy, 31* (2): 221–238.

Troupp, C. (2013). "What do you want to get from coming here?" Distinguishing patient-generated outcome measures in CAMHS from a bespoke sandwich. *Child and Family Clinical Psychology Review, 1*: 19–28.

Trowell, J. (1977). Child sexual abuse. In: N. Wall (Ed.), *Rooted Sorrows: Psychoanalytic Perspectives on Child Protection, Assessment, Therapy and Treatment*. Bristol: Family Law.

Trowell, J., & Dowling, E. (2011). Reflections and thoughts: Learning from the study. In: J. Trowell, & G. Miles (Eds.), *Childhood Depression: A Place for Psychotherapy* (pp. 241–252). London: Karnac.

Trowell, J., Joffe, I., Campbell, J., Clemente, C., Almqvist, F., Soininen, M., et al. (2007). Childhood depression: A place for psychotherapy. An outcome study comparing individual psychodynamic psychotherapy and family therapy. *European Child and Adolescent Psychiatry, 16*: 157–167.

Trowell, J., Kolvin, I., Weeramanthri, T., Sadowski, H., Berelowitz, M., Glasser, D., et al. (2002). Psychotherapy for sexually abused girls: Psychopathological outcome findings and patterns of change. *British Journal of Psychiatry, 180*: 234–247.

Trowell, J., & Miles, G. (Eds.) (2011). *Childhood Depression: A Place for Psychotherapy*. London: Karnac.

Trowell, J., Rhode, M., & Hall, J. (2010). What does a manual contribute? In: J. Tsiantis & J. Trowell (Eds.), *Assessing Change in Psychoanalytic Psychotherapy of Children and Adolescents: Today's Challenge*. London: Karnac.

Trowell, J., Rhode, M., Miles, G., & Sherwood, I. (2003). Childhood depression: Work in progress. *Journal of Child Psychotherapy, 29* (2): 147–170.

Tsiantis, J., Sandler, A.-M., Anastasopoulos, D., & Martindale, B. (Eds.) (1996). *Countertransference in Psychoanalytic Therapy with Children and Adolescents*. London: Karnac.

Tustin, F. (1972). Psychotic depression. In: *Autism and Childhood Psychosis*. London: Hogarth Press; reprinted London: Karnac, 1995.

Tustin, F. (1986). *Autistic Barriers in Neurotic Patients*. London: Karnac.

Ulberg, R., Hersoug, A. G., & Høglend, P. (2012). Treatment of adolescents with depression: The effect of transference interventions in a randomized controlled study of dynamic psychotherapy. *Trials, 13*

(159). Available at: https://trialsjournal.biomedcentral.com/articles/10.1186/1745-6215-13-159

Urwin, C. (2009). A qualitative framework for evaluating clinical effectiveness in child psychotherapy: The Hopes and Expectations for Treatment Approach (HETA). In: N. Midgley, J. Anderson, E. Grainger, T. Nesic-Vuckovic, & C. Urwin (Eds.), *Child Psychotherapy and Research: New Approaches, Emerging Findings* (pp. 157–170). London: Routledge.

Vadera, R. (2014). *What Are Child and Adolescent Psychotherapists' Experiences of Using a Treatment Manual?* Unpublished MSc dissertation, Anna Freud Centre/UCL, London.

Varchevker, A., & McGinley, E. (Eds.) (2013). *Enduring Migration through the Life Cycle*. London: Karnac.

Vliegen, N., Meurs, P., & Cluckers, G. (2005). Closed doors and landscapes in the mist: Childhood and adolescent depression in developmental psychopathology. In: J. Corveleyn, P. Luyten, & S. Blatt (Eds.), *The Theory and Treatment of Depression* (pp. 163–188). Belgium: Leuven University Press.

Waddell, M. (1998). *Inside Lives: Psychoanalysis and the Growth of the Personality*. London: Karnac.

Waddell, M. (2000a). Developmental issues from early to late life. *Psychoanalytic Psychotherapy, 14*: 239–252.

Waddell, M. (2000b). Assessing adolescents: Finding space to think. In: M. Rustin & E. Quagliata (Eds.), *Assessment in Child Psychotherapy* (pp. 145–161). London: Karnac.

Waddell, M. (2003). Coming into one's own: The Oedipus complex and the couple in late adolescence. *Journal of Child Psychotherapy, 29* (1): 53–73.

Waddell, M. (2006). Narcissism – an adolescent disorder? *Journal of Child Psychotherapy, 32* (1): 21–34.

Weinberg, W. A., Rutman, J., Sullivan, L., Penick, E. C., & Dietz, S. G. (1973). Depression in children referred to an educational diagnostic center: Diagnosis and treatment. *Journal of Pediatrics, 83* (6): 1065–1072.

Weissman, M. M., Wolk, S., Goldstein, R. B., Moreau, D., Adams, P., Greenwald, S., et al. (1999). Depressed adolescents grown up. *Journal of the American Medical Association, 281* (18): 1707–1713.

Whitefield, C., & Midgley, N. (2015). "And when you were a child?": How therapists working with parents alongside individual child psychotherapy bring the past into their work. *Journal of Child Psychotherapy, 41* (3): 272–292.

WHO (1992). *The ICD-10 Classification of Mental and Behavioural Disorders.* Geneva: World Health Organization.

Williams, G. (1997a). *Internal Landscapes and Foreign Bodies: Eating Disorders and Other Pathologies.* London: Duckworth.

Williams, G. (1997b). The no-entry system of defences: Reflections on the assessment of adolescents suffering from eating disorders. In: *Internal Landscapes and Foreign Bodies: Eating Disorders and Other Pathologies* (pp. 115–122). London: Duckworth.

Wilson, P. (1991). Psychotherapy with adolescents. In: J. Holmes (Ed.), *Textbook of Psychotherapy in Psychiatric Practice* (pp. 443–469). London: Churchill Livingstone.

Winnicott, D. W. (1948). Reparation in respect of mother's organised defence against depression. In: *Through Paediatrics to Psychoanalysis* (pp. 91–96). London: Tavistock, 1958; reprinted London: Hogarth Press, 1975.

Winnicott, D. W. (1949). Birth memories, birth trauma and anxiety. In: *Through Paediatrics to Psychoanalysis* (pp. 174–193). London: Tavistock, 1958; reprinted London: Hogarth Press, 1975.

Winnicott, D. W. (1958). *Through Paediatrics to Psychoanalysis.* London: Tavistock; reprinted London: Hogarth Press, 1975.

Winnicott, D. W. (1960a). Ego distortion in terms of true and false self. In: *The Maturational Processes and the Facilitating Environment* (pp. 140–152). London: Hogarth Press, 1965; reprinted London: Karnac, 1990.

Winnicott, D. W. (1960b). The theory of the parent–infant relationship. *International Journal of Psychoanalysis, 41*: 585–595. Reprinted in: *The Maturational Processes and the Facilitating Environment* (pp. 37–55). London: Hogarth Press, 1965; reprinted London: Karnac, 1990.

Winnicott, D. W. (1962). The aims of psycho-analytical treatment. In: *The Maturational Processes and the Facilitating Environment* (pp. 166–170). London: Hogarth Press, 1965; reprinted London: Karnac, 1990.

Winnicott, D. W. (1963). The mentally ill in your caseload. In: J. F. S. King (Ed.), *New Thinking for Changing Needs.* London: Association of Social Workers. Reprinted in: *The Maturational Processes and the Facilitating Environment* (pp. 217–229). London: Hogarth Press, 1965; reprinted London: Karnac, 1990.

Winnicott, D. W. (1967). The mirror role of mother and family in child development. In: P. Lomas (Ed.), *The Predicament of the Family: A Psycho-*

Analytical Symposium. London: Hogarth Press. Reprinted in *Playing and Reality* (pp. 111–118). London: Tavistock, 1971.

Winnicott, D. W. (1974). Fear of breakdown. *International Review of Psycho-Analysis, 1*: 103–107. Reprinted in: *Psycho-Analytic Explorations* (pp. 87–95). London: Karnac, 1989.

Wittenberg, I. (1999). Ending therapy. *Journal of Child Psychotherapy, 25* (3): 339–356.

Wynn Parry, C., & Birkett, D. (1996). The working alliance: A re-appraisal. *British Journal of Psychotherapy, 12* (3): 291–299.

Zetzel, E. (1956). Current concepts of the transference. *International Journal of Psychoanalysis, 39*: 369–376.

INDEX

AACAP: *see* American Academy
  of Child & Adolescent
  Psychiatry
Abbass, A. A., 43, 44, 46
Abraham, K., 13, 14, 16
abuse:
  emotional, 17, 89
  physical, 17, 89
  sexual, 7, 42, 61, 89, 172
ACP: *see* Association of Child
  Psychotherapists
acting in:
  as defensive enactment, 147
  and acting out, 194–197
    13-year-old "Michael" [case
    study], 195–197
acting out:
  and acting in, 194–197
    13-year-old "Michael" [case
    study], 195–197
  dangerous, 110, 157
  defensive, for managing anxiety
    and evading pain, 135, 152
  enactment of feelings of rejection,
    116
  by family, 140

preventing, 148
  by professionals, 170, 205
active receptivity, 39
ADAPT: *see* Adolescent Depression
  Antidepressant and
  Psychotherapy Trial
Addis, M. E., 214
adolescence:
  depression in, nature and
    prevalence of, 4–6
  developmental tasks of, 26, 74, 122
  emerging sexuality during, 35, 100
  identity in, 26–28
  individuation in, 26–28
  intense, passionate, polarized
    states of mind in, 186
  oedipal anxieties in, 28–30
  re-emergence of oedipal conflict
    during, 35, 100
adolescent(s):
  with depression, STPP for,
    evidence base for, 47–48
  psychoanalytic work with, 9,
    37–51
    younger, 70
  social world of, 31–32

247

adolescent depression (*passim*):
  as developmental crisis, 27
  genetics of, 216
  psychoanalytic formulation for,
      34–35
  psychoanalytic theories and
      models of, overview of, 8,
      11–35
  psychoanalytic views of, 11–35
  treatment of, 6–7
Adolescent Depression
      Antidepressant and
      Psychotherapy Trial
      [ADAPT], 7
adolescent states of mind, 136, 149
adopted children, working with,
      159–165
adoptive parents, 3, 128, 139, 159
adult(s):
  with depression, 50
    psychodynamic psychotherapy
        for, 43
    STPP for, 8, 43, 44, 50
    treatment of depression in, clinical
        practice guidelines for, 43
agency, sense of, 57, 110, 173, 196
aggression:
  defensive use of, 163
  focus on, in psychoanalytic
      theories of depression, 13
  internalization of, 104
  management of, 21, 54
  passive, 25
  role in genesis of depression, 13
  self-directed, 15
  splitting as defence against, 25
  turned against self, 14
  unconscious, role of in depression,
      12–13
Aghia Sophia Children's Hospital,
      Athens, 47
Ainsworth, M., 39
alcohol abuse, 33
alienation, 20, 204
Almqvist, F., 33
Alvarez, A., xiv, 37, 62, 67–69, 173,
      202

ambivalence, parents', 131
American Academy of Child &
      Adolescent Psychiatry
      [AACAP], 49, 53, 61, 81
American Psychiatric Association
      [APA], 5, 11
anaclitic depression, 23, 24
analytic attitude, 39
analytic situation, 19, 59
Anastasopoulos, D., 22, 40
Anderson, J., 37
Anderson, R., 77
Anderson, T., 214
Andersson, G., 43
anger, conflicted, 25
Angold, A., 4
annihilation anxiety, 18, 34
Ansaldo, F., 48, 216
antidepressant medication, 7, 74,
      204
  fluoxetine, 6, 76
antisocial behaviour, 27
anxiety(ies):
  annihilation, 18, 34
  countertransference, therapist's,
      118
  defences against, 39
  depressive, 14, 108, 135
  disorder, 5
  existential, 20, 21, 35, 100
  intergenerational, 156
  oedipal, 26
    in adolescence, 28–30
    primitive, 107
  paranoid-schizoid defences
      against, 14
  parental, 134, 149, 150, 154, 157
  persecutory, 14
  primary, fear of annihilation as, 18
  somatization of, 175
  unconscious, 2, 159
    child's, containment of, 38
    parents', 128
APA: *see* American Psychiatric
      Association
apathy, sense of, 16
appetite, loss of, 5

Arnow, B. A., 214
art materials, 70–71
assessment:
    free-standing, 79, 86
    for STPP, 79, 87, 192, 193
assessment phase, 90, 96, 98, 142, 146
assessment process, 82, 98, 145
assessment report, in early stages of
        treatment, 98–99
Association of Child
        Psychotherapists [ACP], xiii,
        8, 41, 219–220
    Implementation Group, 217
Athens, Aghia Sophia Children's
        Hospital, 47
attachment(s), 37, 124
    dysfunctional, 42
    insecure, 17
    internal working models of, 39
    and mother–infant relationship,
        19
    patterns of, 17
    secure:
        importance of, 17
        normal, 130
attachment theory, 37
attacks on linking, 175
attunement, in parent work, 130
authoritarian control, excessive,
        early, 24
autistic children, 128
autistic spectrum disorder, 187
autonomy, achievement of, 26

Bailey, T., 136
Barron, J., 214
basic assumption, 32
behavioural problems, 81
Bell, D., 77
Bemporad, J., 16
bereaved families, 136
Bibring, E., 13, 14, 16, 17, 65
Bick, E., 20, 21, 37
Bifulco, A., 33
Bion, W. R., 15, 20, 21, 32, 39, 40, 51,
        58, 59, 68, 69, 77, 82, 148, 202,
        209

bipolar illnesses, 186
Birkett, D., 60
Birmaher, B., 4, 5
Black, L., 215
Blatt, S., 11, 23–25, 27
Bleichmar, H., 13, 22, 23
Blos, P., 26
borderline psychosis, 69
    girl with [case study], 67–68
Boston, M., 51, 58, 68
Bott Spillius, E., 19, 39
Bowlby, J., 17, 39
Bradley, E., 42, 170, 183
Bretherton, I., 39
Briggs, A., 161
Briggs, S., 42, 54
Britton, R., 29, 203
Brown, G., 17, 33
Bruni, G., 46
Busch, F. N., 22, 24, 50, 53, 57, 66, 90,
        92, 97, 104, 215, 216
Buxbaum, E., 125

CAMHS: see Child and Adolescent
        Mental Health Services
cancellations, 88
Canham, H., 51
care coordinator, 74: see case
        manager
carer(s):
    foster, 128, 160, 161, 164
    liaison with, 41, 55–56
    psychoanalytic work with,
        principles of, 127–134
    working with, in psychoanalytic
        child psychotherapy, 40–
        41
Carr, A., 33
Casaula, E., 63
case holder, 74
    see also case manager
case management, 8, 9, 74–78, 80,
        134, 182
case manager/lead practitioner/
        case holder/care coordinator,
        74–76, 78, 136, 200, 201
    as parent worker, 141

case study, composite ["Anna"]:
  early stages of treatment:
    assessment report, 101–104
    establishing therapeutic
      alliance, 97–98
    initial assessment sessions,
      93–96
  first review meeting, 146
  initial meeting, 86
  low mood, underlying dynamics
    of, 122–124
  middle stages of treatment:
    confronting problematic areas,
      111–112
    deepening of the transference
      relationship, 109
    increased trust in therapy, 107
  parents:
    assessment and setting-up
      process, 144
    early parent work sessions,
      150–151
    ending stages of parent work,
      155
    middle stages of parent work,
      153
  post-treatment follow-up session,
    125–126
  referral, 82–83
  summary report, 121–124
  supervision of therapist, 175–
    176
  termination of treatment, 116–
    117
    endings and losses, 119–120
  beyond therapy, 121
case vignettes:
  acting out and acting in [13-year-
    old "Michael"], 195
  borderline psychosis, little girl
    with, 67–68
  container, failure of, and dropping
    out [17-year-old "Tony"],
    209–212
  countertransference, therapist's
    difficulties in understanding
    and bearing [15-year-old
    "Steve"], 178–179

difficulties with engaging parents
    [17-year-old Lucinda], 207
  emotional deprivation and
    containment [16-year-old
    "Priscilla"], 211–212
  impasse [17-year-old "Peter"],
    199–200
  inpatient admission [15-year-old
    "Jack"], 188–189
  looked-after boy [16-year-old
    "Danny"], 162–165
  mirroring, therapist/supervisor
    [adolescent "Millie"], 180
  negative transference, aggressive
    and attacking [15-year-old
    "Jake"], 198–199
  and psychiatric assessment
    [16-year-old "Mark"], 204
  parent work following trauma
    [14-year-old "Thomas"],
    192–195
  play material, use of [12-year-old
    "Jacob"], 71–73
  psychotic symptoms [12-year-old
    "Leah"], 187
  silent patient [16-year-old
    "Becky"], 190–191
  see also case study, composite
    ["Anna"]
Cassidy, J., 54
Catty, J., 60, 216
CBT: see Cognitive Behavioural
    Therapy
Chambless, D. L., 44
child(ren):
  adopted: see adopted children
  autistic, 128
  with depression, STPP for,
    evidence base for, 47–48
  looked after: see looked-after
    children
  observation, 37, 41
  psychoanalytic work with, 9,
    37–51
  therapy with, playroom with toys
    needed for, 38
Child and Adolescent Mental Health
    Services [CAMHS], 217, 218

child and adolescent psychodynamic psychotherapy, 43
   evidence base for, 45–46
child development:
   study of, 37
   theories of, 9
childhood, loss of, 26
childhood depression, 21, 27, 33, 51, 180
   psychoanalytic conception of, 34
child protection, issues of, 40, 56
child psychotherapists, working in multidisciplinary teams, 8
Children and Young People's Improving Access to Psychological Therapies [CYP-IAPT], xvii, 217
Children's Hospital, Helsinki, 47
Cid Rodriguez, M. E., 169
clarification, process of, 65
Climbié, Victoria, 170
clinical techniques, 65–70
   and traumatic factors in patient's history, factors in, 202–203
Cluckers, G., 26
Cognitive Behavioural Therapy [CBT], 6–8, 24, 48
collaborative working, 74–78
college:
   difficulties in, 157–158
   liaison with, 56
Coloma, J., 63
Colzani, F., 63
communication:
   drawings as, 2
   play as, 2
   primitive non-verbal forms of, 40
   silence as, 189
   unconscious: see unconscious communication
concentration, poor, 5
concrete thinking, 34
conduct disorder, 81
confidentiality:
   clarity around, 88, 89, 140
   exception to, in cases of risk, 56, 78, 185
   protecting, 157

and secrecy, distinction between, 55
   in supervision, 169, 171
conflict, unconscious, role of in depression, 12–13
conflicted anger, 25
confrontation, 67
   as technique, 66
Conger, R. D., 136
Connolly Gibbons, M. B., 44
conscious and unconscious anxieties, 38
container, therapeutic alliance as, 59
containing object, in patient's mind, establishing, 68
containment:
   of anxieties, 38
   concept of, 20, 59, 65, 69, 82
   and emotional deprivation, 16-year-old "Priscilla" [case study], 211–212
   failure of:
      and drop-out, 209–212
      17-year-old "Tony" [case study], 209–212
   maternal, 170
   of psychic pain, 68
   in peer supervision, 141
   by therapist, 38, 68, 82, 129, 134, 148–149, 164, 180
contract, in parent work, 137–138
conversation, as free association, 38
Cooper, P., 37
coping strategies, maladaptive, 188
Copley, B., 42
core self, fragility of, 34
Corveleyn, J., 11, 25
Costello, J., 4
countertransference (passim):
   attending closely, 132
   attention to, 66
   difficulties in understanding and bearing, 15-year-old "Steve" [case study], 178–179
   issues, 54
      around ending of therapy, 113, 118–120

countertransference (*continued*):
  monitoring, 87, 105, 108
    in early treatment, 91
  non-verbalized, therapist's use of,
    133
  phenomena, xvi, 40
  scrutiny of, 203
  supervision as safe space for
    processing, 3
  understanding, 134
    therapist's use of, 133
  use of, 170
  working in, towards containment
    of psychic pain, 68
  working through, 179
countertransference anxieties,
  therapist's, 118
countertransference frustration,
  195
countertransference reactions, 66
countertransference response, 169,
  177
couple state of mind, 139
Creaser, M., 173
Cregeen, S., xiii, 26, 51, 198
Crits-Christoph, P., 44
Cuijpers, P., 43
cure, total, omnipotent fantasy of,
  55
curiosity:
  capacity for, 71, 87, 91
    lack of, 63
  infantile, resurgence of in
    adolescence, 28
  therapist's sense of, 67, 147, 168
CYP-IAPT: *see* Children and Young
  People's Improving Access to
  Psychological Therapies

Davanloo, H., 42
Davis, M. K., 59, 60
daydream(s), 39
day hospital treatment, 187–189
dead mother, phantasy of, 21
death instinct, 17
  primitive envy as destructive
    manifestation of, 18
  silent pull of, 19

defence(s):
  against anxieties, 39
  interpretation of, 39
  interpretations, 64
  manic, 68
  omnipotent, 68
  paranoid-schizoid, 14
defensive enactment, 147
de Jonge, A. L., 50
de Jonghe, F., 43
Dekker, J., 43
delusion, analysis of, 201
de Maat, S., 43
denial, 25, 68, 150
denigration, 58
  of self, 35, 100
depression (*passim*):
  in adolescence, nature and
    prevalence of, 4–6
  adolescent, psychoanalytic
    formulation for, 34–35
  anaclitic (dependent), 23, 24
  childhood, 21, 27, 33, 51, 180
    psychoanalytic conception of,
    34
  developmental perspective on,
    25–34
  and diet, relationship between,
    143
  double, 47, 81
  dynamic-interactionist model of,
    25
  endogenous, 20
  essential, 21, 23
  and exercise, relationship
    between, 143
  family history of, 124
  "flop" type of, 20
  guilty, 22
  integrated psychodynamic
    formulation for, areas of,
    24–25
  introjective (self-critical), 23
  narcissistic, 22, 23
  psychiatric definitions of, 11
  psychoanalytic theoretical model
    of, 9, 68
    integration of, 21–25

psychoanalytic theories of, xvi,
        12–25, 37
psychotic, 19–21
reactive, 20
recurrence of, resilience against,
        fostering, 12
self-hatred in, 16
and sleep, relationship between,
        143
sub-types of, 23
and traumatic experiences, link
        between, 17
treatment-resistant, 45
types of, internalizing and
        externalizing, 12
depressive anxieties, 14, 108, 135
depressive apathy, 110
depressive disorder(s), 44
    diagnosis of, 4
    major, symptoms of, 5
depressive position, 23, 29
    working through, 14
depressive-position functioning, 29
descriptive commentary, 65
destructiveness, primary, 18
development, patterns of,
        compromised, 2
developmental considerations,
        regarding depression, 25–34
developmental crisis, adolescent
        depression as, 27
developmental difficulties/deficits,
        2, 37, 91
developmental psychopathology, 37
*Diagnostic and Statistical Manual of
        Mental Disorders* [DSM], 4,
        5, 11
diathesis-stress model, 33
diet:
    balanced, 6
    and depression, relationship
        between, 143
Dietz, S. G., 4
displacement, 61, 66
    interpretations in, 63
disruptive disorder(s), 5, 49
dissociation, 135
Dorta, K. P., 51

double depression, 47, 81
Dowling, E., 34, 35, 47, 58
drawings, 72, 104
    as communication, 2
    as free association, 38
dream(s), 30, 39, 90, 105, 187
    latent and manifest content of, 67
    working with, 67
dream work, 67
Driessen, E., 43, 44, 50
dropping out:
    and failure of containment,
        17-year-old "Tony" [case
        study], 209–212
    implications for parents, 158
drug abuse, 33
DSM: *see Diagnostic and Statistical
        Manual of Mental Disorders*
Dubicka, B., 8
Dulgar, K., 215
dynamic-interactionist model of
        depression, 25
dysthymia, 47

early trauma, 159
eating difficulties, 5
eating disorders, 217
Edwards, J., 42
ego:
    impoverished, 51
    narcissistic fragility of, 23
ego-destructive superego, 15
ego function, disturbed, 51
ego strength, 114
Emanuel, L., 42, 58, 60, 145, 161, 172
Emanuel, R., 20, 58, 60, 145, 161, 172
emotional abuse, 17, 89
emotional deprivation, 209
    and containment, 16-year-old
        "Priscilla" [case study],
        211–212
emotional disorder(s), 49
emotional pain, 163, 204
enactment, 147, 186, 194
endogenous depression, 20
energy, reduced, 5
engagement, in treatment, barriers
        to, 92–93, 104

enmeshment, 33
envy:
    interpretation of, 202
    primitive, 18
Erikson, E., 26
Erkanli, A., 4
eroticized transference, 201
essential depression, 21, 23
Eubanks-Carter, C., 61
evacuation, 77, 209
evenly suspended attention, 39
evidence-based practice, 38, 51, 213
evidence-based treatment, 44
evidence base for STPP for children
        and adolescents with
        depression, 47–48
exercise:
    and depression, relationship
        between, 143
    regular, benefits of, 6
existential anxiety(ies), 20, 21, 35, 100
expectations, idealized and
        devalued, 25
externalizing behaviours, 216
externalizing disorder(s), 49

Fagan, M., 159
false self, 19
families:
    bereaved, 136
    reconstituted, 143
    refugee, 136
    separated, 143
family situations, range of, 139
family therapy, 7, 37
    systemic, 6, 42, 47
fantasy(ies), conscious, 25, 55
    vs. unconscious "phantasy", 8
Fava, M., 11
fear of annihilation, as primary
        anxiety, 18
Fearon, R. M. P., 32
feeling interpretation, 64
Feldman, M., 18
FEST-IT: see First Experimental Study
        of Transference work–In
        Teenagers

FIPP: see Focused Individual
        Psychoanalytic
        Psychotherapy
First Experimental Study of
        Transference work–In
        Teenagers [FEST-IT], 48, 49,
        216, 217
"flop" type of depression, 20
fluoxetine, 6, 76
Flynn, D., 170
Focused Individual Psychoanalytic
        Psychotherapy [FIPP], 42,
        47
Fonagy, P., xiii, 7, 32, 45, 46, 50, 51,
        62, 215
Forbat, L., 215
foster carers, 128, 160, 161, 164
frame:
    in parent work, 137–138
    psychoanalytic, 181, 205
framework, establishing, 88–89
free association, free play, drawings,
        conversation as, 38
Freud, A., 25, 37, 51, 63
Freud, S., 12–19
    "Analysis of a phobia in a five-
        year-old boy", 39
    "Analysis terminable and
        interminable", 17
    Beyond the Pleasure Principle, 17
    Civilization and Its Discontents, 17
    "The dynamics of transference",
        59
    The Interpretation of Dreams, 67
    "Mourning and melancholia", 12,
        15, 18
    An Outline of Psycho-Analysis, 59
    "Remembering, repeating and
        working-through", 14
    Studies on Hysteria, 59
Frick, M. E., 127, 131

Garoff, F. F., 33
Garske, J. P., 59, 60
genetics, of adolescent depression,
        216
genital sexuality, 28, 30

Goldfried, M. R., 214
Goodyer, I., xiii, xv, 8, 17, 42, 47, 51, 213
Gottken, T., 216
GP, liaison with, 78
Grainger, E., 37
Green, A., 21, 23
Green, V., 15, 132, 149
Greenson, R., 59, 60
Gretton A., 34
group therapy, 7
guilt, sense of, 5
guilty depression, 22
Gustavsson, J. P., 50

Hagan, C. C., 216
Hall, J., 173, 213
Halligan, S., 17
Hallowell, E., 16
Hancock, J., 43
Hanley, C., 60
Harold, G. T., 136
Harris, M., 25, 31, 128, 130, 170
Harris, T., 17, 33
Harris Williams, M., 170
Hartnup, T., 88
Haynal, A., 16, 17
Hearon, B., 44
Heinonen, K., 33
helplessness, 14, 22, 116, 150
    and depression, 13
    sense of, 16
Helsinki, Children's Hospital, 47
Henderson, J., 43
Henton, I., 48, 214, 215
Herbert, J., 17
Hersoug, A. G., 48, 216
Hindle, D., 159
Hoffman, L., 216
Høglend, P., 48, 49, 216
holding environment, 81
holiday breaks, 54, 88, 106
Hollon, S. D., 44
hopelessness, 12, 22, 23, 92, 110
    sense of, 5, 14, 16, 26
Hopkins, J., 129
Horn, H., 46

Horne, A., 133, 170
hospitalization, 78, 187–189
Houzel, D., 128, 132
Hughes, C., xiii, 26, 33, 127, 131, 133, 143
Hurry, A., 63, 70

ICD: see International Classification of Diseases
idealization, 25, 35, 58, 100, 202
idealized and devalued expectations, 25
identification(s), 18, 19, 24, 31, 113
    with adolescent states of mind, 149
    parental, 149
identity:
    confusion about, 186
    and individuation, in adolescence, 26–28
    loss of, 35, 100
    sense of:
        coherent, lack of, 66
        effect of maternal mirroring on, 19
        threat to, 17
    sexual, 26, 28, 152
IMPACT: see Improving Mood with Psychoanalytic and Cognitive Therapies
IMPACT–ME: see Improving Mood with Psychoanalytic and Cognitive Therapies–My Experience
impasse:
    pseudo-therapeutic, 203
    therapeutic, 205
        in clinical practice, 198–201
        17-year-old "Peter" [case study], 199–201
impotence, sense of, 16
Improving Mood with Psychoanalytic and Cognitive Therapies [IMPACT], 42, 47–51, 54, 76, 156, 183, 213–217
    trial, and STPP, 7–9

Improving Mood with
Psychoanalytic and Cognitive
Therapies–My Experience
[IMPACT–ME], 48
individuation:
and identity, in adolescence, 26–28
and separation, 103, 122
infantile neurosis, 59
infant observation, 170
information-gathering, 87
and reflection on internal
experience, 90–91
inhibition, sense of, 16
inpatient admission, 78, 187
15-year-old "Jack" [case study],
188–189
inpatient work, function of
supervision in, 170
integrity of self, sense of, injury to, 13
intergenerational anxieties, 156
intergenerational difficulties, 1, 209
in parent work, 156–157
intergenerational experiences, of
loss, 180
intergenerational loss, 32–34, 35, 100
intergenerational trauma, 35, 100,
156
internal experience:
focus on, 90
reflection on, and information-
gathering, 90–91
internalizing disorder(s), 49, 50
internal maternal figure, 107, 122
internal parental figures, 29, 175
International Classification of
Diseases [ICD], 11
interpersonal loss, 13
interpersonal problems, 6
interpersonal therapy, 6
Interpersonal Therapy with
Adolescents [IPT-A], 51
interpretation(s):
defence, 64
in displacement, 63
feeling, 64
four modes of, 61
mutative, 58

patient- and therapist-centred, 63
phrasing of, 67
process, 64
transference, 48, 62, 69, 70
varieties of, 62
interventions, mirroring, 66, 70
introjection, 31
introjective depression, 23
IPT-A: see Interpersonal Therapy
with Adolescents
irritability, sign of depression in
adolescence, 4–5

Jacobson, E., 13
Jarvis, C., 128
Joffe, R., 42
Joffe, W., 16, 17
Jordan, J. F., 63
Joseph, B., 38, 62, 71, 189

Kam, S., 51
Karpf, A., 156
Kazdin, A. E., 214
Keats, J., 39
Keenan, A., 42, 54
Kelleher, I., 186
Kennedy, E., 38, 45, 46, 49, 129
Kernberg, O., 22
key worker, liaison with, 55
kindness, importance of, 171
Kisely, S., 43
Klauber, T., 129, 131, 132
Klein, M., 13, 14, 16–19, 21, 26, 27, 37,
38, 40
Kohut, H., 13, 21, 22, 23
Kolvin, I., 46
Kovaks, M., 33
Krasnow, A. D., 214

Lanyado, M., 55, 112, 118, 124, 170
Laufer, E., 26
Laufer, M., 26
Lazar, S., 16
lead practitioner: see case manager
learning disabilities, 51
Leibing, E., 43
Leichsenring, F., 43, 46

letting go, at end of therapy, 118
life instinct, 17, 18
linking, attacks on, 175
Long, J., 61, 114
looked-after children/adolescents, 3,
        55, 128, 138, 143, 209, 219
    and carers, working with, 159–
        165
    16-year-old "Danny" [case study],
        162–165
loss(es):
    and abandonment, 154
        history of, 54
    early, 35, 100
    and endings, 118
    experiences of, 2, 15–17, 89, 105,
        115, 153, 154, 156, 180
    intergenerational, 32–34, 35, 100,
        180
    interpersonal, 13
    issues around, 2, 4
    management of, 163
    painfulness of, 122
    role of, in depression, 15–17
    and separation, 115, 116, 154
        managing, 17
    transgenerational, 172
    traumatic, 156, 192
lost object, identification with, 18
Luborsky, L., 59
Ludlam, M., 160
Luyten, P., 11, 25, 27

Macmillan, A., 46
Magagna, J., 70, 190
Malan, D. H., 42
Malhi, G. S., 43
Maltby, J., 42
manic defences, 68
manic state of mind, 179
Martin, D. J., 59, 60
Martindale, B., 40, 169
maternal containment, 170
maternal figure, internal, 107, 122
maternal mirroring, 19
    failures of, 23
Mathes, L., 26

Maxwell, M., 42, 54
McGinley, E., 156
medical consultation, and negative
        transference, 203–204
medication, 92
    antidepressant, 6, 75–78, 204
        use of, and concurrent
            psychiatric treatment, 75–76,
            80, 203
    fluoxetine, 6, 76
    use of, 7, 75, 78, 186
melancholia, 163
    dynamic combination in, of severe
        superego and narcissistic
        identification, 18
    vs. normal mourning, 15
Meltzer, D., 18, 27, 31, 59, 60, 70
memory or desire, being without, 39
mental health:
    parental, 32–34
    problems, history of, 81
mentalization, 32
Meurs, P., 26
Midgley, N., xiii, 2, 5, 26, 27, 33, 37,
        38, 45, 46, 48, 49, 51, 129, 131,
        134, 136, 149, 214–216, 218
Mikulincer, M., 33
Miles, G., 21, 34, 127, 132, 172
Miller, L., 58, 131, 161, 172
Milrod, B. L., 50, 215, 216
Milrod, D., 23
mirroring, 66, 70
    maternal, 19
        failures of, 23
    therapist/supervisor, 179
        adolescent girl, "Millie" [case
            study], 180–181
mirroring interventions, 66, 70
missed sessions, 88, 91, 96, 200, 204,
        205
Mitrani, J., 62, 68
Molnos, A., 4, 54
monitoring countertransference, 87,
        91
Moreau, D., 51
Morgan, M., 139
Morner, M., 169

mother:
  dead, phantasy of, 21
  early relationships with, 13–14
  –infant relationship, 14, 19
    and attachment, 19
    earliest, 14
  internal, 128
  see also: parents(s)
mourning, 12, 116, 123, 152
  difficulties with, 105
  "healthy", 16
  vs. melancholia, 15
  normal, 15
  pathological, 15
multidisciplinary clinic(s), 9, 41, 71,
    74, 82, 200
multidisciplinary team(s)/service, 6,
    74–76, 79, 98, 176, 180, 203
  child psychotherapists working
    in, 8
  support from, 40
  working with, in psychoanalytic
    child psychotherapy, 40
Muran, J. C., 61
Muratori, F., 46
Murray, L., 17, 37
mutative interpretation, 58

nameless dread, 20, 39
Napier, J., 169
narcissism, 18
  "thick" and "thin skinned" forms
    of, distinction between, 203
narcissistic depression, 22, 23
narcissistic fragility, 23, 24
narcissistic identification and
    severe superego, dynamic
    combination of, in
    melancholia, 18
narcissistic personality states, 100
narcissistic vulnerability, 21, 24, 100,
    110
National Institute for Health and
    Care Excellence [NICE], 6,
    27, 49
  guideline on depression in
    children and young people,
    76

negative capability, 39
negative therapeutic reaction,
    198–201
negative transference, 58, 60, 61, 68,
    92, 145, 191
  aggressive and attacking, 15-year-
    old "Jake" [case study],
    198–199
  in clinical practice, 198–203
  and medical consultation, 203–
    204
  in middle stages of treatment,
    108–109
  and psychiatric assessment,
    16-year-old "Mark" [case
    study], 204
Nesic-Vuckovic, T., 38
neuroscience, of adolescent
    depression, 216
neuroses, infantile, 59
neurotic personality organization,
    50
NICE: see National Institute for
    Health and Care Excellence
Nicol, A. R., 46
nightmares, 187
non-attendance, and STPP time
    frame, 204–206
Norcross, J. C., 59, 60
Novick, J., 129
Novick, K. K., 129
Nuttall, J., 59

object, lost and hated, identification
    with, 18
object loss, 24
  role of, in depression, 15–17
object-related functioning, 49
observation:
  child, 37
  infant, 170
    and young child, 41
oedipal anxiety(ies), 26
  in adolescence, 28–30
  primitive, 107
oedipal conflict(s), 149, 159
  re-emergence of, during
    adolescence, 35, 100

oedipal development, 29, 30
oedipal dynamics, 96, 151, 152, 206
oedipal issues, xvi, 100, 208
Oedipus complex, 130
omnipotent defences, 68
omnipotent fantasy, of total cure, 55
omnipotent possession, phantasy
    of, 116
open-ended psychotherapy, 2, 54
O'Shaughnessy, E., 15, 18, 38, 40
Osimo, F., 42
outcome monitoring, 60, 80, 89, 99,
    142, 145

PaCT: *see* Psychoanalytic Child
    Therapy
panic attack(s), 75, 117, 155, 203
panic disorder, 50, 216
parallel process(es), 137, 177
    in supervision, 179–181
paranoid-schizoid defences, 14
paranoid-schizoid position, 14, 29
parent(s):
    adoptive, 3, 128, 139, 159
    ambivalence of, 131
    and carers, working with, 127–
        165
    difficulties in engaging, 17-year-
        old "Lucinda" [case study],
        207–209
    emotional distress of, five core
        elements of, 130
    good-enough, 132
    liaison with, 41, 55–56
    need for help in their own right,
        158–159
    psychoanalytic work with,
        principles of, 127–134
    relationship to therapist, service,
        and parent worker, 128–129
    therapeutic alliance with, 128
    working alliance with, 132
    working with, in psychoanalytic
        child psychotherapy, 40–41
parental anxiety(ies), 134, 149, 150,
    154, 157
parental couple relationship, 139
parental figures, internal, 29, 175

parental functioning, 130, 142
    disturbed, 136
parental identifications, 149
parent–infant relationships, 32–34
parental mental illness, 1, 6, 32–34,
    35, 100
parental projections, 148
parental psychopathology, 33
parental rejection, 24
parental transferences, 32
parent work/parental therapy:
    aims and objectives, 135–136
    assessment and setting-up,
        142–144
    changing parental functioning, as
        primary aim of, 136
    common themes, difficulties,
        variations, 156–159
    early stages of, 148–151
    ending stages of, 153–155
    frame, setting, contract, 137–138
    five areas of focus in, 131
    following trauma, 191
        14-year-old "Thomas" [case
            study], 192–195
    four main categories of, 129
    initial joint meeting, components
        of, 142
    intergenerational difficulties in,
        156–157
    maintenance of therapeutic
        boundaries in, 157
    middle stages of, 151–153
    primary aims of, 135–136
    primary focus of, 136–137
    process of, 129, 146
    STPP, 134–142
        aims and objectives, 135–136
        frame, setting, contract, 137–138
        primary aims of, 135–136
        primary focus, 136–137
        therapeutic technique in,
            146–148
    supervision of, 181
        forms of, 182–183
        triangulation in, 182
    use of transference and
        countertransference in, 133

parent worker:
    as case manager, 141
    consultation with, for risk
        management, 177
    liaison with, 187
    primary role of, 135
parent-work supervision, 182
passive aggression, 25
Patarnello, M., 46
patient, communications of,
        understanding, 168
Peen, J., 50
peer supervision, 3, 182
Penick, E. C., 4
Perepletchikova, F., 214
persecutory anxieties, 14
personality, psychotic part of, 77
personality disorder(s), 5, 11, 44, 45,
        217
personal mental space, sense of, 202
Pesonen, A.-K., 33
phantasy(ies), unconscious, 28
    acting out, 27, 69
    vs. conscious "fantasy", 8
    of dead mother, 21
    interpretation of, 62
    of omnipotent possession, 116
    parental, 130, 150
    vs. reality, 57, 69, 110
    underlying young person's
        relationship to self and
        others, 39
    sexual, 30
    understanding, though
        countertransference, 2
physical abuse, 17, 89
physician, liaison with, 78
Picchi, L., 46
Pick, I. B., 179, 202
play:
    as communication, 2
    as free association, 38
    undirected, as source of clinical
        facts, 38
play material(s):
    use of, 70–73
        with younger adolescent,
            "Jacob" [case study], 71–73

postnatal depression, 208
post-treatment contact, 124–126
primary anxiety, fear of annihilation
        as, 18
primary destructiveness, 18
primitive envy, as destructive
        manifestation of death
        instinct, 18
problematic areas, capacity to
        confront, 110–112
process interpretations, 64
process notes/process recordings,
        167, 173, 174, 177, 181
Professional Standards Authority
        [PSA], 219
projection(s):
    benign (communicative) forms
        of, vs. malign (destructive)
        forms, 40
    communicative and evacuative
        forms of, distinction between,
        202
    of dangerous destructiveness, into
        therapist, 186
    from family members, 202
    holding, 68
    negative, holding, 173
    parental, 148
    of parts of self, 23
    into therapist, of irritation and
        disappointment, 191
    unconscious, 3
    young person's, into parents, 147
projective identification(s), 40, 57,
        197
    pathological, 116
Prout, T., 216
PSA: see Professional Standards
        Authority
pseudo-therapeutic impasse, 203
psychiatric assessment, 78, 203, 204
psychiatric difficulties, management
        of, 185–189
    psychotic symptoms, 186–187
psychiatric disorder(s), 186
psychiatric issues, 74–78
psychiatric treatment:
    concurrent, 75–77

and medication, use of,
     concurrent, 75–76
psychic death, fear of, 196
psychic experience, 120
     openness to, 39
psychic pain:
     containment of, 68
     defences against, 100
psychic retreat, 14
psychoanalytic assessment, for STPP,
     83, 86, 87
psychoanalytic child
     psychotherapists, training
     of, 41
psychoanalytic child psychotherapy,
     37–51
     basic principles of, 38–40
Psychoanalytic Child Therapy
     [PaCT], 216
psychoanalytic formulation, in
     early stages of treatment,
     99–100
psychoanalytic frame, 181, 205
psychoanalytic models of
     depression, 37
     integration of, 21–25
psychoanalytic parent work/
     psychotherapy of
     parenthood, 9, 48, 127–165
     in STPP, 134–142
     see also parent work
psychoanalytic psychotherapy,
     evidence for, 42–51
psychoanalytic supervision: see
     supervision, psychoanalytic
psychoanalytic work with parents
     and carers, principles of,
     127–134
psychodynamic child/adolescent
     psychotherapy, 6, 49
     evidence base for, 45–46
psychodynamic psychotherapy(ies)
     (passim):
     for adults with depression,
          evidence base for, 43–46
     child, 6, 49
          and adolescent, evidence base
          for, 43, 45

short-term, 43, 44, 46, 50
suitability for, 49–51
psychological-mindedness, 81
psychopathology, 25, 27
     developmental, 37
     parental, 33
     severe, 186
psychosis(es), 20
     borderline, 67, 69
          girl with [case study], 67–68
psychotherapy, open-ended, 2, 54
psychotherapy of parenthood: see
     psychoanalytic parent work
psychotic depression, 19–21
psychotic disorder(s)/illness(es),
     186, 187
psychotic part of personality, 77
psychotic symptoms, 51, 75, 76
     hearing voices, 186
     12-year-old "Leah" [case study],
          187
psychotic thinking, 74

Quagliata, E., 113, 116
questioning, 66

Rabung, S., 43, 46
Rado, S., 12
Rance, S., 51
Randomized Controlled Trial(s)
     [RCT(s)], 1, 7, 8, 42–45, 47, 213
Ratey, J., 16
RCT: see Randomized Controlled
     Trial
reactive depression, 20
reality, testing, 40
real relationship, 59
reenactment, in analytic work, 202
referral, for STPP, 78–83
     considerations in, 81
referral process, 79–80
reflectiveness, 169
Refseth, J. S., 46
refugee families, 136
regression, 169, 203
relational trauma, 35, 100
reparation, 14
     centrality of, 17

reparative hope, parents', 132
residential unit manager, liaison
     with, 55
resistance, 60, 131
   in middle stages of treatment,
        108–109
reverie:
   state of, 39, 40, 68
   therapist's, 39, 40, 68
review appointments, 121
review meetings:
   with parents and carers, 41, 89,
        128, 140, 162
   purpose of, 145
   setting up, 143, 145
Rhoades, K. A., 136
Rhode, M., xiii, 21, 34, 58, 70, 100,
        170, 172, 173, 180, 213
Rice, T., 216
Richardson, P., 89
Richmond, T., 5
rigidity, 135
risk assessment, 77–78, 98
risk management, 9, 74, 136, 176–177,
        185–189, 195
   deliberate self-harm, 185–186
   suicidal ideation, 185–186
risk-management protocol, 176
risk-taking behaviour, 116, 177, 182,
        186, 205
   unconscious communication in,
        185
Riviere, J., 201
Rosen, S., 5
Rosenfeld, H., 18, 19, 23, 27, 202, 203
Roth, P., 62, 69
routine outcome monitoring, in
        parent work, 145–146
Rudden, M., 22, 24, 50, 53, 57, 66, 90,
        92, 97, 104
Rustin, M., xiii, xv–xviii, xviii, 26,
        38, 40, 51, 58, 62, 67, 71, 124,
        128–130, 134–137, 147, 159,
        161, 170–172, 183
Ruszczynski, S., 131
Rutman, J., 4
Ryz, P., 113, 118

sadomasochistic relationship, 202
Safran, J. D., 61
Salminen, J. K., 43
Salzberger-Wittenberg, I., 42
Sandberg, L. S., 215
Sandler, A. M., 40
Sandler, J., 16, 17, 58
Schachter, A., 46
Schmidt Neven, R., 42
Schoevers, R., 43
school:
   difficulties in, 157–158
   liaison with, 55–56
secure attachment, 17
Sedlak, V., 169
Segal, H., 18, 64, 189
self:
   integrity of, 13
   sense of, 15, 16, 19–23, 26, 28, 103,
        110
   unstable sense of, 21
self-esteem:
   loss of, 16
      and depression, 13
   low, 5, 26
self-harm, 3, 74, 193, 217
   assessment of risk of, 77–78, 98,
        176, 185–186
   as coping strategy, 188
   cutting, 48, 180, 185–186, 192, 200
   deliberate, 3, 89, 176, 185–186
   history of, 89
   relief through, 20
   risk of, in depression, 5, 118
sense of self, 15, 16, 19–23, 26, 28, 103,
        110
separation, conflicts around, 105
sessions:
   frequency and length of, 88
   missed, and 28-session time frame,
        88, 91, 200, 204–206
   number of, 88
   regular time for, 88
setting:
   consistent, 88
   establishing, 88–89
   in parent work, 137–138

predictability and reliability of, 53
therapeutic, 88, 91, 104
    reliability and constancy of, 89
treatment, establishing, 88–89
severe superego, and narcissistic
        identification, dynamic
        combination of, in
        melancholia, 18
sexual abuse, 7, 42, 61, 89, 172
    child, 170
sexual abuse cases, work with,
        function of supervision in,
        170
sexual identity, 26, 28, 152
sexuality:
    developing, during adolescence,
        35, 100
        anxiety about, 68
    genital, 28, 30
sexual transference, 107
Shapiro, T., 22, 24, 50, 53, 57, 66, 90,
        92, 97, 104, 216
Shaver, P. R., 33
Shedler, J., 43
Sherill, J. T., 33
Sherwood, I., 21
Shortt, A. L., 33
Short-Term Psychoanalytic
        Psychotherapy [STPP]
        (passim):
    for adults, 8, 44
        with depression, 43, 50
    assessment for, 79, 87, 192, 193
    based in psychoanalytic child
        psychotherapy, 37
    breaks in, 54, 106
    case management, 9, 53–83
    for children and adolescents with
        depression, evidence base for,
        43, 47–48
    in clinical practice, 185–212
    collaborative work in
        multidisciplinary clinic, 9,
        53–83
    development of, 41–42
    difficulties arising in, 9, 185–212
    effect on depression, 43

effective for depression, 44
empirical evidence for, 42–51
ending stages of, 112–124
    countertransference issues,
        118–119
framework and process, 53–83
and IMPACT trial, 7–8
key principles of, 9, 85–126
vs. open-ended psychotherapy, 2
parent work in: see parent work
principles, aims, techniques of,
        53–73
psychoanalytic assessment for, 83,
        86, 87
psychoanalytic parent work in,
        134–142
referral for, 9, 53–83
    considerations in, 81
stages of treatment, 9, 79, 82,
        85–126, 203
    early, 86–104
    ending, 112–124
    middle, 104–112
supervision for, 9, 167–183
    framework and process,
        173–176
therapeutic frame for, 90
time frame of, 53, 204–206
time-limited nature of, 1, 7, 42, 55,
        58, 62, 87, 91, 92, 105, 106, 118,
        154, 170, 172, 176, 180, 201,
        216
transference in, role of, 57–61
28-week/session structure of, 4,
        53, 54, 72, 83, 86, 88, 101, 112,
        163, 204
for young people with depression,
        aims of, 56–57
Shulman, G., 159
silence as communication, 189
silent patient(s), 189–191
    16-year-old "Becky" [case study],
        190–191
Sinason, V., 51
Sinclair, D., 37
sleep and depression, relationship
        between, 143

sleeper effect following therapy, 7, 46, 47
sleep hygiene, 6
sleeping, difficulty in, 5
Slinger, M. B., 50
Smadja, C., 21, 23
social worker, liaison with, 55
Sodre, I., 18
Soenens, B., 24
Sorenson, P. B., 65
Specialist Clinical Care, 8, 48
Spence, S. H., 33
Spillius, E., 19, 40
splitting, 135, 189, 204, 210
　as defence against aggression, 25
　of good and bad, as defence, 14
Sprince, J., 161
Stasiak, K., 145
states of mind, infantile and adult, distinction between, 130
Steele, H., 32
Steele, M., 32
Steiner, J., 14, 63, 93
Stern, D., 37
STPP: see Short-Term Psychoanalytic Psychotherapy
Strachey, J., 58
Strupp, H. H., 214
substance abuse/misuse, 5, 6, 33, 209, 210
suicidal attempts, 89
suicidality/suicidal ideation, 3–5, 24, 77–78, 80, 98, 103, 176, 185–186
suicide, xvi, 5, 7, 19, 24, 33, 77, 110, 118, 148, 178, 185, 189
Sullivan, L., 4
superego, 128
　early, destructiveness of, 18
　ego-destructive, 15
　harsh, 18
　severe, 19, 25, 35, 100
　　and narcissistic identification, dynamic combination of, in melancholia, 18
supervision, psychoanalytic, 2, 9, 55, 167–183

framework and process, 173–176
importance of, 3, 183
　in supporting therapists' management of countertransference, 177–179
　in supporting therapists and parent workers, 3
management in, problems of, 177
meeting, first, topics in, 174
parallel process in, 179–181
of parent work, 181–183
peer, 3, 182
principles and aims of, 168–173
of time-limited psychotherapy, 172
work discussion group, 183
supervision group(s), 96, 107, 119, 174–176, 179, 180, 198–200, 210
　tasks of, 174
supervisor:
　liaison with, 140–142
　parent worker's liaison with, 140–142
　stance of, features of, 168–169
Sutton, A., 127, 131, 133, 143
Svanborg, P., 50
symbolic capacity:
　annihilation of, 172
　lack of, 69
symptomatic improvement, 12, 57, 104
systemic family therapy, 6, 42, 47
Szapocznik, J., 129
Szur, R., 51, 58, 68

TADS: see Tavistock Adult Depression Study
talking cure, 48
Target, M., xiii, 46, 48, 216
Tavistock Adult Depression Study [TADS], 45, 50, 51, 215
Tavistock Centre, London, 47
Taylor, D., 89, 213, 215
technique(s):
　clinical, 65–70
　for STPP, 61–62
　with younger adolescents, 70–73

termination of treatment:
consideration of possible need for
further treatment, 120–121
eliciting feelings about, 113–117
reactions to, working through,
113–117
therapeutic alliance/relationship:
aspects of, 59
as container, 59
concept of, 59–61
establishment of, 97–99
with parents, 128
role of, 24, 57–61
ruptures in, 61
and therapeutic outcome,
associations between, 60
and transference, dynamic
interaction of, 60
therapeutic boundaries, maintenance
of, in parent work, 157
therapeutic frame, 104, 149, 183
for STPP, 90
therapeutic intervention(s):
modes of, 61–62
replicable and systematized
approach to, treatment
manuals as, 213
therapeutic outcome and therapeutic
alliance, associations
between, 60
therapeutic relationship: see
therapeutic alliance/
relationship
therapeutic setting:
establishing, 88
reliability and constancy of, 88, 89,
91, 104
therapeutic technique, in STPP
parent work, 146–148
therapeutic work, boundary around,
146
therapist(s):
analytic attitude of, 39
being without memory or desire,
39
containing function of, 68
empathy and warmth of, 60

liaison with, 140–142
parent worker's liaison with,
140–142
reverie of, 40, 68
"taking" transference, 68
trust in, increasing, in middle
stages of treatment, 105–108
therapist-centred interpretation, 63
therapy:
breaks in, 54, 106
developmental aspect of, 124
events and changes during,
review of, 113
internalized experience of, 115
outcomes of, 57
time-limited: see time-limited
treatment
therapy box, 12-year-old "Jacob"
[case study], 71–72
thinking space, therapy box as, 72
time-limited treatment, 4, 53, 54,
105–107, 117, 176, 203, 205
use of, 2
scope of, 87, 91–92
supervision of, 172
Todd, R. D., 33
Town, J., 44
transference(s):
attending closely, 132
/countertransference
understanding:
non-verbalised, 133
in parent work, 133
elements, systematic observation
of, 39
eroticized, 201
"gathering", 59
grandparent, 172
idealization in, tolerance of, 202
interpretation of, 38
negative: see negative transference
parental, 32
positive, 59, 61
resolution of, 124
role of in STPP, 57–61
sexual, 107
"taking", 68

transference(s) (*continued*):
  and therapeutic alliance, dynamic
    interaction of, 60
  unconscious communication
    understood through, 38
transference interpretation(s), 48, 62,
  69, 70, 134, 217
transference relationship, 2, 39, 58,
  59, 104, 108, 109, 206
  attention to, 2
  central to STPP, 57–60
  deepening of, 104, 108, 109
    in middle stages of treatment,
     108–109
  evolving, 105
transferential elements, 87
  emergence of, in early treatment,
    91
transgenerational loss, 172
transgenerational trauma, 172
trauma:
  early, 2, 3, 159
    relational, 4
  intergenerational, 35, 100, 156
  parent work following, 191–194
    14-year-old "Thomas" [case
     study], 192–194
  relational, 35, 100
    early, 4
  transgenerational, 172
  work with cases of, function of
    supervision in, 170
treatment:
  outcomes of, 57
  termination of, eliciting feelings
    about, 113–117
treatment alliance, 59, 108: *see*
    therapeutic alliance/
    relationship
treatment manual(s), xv, 8–10
  rationale for, 8–9, 213–218
  as replicable and systematized
    approach to therapeutic
    interventions, 213
Trevatt, D., 128
triangular space, 29, 206
Troupp, C., 145

Trowell, J., xv, 7, 11, 12, 21, 34, 35, 42,
  46, 47, 49, 51, 53, 58, 61, 77,
  81, 106, 114, 120, 170, 172, 180,
  213
Tsiantis, J., 40
Tustin, F., 20–23, 37

Ulberg, R., 48, 216
unconscious anxiety(ies), 2, 159
  child's, containment of, 38
  parents', 128
unconscious communication, 105,
  194
  interpretation of, 51, 194
  in risk-taking behaviour, 185
  role of in STPP, 57–61
  through transference, 38
unconscious phenomena,
  attentiveness to, 39
unconscious projections: *see*
    projection(s), unconscious
undirected play, as source of clinical
    facts, 38
unstable sense of self, 21
Urwin, C., 38, 60

Vadera, R., 214, 215
validation, 65–66
Van, H. L., 50
van Oppen, P., 43
van Straten, A., 43
Varchevker, A., 156
Vidit, J.-P., 169
Vliegen, N., 26
voices, hearing, as psychotic
    symptom, 186
von Klitzing, K., 216

Waddell, M., 26–28, 31, 37, 90, 186
Weinberg, W. A., 4
Weinryb, R. M., 50
Weissman, M. M., 5, 6, 51
Wexler, M., 59
Whitefield, C., 48, 131, 134, 136, 149
WHO: *see* World Health
    Organization
Williams, G., 37, 51, 170, 189

Wilson, J., 89, 113, 118
Winnicott, D. W., 19–21, 23, 37, 51,
        55, 81
withdrawal, social, 5
Wittenberg, I., 113, 115, 116, 118
Wolfe, B. E., 214
working alliance, 59, 132: *see*
        therapeutic alliance/
        relationship

World Health Organization [WHO],
        11
Wrate, R. M., 46
Wynn Parry, C., 60

younger adolescents, technique with,
        70–73

Zetzel, E., 59